WALKING WITH THE FOOL

A Leap Of Faith

TAM DILLON

Cherise Wilson, PR Divas

Spiritually Mindful LLC www.spirituallymindfulllc.com Greenville, South Carolina

First Printing, 2021

Edited by PR Divas
Cover and inner art by Cherise Wilson

Publisher Spiritually Mindful LLC
www.spirituallymindfulllc.com

WALKING WITH THE FOOL

Contents

I

HALLUCINOGENIC HIGH PRIESTESS

1 The Makings of a Witch 10

2 Ten Years on the Cliff Edge 18

3 Time to Leap! 26

4 Soul Fire 34

5 The Magician's Couch 43

6 The Shadow Rises 51

7 Questions of Faith 59

8 Surviving in Limbo 69

9 Goddesses and Cats 86

10 Finding Sanctuary 102

11 Becoming High Priestess 113

2

THE DRUNK MAGICIAN

12 The Gift 126

13 Base 136

14 Initiation Training 144

15 The Goddess Rises 153

16 No Strings Attached 164

17 Ancestors At My Door 174

18 Deported 182

19 Stepping Into Shaman 199

20 Trip to the Future 211

21 Declined 225

22 Liminal Skills 240

23 The Mindful Spider - Lessons in Toxicity 257

24 Owning the Crone 269

25 Toxic Christianity 284

26 Stepping Back into Alignment 301

27 My Insights into the Shift and Final Thoughts 312

Introduction

What you are holding in your hands is my spiritual journey. A journey that was originally written in two separate parts. Knowing what I do now about authenticity and duality, I've chosen to combine these two parts into what was always meant to be a single journey - the journey back to myself. A journey that has involved stripping away aspects of myself, mind-altering shamanic experiences, and insightful interactions with those beyond the veil. This has led to me integrating my natural gifts and learning to live between worlds; all while navigating everyday life. A big aspect of my journey has been the struggle to step into and own who I am – and how, at the times where I have done this, I have struggled to maintain this space. Having fully understood the reasons and barriers for this, I am ready to share my full story. I'm ready to share in the hopes that it could assist someone else with their journey, coming into their gifts, or just simply to help them find their place in the world.

If you have previously read the first edition of either part of this book, you will note that this edition has some amendments; some chapters have been moved or expanded upon, new insights have been shared and the parts that are no longer relevant have been removed. I believe that everything in life happens for a reason. That includes the idea that if you have picked up this book, it is not by chance! One of my greatest hopes is that this story will inspire you to either make the changes you desire, assist you greatly on your path of transformation, or help you navigate your own shamanic or spiritual journey.

I have known for many years what my purpose is, and I take every opportunity to live that purpose. However, something has always felt 'in the way'; limiting me from really stepping into who I am. It has only been in recent months that I have fully come to understand what has stopped me from stepping fully into my purpose: the massive disconnection to authenticity and from the ancient ways that is plaguing the Western world. A plague that has sadly infected many cultures that still had a strong connection to the old ways. The ramifications of colonization, the slave trade, and the near obliteration of the First People runs far deeper than we believe! They run right into the heart of Spirituality, our connection with the divine, and our connection with ourselves. The Western world's disconnection has been around for centuries and has become so ingrained in what is left of this muddied culture. Where this ancient disconnect has left us is as a culture of lost, gifted Westerners that do not understand what is happening to them, often leaving many feeling terrified, confused, and questioning their sanity - while many others turn to varying forms of addiction in order to help them cope or feel connected to something. With the systematic indoctrination of this cultural disconnect on Westernised societies, I have witnessed a painful disconnect in those still closely connected to Spirit. The more these cultures Westernise, the more disconnected they become. I fear we may lose these cultures altogether if the influence of disconnected Western society continues to erode the wisdom of these ancient cultures.

The impact for me personally, has a been a bad case of Imposter Syndrome - who am I (some white girl) to claim that I'm gifted, that I have been given profound insights from beyond the veil, to claim that I am Shaman? I have no tribal elders I can turn to for validation of these things. I have no culture to explain what has been happening on my path. I have no shaman from my people to give me guidance. This has left me to walk my path alone, finding my own guidance and re-establishing my culture for myself. In seeing this for myself, I cannot stop seeing it for others. Nor can I stop seeing the impact on other cultures; cultures that still have a connection to their ancient ways. So many people have become unsure and unfamiliar with the deep wisdom of their own cultures; with many turning away to embrace the idealistic vision of the Western way. The Western culture hasn't completely disconnected, however. Instead, it has become so mixed and integrated with other ways that it has all but lost its core. The West was not always this disconnected, however, and some remnants of that connection remain - many turning to the old pathways of the Pagans, Druids, Hermetics and Witches. Our Eastern and African counterparts are mostly still firm in their ways, but much has been lost due to Colonization and the forced conformity by the Christian Church. This has left much of today's younger generations disinterested in or unfamiliar with the ancient wisdom of the cultures that they have inherited as their birthright. Instead, many have turned to a more Westernised way of life, either following suit with the disconnection of their spiritual aspect, or choosing to follow the ways and philosophies of the more popularised Ancient West.

Coupled with my understandings of the impact of Westernisation, has been the understanding that we have become so focussed on our duality that we have disconnected ourselves from the truth that we are in fact whole. In addition, with the insights into an emerging worldwide consciousness; came the understanding that we are destined to become unified once more. Yes, we have been unified before and we can be again. I know this unification has started already and it is stemming from the individual level. Some of these insights date back to my childhood. The majority, however, have come about within the last few years. The last few years have seen some tumultuous changes and experiences in my life. Little did I know that when I started this journey, I would be stepping into a real-life adventure - an adventure that would result in the full opening of my gifts, me stepping back into myself and channelling insights into the New World Consciousness along the way. At times a terrifying, yet oddly humorous journey, this journey has become my gift to you.

The main portion of my journey began in December 2015. My beautiful friend and personal reader, Leo, did a Tarot reading for me. Two very specific cards were drawn that day. The High Priestess - the ultimate spiritual guide and teacher; and the Queen of Cups - deeply empathetic, intuitive, and a natural caregiver. I was told that it was time for me to embrace my mission as High Priestess and emulate the qualities of the Queen of Cups. And the time was now. As I understood immediately what was required of me, it sounded easy enough right? After all, I believed I was almost there already. Having worked with the High Priestess archetype for a number of years and understanding her implicitly, I believed stepping into that aspect of myself would be a breeze. I can now safely say how very, very wrong my assumptions were! In reality, I was far from who and what I needed to be. One does not just simply step into High Priestess power. So what did the journey require? It required a journey of transformation, deep faith and learning to live intuitively in every waking moment. It required learning to live between worlds and the interpretation of often confusing insights and visions from beyond the veil. It would also require me to take numerous long, hard looks deep within to fully understand the layers of pre-conditioning, addiction, and aspects that were never truly me.

Shortly after my reading with Leo, I received a call from a national TV station inviting me to do a live Tarot reading for South Africa for the upcoming year. This was a 'first of its kind' opportunity and I did not hesitate in accepting the offer. I have looked back on that reading a number of times and more so in recent weeks. That reading was a foundation

- a 'how-to' guide for moving us forward. At the time I saw this, but not to its full capacity. There is still much that I stand by in my original reading and the additional insights... well you'll need to keep reading. Later that year I would make a decision that would spark a five-year-long experience, one that has spanned three continents and seen me experience firsthand insights from East, West and African ancients.

In order for us to fully understand the main part of my journey, I believe it will be helpful to start back in the beginning. Back to where my insights started and my gifts began to switch on...

I

Hallucinogenic High Priestess

I

The Makings of a Witch

"Tamaryn, for goodness sake! Close your curtains. Sleeping with moonlight on you is not good for your sleep my love." The semi-frustrated sound of my mother's voice. I can still hear her clearly. My fascination with the Moon and my peculiar desire to sleep under Her luminescence began around age seven. Much to my mother's frustration, it was something I continued to do for several years. My fascination with the Moon, however, has never dwindled. By age nine my ability to perceive the veil developed. It would be years before I would understand that the veil I could perceive back then, was the same light-sparkled grid that others would see and experience with psychedelics and plant medicine journeys. I then began having lucid dreams of spiders and wars. Terrifying dreams I would only come to understand as an adult. At the age of fourteen, the ancient ways of magic and wisdom opened up to me; along with the pathways of drugs and addiction as my older brother Jadie became my first Spiritual Mentor.

My brother and I were similar in that we both strove to be unique and non-conformist. We shared a common thirst for ancient and occult knowledge and we were both insatiably curious. Perhaps it was Jadie's curiosity that led him to his journey with addiction. I cannot say for sure. What I do know is that observing the rough impacts of his path, I saw the dark side of substance abuse from a young age. The early impact of Jadie's addiction was that it made me very 'uncurious' about experimenting with drugs. I did not understand back then, however, that addiction could come in many forms. As I progressed into my mid-teens, I focused on learning, understanding, and absorbing knowledge. My spiritual world was expanding and I had a growing collection of books lining my shelves. On Jadie's 'clean runs', we would sit and talk for long stretches. We talked on philosophies, beliefs, and ancient occult ways. Jadie fully supported my studies and developing practices. He would openly share his knowledge, books, and experiences with me. It was not before long, however, that I found myself more drawn to follow the ways of the Wise Ones. The Witches. More specifically I was drawn to the Solitary Witch's path; that of a solitary practitioner that tends to the various ailments of the community. Working across the full spectrum of a person's psyche, particularly the soul, this Wise One understands the link between the multifaceted aspects of a person. Working through various mediums, the Witch seeks to assist the healing process of the person in need. This includes connecting with the spirit realm to seek solutions. These solitary souls resonated with mine.

As I pursued the path of Solitary Witch, a sense of purpose grew. It was during one of Jadie's 'clean runs' that he introduced me to the Tarot, Shamanism, Collective Consciousness, and the Global Shift. Aspects that would become pivotal later in life. I have a recollection of him explaining the Shamanic way. He shared about a unique individual within the ancient cultures that still exists today. A practitioner with the ability to connect and interact with the Ancestral and Spiritual realms to assist with any ailments a person may experience. Each culture has its title, but the core of the practitioner remains the same. My brother's insights into Shamanism resonated strongly with my knowledge of the Wise Ones. He then shared his insights into altered states of consciousness. Being an integral part of many rituals and ceremonies, the ancients partook of varying natural substances, all found within their environment and each unique to their part of the globe. He then divulged parts of his own altered experiences with psychedelics. Jadie had always been open with me regarding his substance use and abuse. He then went on to share how some of the ancient civilizations had not shifted and were now lost. He expressed his concern regarding humanity heading the same way. His concern stemmed from the way the world was: full of war, imbalance, and intolerance. Humanity had spent decades destroying the planet and itself. He felt that the power of the Collective Consciousness and the ancient ways of Shamanism and ancient cultures could be the solution to restoring the world back to where it should be. I was then handed a set of Tarot cards and given a brief overview of all that he had learned to that point. This included an explanation of the Soul's Journey and how the cards appeared to be a map for the journey. With this new influx of information, my spiritual world shot open and my sense of purpose heightened. My journey with Tarot had begun and my book collection expanded. Still aligned with the ways of the Solitary Witch, I researched further. I sought to understand fully, these new ideas and concepts that had been introduced to me. More importantly, why they resonated so strongly. I began to see definite links between the ancient ways - commonalities that resonated with my soul. This is where I built my traditions and beliefs. The systems that have now become my teachings; refining them over the years as I have acquired deeper understandings; building my path from the teachings of East, West, and Africa ... I forged my connection with the spirit realms.

At sixteen I had what I believe to be my first Shamanic initiatory experience; alternatively known as Shaman Sickness within many cultures.

It is believed that when one is called to the Path, they acquire a sickness. A sickness the initiate can only heal by taking up the calling of their Path. This sickness can manifest as a severe physical ailment or mental dis-ease; often misdiagnosed or not diagnosable by Western medicine. As a young 'witchling' still fresh on her path, I had no understanding of such things. I was also not born into a culture with elders who could accurately explain and manage what was happening to me. It has been said that initiations are like being dismembered and rebuilt. My sixteen-year-old body was inclined to agree. For a couple of days my legs and lower body were wracked with severe pain - pain that felt as though I was being stabbed continuously by hundreds of knives; leaving me almost incapable of walking. I sobbed my way through the process. My mother, desperate to comfort me and ease my pain, could only hold me as I cried through the experience. My doctor could only tell us that I had some type of infection. The Universe then sent me a healer that could help: Tamsin, a very close friend of Jadie's who had qualified as a Reiki Practitioner and offered to give me a session for free. It was not long after my session with Tamsin that my body began to ease and heal. However, this was not to be my last experience. Looking back over my spiritual journey so far, I can clearly see the initiator periods. I can see where sickness set in due to me not fully following my path and what were essentially initiations into new stages of awareness. It has taken a bit of effort to work out what was me leveling up (in a sense) and what were the backhands from the Ancestors and Spirits. Both seem to incur a sickness of some form. However, the more I progress and more mindful I am of certain factors, the less intense the initiation stages have become. I would like to note here that Shamanism is not about achieving a master level. The only thing one can master is oneself. Shamanism is a way of life and a way of being. It was around this time that my interest in Psychology and human nature began to peak. I cannot say what sparked my interest specifically. Perhaps it was my intrigue with history and why humanity had done the things they had and seemed to be stuck in a cycle of repetition. Nevertheless, a side study of simple principles began and I learned to observe human nature in order to understand.

When I reached eighteen, I had my first Tarot reading experience. I was fortunate to grow up in a very open-minded home. My parents never fully understood my practices or ways, but they supported me nonetheless. My mom took a keen interest and would often chat with Jadie and I. It was my mother that took me for my first reading. It was an impulse decision by both of us. The reader looked legit with her crystals and gold rings and her sign advertised her as Madame I - Psychic. My mother and I were also curious as hell! Insisting I go first to 'see what it's like', my mom took up a seat next to me and observed my reading with intrigue. More than fifteen years later and Madam I's predictions are still falling into place. She spoke of me standing at a grave in coming weeks, but that only my father and I would attend. The passing of a relative on my dad's side weeks later and a funeral attended by only my father and I was the first of her accurate predictions. She spoke of my passion for Psychology but warned that if I did not begin my studies before twenty-one, I would likely never receive my Masters. She assured me however, that it was an ideal profession for me. She then pointed out my blatant laziness with school, but guaranteed my mom that I knew what I was doing and that I would pass my final year without concern. She also spoke of me travelling to a foreign land on my own. Here I would meet a man with a ring on his little finger. "This is the man you will marry," were her words to me. I recall my mother and I looking at one another, clearly both thinking the same thing. We shared an amusing 'vision' of a rich, exotic 'hotty', with a gold signet ring, luxuriating in a tropical paradise. Hey! A girl and her mother can dream, you know. However exotic this foreign man was, neither of us quite saw me going that route. Madame I then mentioned that I would move and settle in another country, but assured my mother that visiting would not be a problem. Madame I shared many insights with me that day - many of which I have forgotten over the years, but some I can recall with absolute clarity. Overall, my first experience with an authentic Reader was truly awe-inspiring. Madame I was batty as a fruit cake, but gifted as hell. Her assurance of my own natural psychic and healing abilities is what lit the spark for me. It was the spark that led me to pursue the path of Spiritual Therapist.

By my early twenties, I had a sound understanding of the workings of ceremonial magic and divination. Along with this came the knowledge that ceremony was not necessary in order to manifest. I understood that it helped to achieve the required state of being, however, it was not always essential. As long as what I did was in alignment with myself and had no ill intentions or harmed another being, I created as I wanted. My passion and relationship with Tarot had grown exponentially. I had been working with the cards for a couple of years already and I knew, without question that the Tarot was integral to my path. It resonated strongly with purpose. I was drawn more and more to read for others and my path of Guide opened up. Around this time Jadie introduced me to the Twelve Steps and the Serenity Prayer. The Twelve Steps is a program followed by addicts in recovery. Based on spiritual principles and philosophies, the steps resonated with me and soon were incorporated into my belief system. The Serenity Prayer can be heard frequently in AA and NA meetings, as well as in recovery centers around the world - a simple set of words with a deep meaning. The first time I heard the words, they sang to my Soul and the prayer has never left me.

The Serenity Prayer
Grant me the Serenity to accept the things I cannot change,
the Courage to change the things I can,
and the Wisdom to know the difference.

During my time of early spiritual growth, I began to be more outspoken on topics of inequality, intolerance and the imbalances of society. As a child I had always spoken my mind; often to the dismay of my parents. If I knew something was not right or untrue, I spoke up. As I progressed on my path, my outspoken nature grew. Along with the knowing that I was meant for something bigger, I knew I had purpose; that it concerned the world at large and a massive Shift in Consciousness was on the way. I soon took the step and began reading for others on a more formal level. I took up alternative therapy courses and eventually began a three-year Diploma in Metaphysics. I felt whole and fulfilled. It was during my time at the Metaphysical Academy that my purpose was confirmed. The third-year students required volunteers for their Past Life Regression class. Curious as always, I willingly volunteered. I was introduced to my trainee facilitator and the process was explained. I was placed under light hypnosis and taken backwards. She guided me back through various memories, allowing me to share what I was experiencing. I regressed back into early childhood and into the womb. She let me 'hang' there for a moment before taking me back into my last lifetime. My facilitator guided me through the experience of my last life to the moment of my death. From here she took me to what she termed, 'Life Between Lives'. With crystal-clear clarity I can still see the massive cavern. Thousands of souls and energies moving in and out. I was then moved forward to a moment that stood out for me. I found myself before a cluster of twelve beings. Beings of brilliant light, with no shape or form - beings I referred to as the Council. A council I was having an intense argument with. They were insisting that I return to the earthly plane; that what was happening there needed to shift. I was having none of it, and standing my ground, I protested further. Clearly being outspoken is a soul trait! My protests however, fell on 'deaf ears' and I found myself back in the womb. My knowing of having a higher purpose had been confirmed. More than this,

I understood what the purpose was. The 'how' is something I have only in recent years come to understand correctly. The explanation for my intense disapproval for being on the earthly plane also made far more sense. As far back as I can recall, I have had a resentment towards the Universe. I never understood where this came from. I just knew that it was there. I guess being forced into a lifetime as a stubborn soul would set something like that off. However, I also understood that my fulfillment came from being on my path and living my purpose. A Universal catch twenty-two. However, the fulfillment outweighed the resentment and I formed an agreement of sorts with the Higher realms. Most importantly though, it affirmed another knowing I had always had. The knowing that I'm here to help change the world. To rectify the imbalances, teach the ancients ways and assist the world in becoming unified once more. Sounds a rather tall order, I know. However, I have over the years come to learn and understand where and how I can assist to make these changes; and it begins with the Self! I was well into my metaphysical studies, I had clear direction and purpose and my gifts were progressing. Then I met Ryan and took a ten-year-long detour on my path.

2

Ten Years on the Cliff Edge

The Fool is a remarkable card in the lessons he teaches. His core lessons are authenticity and how to do it, and once one has stepped into that authenticity, they find an insurmountable amount of faith in themselves - faith so strong they would willingly step off a cliff edge into the unknown, and know that they will grow wings and soar. For a good ten years I sat at the cliff edge, never fully having the faith to step off. My ten-year detour at that proverbial cliff edge, as much as I spent more time there than was necessary, wasn't all a waste! This stint at the edge gave me space to step into reading Tarot full time and begin teaching, but I never truly stepped fully onto my path. Instead, I lived almost parallel to my path, close enough to read with accuracy, but with enough distance to avoid external judgment and criticism. In the early days of this ten-year stint, my relationship with marijuana began and I experienced the realm of hallucinogens for the first time. It was here that I learned quickly that hallucinogens worked differently for me; or rather they didn't. Instead of the commonly experienced sensory and perception effects commonly experienced, they just made me tired. I did find a marked increase in my intuitive abilities, though, but I never 'tripped' as such.

Ryan was always a deeply spiritual person at his core, his home environment, however, had not allowed him the space to explore this or embrace it. Ryan's parents were mostly the opposite of spirituality. As much as their business was metaphysical in nature, they found the realm of spirituality to be mostly a bunch of "woo" and didn't believe in much of what they were selling. I always felt I had to hide a lot of who I was around Ryan's family. I was fully aware of the gifts I had and I knew without question that they were well developed; I just could not bring myself to own this side of myself. My fear of ridicule kept me running parallel to my path and forced me out of alignment with my authentic self. As much as my readings were on point, the visions I had developed as a child had stopped. I would only understand years later that this was due to my relationship with marijuana. As my relationship with Ryan progressed, my spirituality and physical health began to take a backseat and that left me only half pursuing my purpose and distancing me further from my power. As the years wore on, my depression intensified and my sense of self dwindled. My fulfillment moved from my spirituality to Ryan and a feeling of emptiness grew. Then my readings began to slow down and I found myself back in a corporate environment - my Tarot falling to the wayside. The decline in my physical health and the stresses of working in corporate environments were the catalysts for me to introduce a simple yoga practice into my life. My practice, however, was inconsistent and was coupled with a lack of a healthy diet and lifestyle in general. It was our move from Johannesburg to Cape Town about five years into our relationship, that shifted things for me and that's when the spirit realm began to get loud!

When Ryan and I moved to Cape Town, we chose to stay with his biological father while we found our feet and got settled. It was here that I had my first waking vision in years. This is where I learned that marijuana had been halting my visions. When we moved in with Ryan's dad, I chose to stop and within a couple of weeks, my visions returned. The first was a rather terrifying vision! I was restless and struggling to fall asleep. I turned to face away from Ryan and something made me open my eyes. Standing next to my side of the bed was a man. It was definitely not Ryan's dad nor anyone else that was living in the house. He was tall and wearing a heavy coat with a hood up over his head. Something drew my eye to his hands, which were bound with what looked like rope. I took this image in for a split second before my human instincts kicked in and believed we were being robbed. I quickly shut my eyes and pretended I was still fast asleep. It took me a few seconds to digest what I had seen. When the penny dropped, I realized we were not in fact being robbed; well not unless this spirit was a 'klepto' in his last life - which I somehow doubted... rather it was my first visual encounter with the spirit realm after many years.

After that night, things down-spiraled quickly between Ryan and I. Ryan became unbearably depressed and we seemed to lose track of our initial plan. I suddenly found Ryan ending things with me and telling me I had to leave. I moved in with my parents temporarily, who were in turn in the process of moving to another part of the country. My time there was limited and I needed to figure my life out quickly. Looking back in retrospect, I knew that was the Universe attempting to shove me off the cliff. At the time, however, it felt horrible. But when one sits idly at the cliff edge and does nothing, the Universe seems to think a nudge or kick will help - it usually does if you flow with it – which I certainly did not do! Instead, a couple of weeks later, Ryan moved out of his dad's house and we moved back in together. We found a room in a shared house in the pretty Southern Suburbs of Cape Town, and I found myself a space to read Tarot. I can assure you none of this was correct.

I found myself reading Tarot from a space that did not line up with my core values as a Tarot Reader. I had landed a reading space in a well-known Cape Tonian psychic's retail space. She had a quaint little shop with crystals and potions and space for two readers. The one was connected to the shop space, while the other was based across from the shop and ran under a slightly different name and theme. Hell, who am I kidding - the one side was angels and fairy dust and the other was named the Fortune Teller. Yes, I had landed a space reading as a Fortune Teller. Not only this, the owner of the space would insist that we dress a certain way and work in a certain way. I lasted a few months until I found my self-respect and left. Reading again after such a long while felt wonderful though. I realized how much I had missed it. It was here that I also had my first experience as a medium. I had never pegged myself as a medium before, I would somewhat willingly use the term psychic, but even that was rare. A middle-aged gentleman came to see me - he was not there for anything specific, he just wanted to see what would come up. It was while reading for him that I kept seeing a lavish house atop green rolling lawns and the name of a popular South African TV show leapt to mind. I shared with him what I was seeing and the show it reminded me of - "My mom loved that show, especially the fancy houses. She passed away a few years ago."

I felt what I can only describe as nostalgia; that feeling one gets when you think back on fond memories. Then the messages started to flow, mostly as thoughts that were not my own. For my first experience as a medium, I was lucky to get a gentle one, and what a beautiful experience to be a part of! Sharing and feeling a mother's love for her son, I could feel her sense of pride from the other side, for the man he had become. My ability to 'see' and 'know' things had grown and improved. With the increase of my gifts came an increase in my need to be healthier and more connected with myself. My eating habits changed drastically as I shifted to a full vegan diet, regular exercise and my yoga practice returned. My depression decreased exponentially and my relationship with Ryan improved tenfold. My use of marijuana had returned, however, and my visions dwindled again, but my connection to my gifts grew stronger and I felt far more aligned to my path than I had ever experienced before.

Ryan and I spent a total of three years in Cape Town before we moved back to Johannesburg. A massive decline in Ryan's physical health due to a surgery was the catalyst for us returning to Johannesburg and moving in with his mother and step-father. By the time we moved back to Johannesburg however, I was more than confident to pursue my readings and therapies as a full-time job once more. The two years that followed saw me grow and blossom in my work. I felt less concern around other people's judgments and accepted an open space at the metaphysical shop that Ryan's parents owned. It was during this time at the shop that I would first 'hear' Ancestors, witness the frightening effects of African magic and my sense of anxiety around my relationship with Ryan would begin to really rear its ugly head.

From the moment I took up space in the shop, I was busy! It was the busiest I had ever been up to that point. My readings flowed, my medium work grew, and more and more highly awakened souls came to see me. My work became a bizarre mix of "What's my future spouse's star sign" to people who were highly gifted and held important life purposes. The students that filled my classes were seeking a Higher Level education. My knowledge of the Tarot flourished and I pursued Energy Healing as an additional modality to use with the people who came to see me. As I grew more popular, offers from local and nearby Sangomas[1] would arise to tempt me, but something deep within me said, "That path is not for you." Then May came to see me. She sat down in front of me, introduced herself, and then said, I've seen you before."

"I don't believe you have, I'm sure this is my first time seeing you?" I questioned.

"No. I've SEEN you before. In a vision. I don't know what connection I have to you, but I know you," was her response.

It took me a moment to wrap my head around what she had just said. This was indeed a first for me! I took a breath and began pulling cards; then my little reading room started to get a little crowded. Other energies in the room started becoming clearer, but once they were out in the open... it was like a sardine tin party in there! "She must walk her path." It took a minute for me to fully catch the words. Then the connection fell into place and flow happened. May's ancestry line was soft but firm. It was like being held in a big Mama's embrace: gentle, soothing, and nurturing. They held firm on her purpose, though. There was no negotiation room. May had little resistance to stepping onto her path; she then sought guidance on the way forward and once more, the messages flowed. Since meeting May, more clients and their ancestors arrived - I had clearly opened up something.

A few months after seeing May, I witnessed the effects of magic. I received a call from a woman asking if I would be willing to see her dad. She explained that he was a healthy 56-year-old man but was now bedridden and no doctor or Sangoma could help them. I agreed for her to bring her dad in to see me, and the man she brought with her looked far from a healthy 56-year-old. He looked closer to his nineties and smelled like death. I had never smelt death before, but I knew without question that was the smell now permeating my therapy room. She took a moment to ensure he was comfortable and she took up a seat next to his wheelchair, her stress, and exhaustion vastly apparent on her face and in the energy she gave off. I asked her a series of questions to get a better idea of what I was dealing with and the general consensus up to that point was that no one knew what was wrong or what had happened. Looking at her dad, I could clearly see he was not even there anymore. His soul had already detached itself from his body. I offered to do what I could, but I knew without question there was nothing I or anyone else could do. As I worked around him, I saw a sibling of his had given him a root of some sort in his food which had caused the rapid deterioration of his body. Over the span of a month, he had gone from being fit, healthy and happy to standing at Death's door. I worked to make him comfortable and came to stand at his side for one last bit of work, when he grabbed my hand, looked me straight in the eyes and I could tell his soul was back. He looked at me as tears filled his eyes and a sense of gratitude washed over me. The moment passed within seconds and his soul was gone again. I shared the insights I had received about him being poisoned. Sadly, she was able to confirm a dispute between him and his sister and also shared with me that she was not surprised to hear what I was telling her. She called me two days later to let me know of his passing.

As the months progressed, my work continued to expand while my relationship with Ryan began to take a toll on me. Ryan had not fully recovered from his physical knock and took strain daily, not just physically, but mentally and emotionally as well. My role in our relationship became one of caregiver with very little energetic exchange in return from Ryan. I was persistently sitting with the intense knowing that I was meant to leave him. I was persistently wracked with fear and guilt, however. Where would I go and what would I do? How would Ryan manage without me? I felt that there was nothing for me outside of the life that I had created and I felt obligated to stay with Ryan. I then had my reading with Leo and was told to step up and step into my power. My reading on national TV followed shortly after, along with an intense anxiety around

Ryan. We had discussed getting married a while back and had agreed that December 2016 would be our date. Shortly after my TV experience, I sat down to begin planning our wedding and was met instead with an intense panic attack. I put our wedding plans on hold, but that anxious feeling only continued to grow. I let this anxious feeling hang around for six more months before I reached my breaking point.

3

Time to Leap!

I was in a very specific situation where I needed to make pivotal decisions about my life. One of my most consuming decisions was regarding my ten-year relationship with Ryan. That day sits so clearly in my memory. The intense anxiety I felt. The heaviness that sat with me. I could not carry on like this anymore. For months I had been asking myself the same questions over and over. Is this where I want to be? Am I here for the right reasons? The answers were always the same. It was clear I was not there for the right reasons. This was not where I wanted to be nor where I should be. At the same time, I felt incredibly stuck. Fear of the unknown had always held me back. I was in a deep comfort zone. As much as my work was fulfilling, my relationship was unbalanced and my day-to-day life had become dull and monotonous. I felt like I was going nowhere. I wasn't living; I was merely existing. I had to get out! A shift and a change was imperative in order for me to move out of that space permanently. This was the reason I went to visit Nikki, one of my closest friends. My head was a complete mess and it was now time to find order in the chaos. I opened up to her about everything. I told her how I was feeling and about the questions I constantly asked myself. Nikki listened and asked questions as we spoke. She shared her perspective about things. Being completely honest with me, she told me that I could achieve anything I set my mind to. She acknowledged the strength that was inside me which was necessary to make the changes I needed to.

Nikki showed me a glimmer of the strength I needed in order to do what was necessary. Her comforting words were a stark reminder that I would be okay no matter what. It required faith in myself and my strength was the foundation for that faith. I still hold so much gratitude for Nikki and for her showing me that glimmer. I believe this was the moment I started to search for my courage. It was the courage to step off the cliff and begin my journey of full transformation. It was time to stop dancing at the cliff's edge and leap. The conversation with Nikki buzzed around in my head for the next couple of days. First on the agenda? I needed to find the strength to tell Ryan I was leaving him. I kept trying to find the right time and way to do it. However, Ryan beat me to it. He picked up that something was seriously amiss with me and finally asked me what was going on. The moment had presented itself and it was now, or probably never. This was the moment that I had to be open and honest with him and tell him that I did not want to be there anymore. I explained that this was not the life I wanted. He asked if we could try again. I intuitively knew that the relationship was long over. However, I ignored my inner voice and agreed to give it another chance. Over the next couple of days, I felt myself growing further and further away from Ryan. I could tell he could feel the distance as well. My intuition continued to tell me that life-changing events were going to happen no matter what. Yet again I ignored my inner voice. I carried on with life. I was, in fact, burying my head in the sand.

During this tumultuous time, I happened to stumble across a very interesting soul. A soul sitting on the other side of the world. A soul I have still yet to meet in person. Danny stepped onto my path at the right time and he became my first clear lesson on how far the Collective Consciousness could reach. My tap dance at the cliff edge was becoming a frustrating one, but my fear held me there. So the Universe sent me a nudge via an online game of all places! When the Universe wants to chat, it makes a plan. Danny evolved into a presence who passed on the most outrageously accurate, divine messages and lessons. At times, it was just so damned annoying that I nicknamed him Nuisance. He would tell me what I already knew to be true, but would have preferred to ignore, yet he made it all sound so simple at the same time. I understood his mantra to be, "It's easy, just make it happen." In truth, it is that easy, which made it even more frustrating. Danny and I clicked almost instantly. It was like meeting a long-lost friend after many years. It was almost as though we had automatically picked up from where we left off. My question was from where? My intuition quickly told me he had wandered onto my path for a very good reason. I just wasn't sure what that reason was. It was a Sunday night and I had taken to being a little flirty with some of the other friends Danny and I had made online. Danny, who had given me the nickname Princess, joked about how I would need to choose one of them as my prince. His exact words were, "You need to make a call." At the time it did not spark anything huge for me. Two days later Ryan said the same words to me! Then it hit home and it hit hard! Having been told the same thing just a few days apart snapped and awakened a realization within. Do Universal messages get passed along in seemingly random ways like this? What were the chances of being told "I need to make a call" twice in such a short space of time? I could not afford to ignore my intuition any longer. It was now speaking to me through other means to get the message across. Although the first time I heard these words was in a light-hearted vein, the words had still been spoken. I did need to make a call.

Earlier that morning I had done a reading for myself for some guidance. This added to my intuitive wake-up call. I randomly pulled seven cards. After laying them out and looking at what I had pulled, I knew them to be a 'timeline' of events. The first card was The Two of Swords; I was avoiding my feelings and emotions and what I knew to be the truth. I was fearful of officially ending my relationship and taking that step out of my comfort zone. The second card was the Death card which I instantly understood to be the necessary 'death' of my relationship and current way of life. No one can escape inevitable death. To progress in life, we need to let go of the old, to make room for the new. The Tower card landed next to the Death card. Immediately I recognized the inevitable path of the 'shit storm' that would end my relationship and the breaking down of my life into nothing. Some serious change was going to happen and I knew it was not going to be easy. The light at the end of the tunnel was revealed through the next cards I chose. The Chariot card was an interesting one - I had known for a while where I was on my spiritual path. I knew I had been learning the lesson of the Chariot card - the lesson of self-mastery. This card teaches you about stepping into who you are. I had to choose my path and master it. The World card came up next. Always a positive card to pull, particularly in situations like mine. If I could master the Chariot, I would see the positive aspects of the World card. I would experience a sense of completeness. I would be able to reach a place where I could achieve anything. The Sun card landing next to the World confirmed this for me. I knew that along with that sense of completeness, I would also have a higher state of enlightenment. The last card was the Star card which represents clarity and having a full understanding of everything we need to know. I took a few minutes to absorb my reading and understand it fully. What I received at the time was what I required to let go of my fears and of what no longer worked in my life. Things were going to get messy and very unpredictable. But I also knew that it would be worth it in the end. I had received the clarity to end my relationship. There was no longer a choice. The change was inevitable.

Now it was time for me to step out of the Two of Swords mindspace and embrace the impending Death card. There was no room for fear anymore.

Ryan agreed to move out for a week and give me the time and space to make my decision. It was possibly one of the greatest gifts he had given me in our ten years together. It was my first taste of freedom. That week when he was away, I didn't need to think or do anything for anyone but myself. This was something I had not been able to do in years. Ryan had been very demanding of my time and energy. I had put all of my energy into the business I had. There was nothing left to give to myself. I was depleted. My continued healthy diet and consistent yoga practice that I had maintained since Cape Town, I believe are what kept me going those last few months. On the first day, after years, I woke up alone. I wandered around feeling at a loss with what to do with myself. My emotions were swinging between contentment with my new-found freedom and mourning the loss of my relationship. That was the day that the Death card came into play. I gave myself permission to mourn the loss and allow the death of an aspect of myself to start taking place. It was in that week that the Universe and my intuition spoke loudly to me. Louder than I have ever experienced. I don't fully know if it was the space from Ryan or the sudden shift toward focussing on myself, but I felt more 'switched-on' than usual. I felt more open to seeing and hearing the messages from the Universe. This openness allowed the Universe some space to get funny. I was googling images for a project I was busy with. Scrolling through the pictures, an image leapt out at me with the words "Goodbye Ryan" on it. All my mind said was, "What the fuck?" And all I could do was laugh! The Universe was now being blunt and to the point and clearly trying its hand at humor. I definitely could not dispute the fact that my relationship was over and that I needed to move on. I simply could not ignore my intuition any longer. That day I chose to start living in full intuition. I chose to trust my inner voice and follow the direction it took me in. I would no longer hide from my purpose and my path. My intuition was required if I was to fulfil the role of a High Priestess. More importantly, I needed to trust that intuition. It was time to choose myself and my path. Where was I meant to go next?

The answer to that came via a very close friend of mine and Ryan's. Ollie had arrived from Cape Town the week that Ryan had moved out. He was spending a few days in Johannesburg on his way through to Mozambique. Ollie was devastated at first by the news that I wanted to leave Ryan. I carefully explained to him why I wanted to end things. He heard me and felt I was making the right decision. As much as it saddened him, he understood. While he was there, he chatted with me about Vietnam. He had mentioned Vietnam to both Ryan and I a few weeks before. He had told us that he and his girlfriend, Tracy, would be heading out there to teach English shortly. He had made the offer for Ryan and I to go with them. Ryan almost instantly declined, stating his health as the reason. Something about Ollie's offer had stuck with me. Now he was talking to me about it again and I listened intently. He explained what was required to do this, as well as the costs. It was not exactly cheap and certainly not the kind of funds I had access to. However, the conversation resonated strongly with me. After he left, I started researching teaching English there. I remember so clearly looking at all the information and pictures of Vietnam. Intuitively I knew that this was where I needed to go. My soul yearned for this place that I had never been to. My direction started to make sense and it was almost as if I could see my path being laid out before me. I had a clear direction. Intuitively, everything felt perfectly correct. I knew I would be getting on a plane to Vietnam in the coming weeks. I knew I needed to go and teach in Vietnam. It was now just a matter of starting the process and finding the money to make it happen. I had no questions or doubts about making it happen, though.

Ryan arrived back on Friday afternoon. I told him that I had made my decision. I also told him about my plans to head to Vietnam to teach English there. I could see he was saddened by this and a part of me felt guilty for ending the relationship. It seemed on the surface that the conversation ended on good terms. I told him that I wanted to fly down and see my parents the next day. I had not seen them in months. I also needed to tell them what was happening face to face. Intuitively, it felt like the right thing to do. It was the phone call to my mom on Friday evening that confirmed that feeling for me. I called and asked her if I could come down for a visit the next day. Her response was so positive and welcoming. There were no questions of, "Why what's wrong?" She was just so happy to hear I was coming to visit. Now, this is not the norm for my mother at all! Her response would usually have been the latter. Her instant positive reaction was just the confirmation I needed. I booked myself a flight for the next afternoon without issue. Next, I had to find a way to get to the airport. I happened to be seeing Leo that morning and intuitively I knew she was meant to take me

I had not seen Leo in quite some time. It was the perfect time for a catch-up. I told her about everything that had been happening. She was beyond happy to hear my news about Vietnam and fully supported my decision to leave Ryan. The positive energy that radiated off her seemed to double my faith levels. I asked her if she would be able to drive me to the airport later that day. When she said that she would love to, I could no longer doubt that I was on the correct path. Everything was unfolding smoothly - just as I knew it would. My intuition had reached a new level, a heightened one. My faith was high and I was super 'plugged in'. This was a new space never before reached in all my years of doing intuitive work. I arrived safely at my parents on Saturday evening. I chatted with them about what had happened and my plans for heading to Vietnam. They were incredibly supportive. They were proud of me for the decisions and choices I had made. I knew without a doubt that I was destined for Vietnam. The next question was where and how would I find the finances to do it? This was the missing piece of my puzzle. I was also working against the clock. I had planned when to book everything that was required for things to unfold exactly as they were meant to. My levels of faith were so high that I just knew I would find the means to make it all happen.

4

Soul Fire

"Danny, I think I've worked out why you've stumbled onto my path. It's a lot more complex than what I'll tell you, but essentially to light a fire and as usual, Universal timing is perfect."

Ayurvedic philosophy speaks about Agni - an inner fire and intelligence that lives within each cell in the body. It is believed that this intelligence facilitates what is absorbed and rejected by each cell. It has been referred to as the Gatekeeper of Life. I have no doubts that the fire Danny had sparked was my inner Agni, and my Gatekeeper was now awake and on guard, ready to reject any rubbish that came my way. I arrived back home on Monday afternoon and Ryan had agreed to pick me up from the airport. As I walked out into the parking, I knew straight away that something was up. His energy was very intense, yet he was shut down. When I asked him about it, he told me not to worry and that everything was fine. I knew this was not the case at all, but I dropped it. Later that evening, he decided to be 'honest' with me. He told me exactly how he felt about me leaving him. That good space we had left one another with on Saturday had gone out the window. I was told that I was being unfair and that I was breaking his heart. Something shifted inside me during that conversation. The newfound fire in me sparked, burnt brighter and I found myself standing my ground with Ryan. This is something I had never done before. Most of the time I would back down and step into a submissive role. Not this time. I told him that it was my decision and there was no turning back. He needed to accept this and respect it. The conversation was dropped quickly after that and no more was said about it. We sat in stony silence for the rest of the evening.

Fortunately, I had to drive out later that night to fetch Ollie. He was returning from Mozambique and would be staying with us for a couple of days. It was a neutral energy I welcomed happily, as I knew it would help to break the mood back home. The following day we all had things we needed to sort out. One of the places we needed to go to was the mall where Ryan's family had their shop. This was the opportunity I needed to tell the ladies that worked there what was happening. One of the ladies, however, had something to tell me. Ryan had been openly flirting with various women that came into the shop and this had been going on for a long time. I had been unaware of this as I trusted him. One woman in particular had been hanging around the shop recently. This was an issue Ryan and I had had before - both in Johannesburg and Cape Town. I assumed that it had been resolved and put to rest. Now, years later, it was back again. I felt an incredible anger welling up inside me. After telling me the night before about being so heartbroken, he had, unknown to me, been chatting up these other women! The fire inside me was raging by the time the lady had finished telling me about the situation. Amazingly enough, it was also after that conversation that I learned how strong my connection with Danny had grown. About an hour after that conversation, I received a message from him asking, "How's the ex been today?" It was a direct question and I had said nothing to prompt it. I told him what I had learned and that I was pissed!

"It couldn't be! I mean if it is, then WOW! Around an hour ago, all of a sudden, I felt a huge surge of anger and hate. No reason at all. I just felt so angry. One of the guys I work with asked if I was ok cause it looked like I wanted to kill someone. I just walked away. I couldn't explain it in words."

This situation was mind-blowing to me. This was the first time anyone else had been able to pick up my emotions and energy like I had done for others for so many years. Never mind that I had never met this someone and that they were in a completely different country. I am very aware that connections like this can and do exist, but experiencing it for myself was awe-inspiring. It gave me the certainty now, more than ever, that Danny had stepped onto my path for very specific reasons. I knew our connection ran a lot deeper than I had originally thought. That evening, Ryan added more fuel to my already raging fire. He told me he was going out for dinner with another woman. He wasn't taking her just anywhere though, he was taking her to a place that we would always go to on a Tuesday night. Ryan was now playing spiteful. To say I was furious at this stage was an understatement, particularly after what I had been told earlier that day in the shop. Although I didn't say anything to Ryan about it, I did feel there was a 'war' of sorts coming and my inner fire burned hot.

At this time, a particular plant medicine appeared in my life that was pivotal to what was about to unfold. Ollie was due to leave the next day and before he left, he chatted to me about micro-dosing with psilocybin mushrooms (magic mushrooms). This plant medicine has been used for eons by medicine men, shamans and other healers to facilitate deep spiritual journeys and the healing of a myriad of ailments ranging from chronic depression to post-traumatic stress disorder and a lot in between. Ollie told me about the research that was being done on the subject and the benefits that people were reaping from the practice of micro-dosing. He handed me a bag of mushrooms and I was intrigued to say the least as I had never done micro-dosing before. Some of the benefits found through research include heightened levels of awareness, as well as a reduction in depression and low energy moods. The plant medicine has also been found to enhance mental focus as well as stimulate high levels of creativity. In the days that followed, I had my first experience with micro-dosing. The impact it had on my journey and intuition levels was astounding! That 'plugged in' feeling was heightened even further and my intuition levels soared. I could also feel that the balancing of my fire within was developing.

Later that week, the inevitable blowout with Ryan occurred. War was coming and the Tower card was making its appearance. Everything that had happened over the past ten years came pouring to the fore. Ryan had asked me to fetch him from the shop. I arrived to see him walking out with whom I presumed was the woman that he had taken out for dinner earlier that week. The ladies that worked at the shop looked at me and I instantly felt and saw the discomfort in them. The fire within started to rage again and then the inevitable happened. On the way home, you could say I lost my shit with him. He pulled over on the side of the road and we had it out with one another for a good twenty minutes. All the issues, all the blaming and all the years of things left unsaid spewed out right there parked on the side of the road.

Throughout the argument, Danny kept sitting in the back of my mind. I just knew he was feeling everything that was going on, and he was. When we got back home, I left Ryan in our lounge and went to find space in the bedroom. Danny offered me a space to vent my frustration. And vent I did! He gave me such a safe space that I was able to let everything out. This man was an absolute blessing and he felt like a gift from the Universe. I let forth a string of expletives, telling Danny how I felt Ryan had thrown the ten years of our relationship down the drain; pretending he was heartbroken when in truth, what I was seeing was someone who had already moved on quite contentedly. I felt I had wasted so many years of giving and giving, going through hell and back and all I had done was waste my life. Danny expressed that he felt it was a low blow. I continued to tell him that the worst part of it was that I was still being so nice about the whole situation and was prepared to walk away with nothing. All I felt like was a first-class idiot. Danny expressed that Ryan should grow a pair of balls and man up. He ended off by saying, "Split the shit, it's only fair!"

So I stepped back fully into my power: split the shit I would! Suddenly the clarity of where I had placed myself for the past ten years hit me full force. The restoring of the balance at that moment made the path even clearer. I knew where I would be getting the finances I needed to go where I was meant to go next. For more than ten years I had sat in a submissive 'people pleaser' role. I just took whatever was handed to me. That raging fire seemed to burn through that side of me; and like the proverbial phoenix rising from the ashes, a different side of me stepped out. It was a side I had not seen in years! A side I didn't realize how much I had missed. The side that took no shit and didn't allow people to walk all over me. I had found my authentic self and I was good and proper pissed and ready to take on any challenge that was laid before me. This was the night that I would take back my power from Ryan.

Before I could carry on my 'vent' conversation with Danny, Ryan stepped into the bedroom and within seconds, another fight had broken out between us. Ryan had picked the wrong moment to start with me. I was not going to back down this time. I made it clear to Ryan that we would be splitting everything. I gave him the choice to either sell everything and split the money or he could pay me out my portion of the value. Either way, I was not walking away empty-handed. I had invested so much more than just financially, I knew intuitively that this was the way things were meant to go. Ryan, having never seen this side of me before, was flabbergasted. When he met me, I had lost a lot of my fire years before. This was due to high levels of depression and anxiety sparked from working in toxic corporate environments. The work I had started in my Metaphysics studies was setting this straight, but then I detoured. This night however, I was standing my ground.

The next morning the submissive side of me had managed to creep in again. Old patterns die hard! I did not realize at the time that stepping into your power after so long needs some practice. I landed up feeling quite bad about what had unfolded the night before with Ryan, especially about me not leaving empty-handed. That day I had arranged to have tea with two different people. These were arrangements I had made much earlier in the week. Both arrangements came out of pure intuitive knowing. I knew I had to see both of these people. The first was my dad's sister, my lovely Aunt Coll, who seems to share a lot of similar gifts with me. I've always enjoyed sitting in her space. That day was no different. I told her about everything that had been going on with Ryan and that I was planning to go to Vietnam to teach. She was so happy to hear my news. However, it wasn't her enthusiasm for my decision that stuck with me, it was the advice she gave me that day. I spoke to her about splitting everything with Ryan. I asked what she thought about it and her words to me were, "Don't be a Fool and leave empty-handed. Never walk away with nothing." She had confirmed what Danny had said the night before. I left her with a lot more surety on what I needed to do and understood why I needed to have tea with her that day. Part of me still felt guilty about splitting everything with Ryan despite everything that had happened that week.

My next tea appointment was with an amazing friend of mine, Brigitte who owned a healing center that I would sometimes work from. She was the third person that week who expressed my need to split everything with Ryan and this put my mind at ease that I was making the right call. She mentioned that one of her clients had been to see her a few weeks before our meeting and had asked her about Ryan. She said that she was sure that he was engaged to me. But she said she felt confused because of how excessively flirty he was with other women that came into the shop. On hearing this, I didn't think my fire could rage any hotter than at that moment. Two completely different people told me the same thing about him. These were two people who did not know one another at all. It was the final blow for me to make up my mind about definitely splitting everything with Ryan. I could not ignore the Universal nudging on what I was meant to do. This is where I would be getting what I needed in order to get to Vietnam. At the same time, I also understood why it needed to come from where it did. It was about restoring balance. It was me taking back my power. I couldn't dispute my intuitive feelings about it. I didn't need any further clarification.

That evening when I got home, I told Ryan about what I had learned that week. This time I had no guilt or bad feelings about saying what I needed to say. He agreed to pay me out for half of everything we owned together. I just needed to work out what the amount was. When I sat down to do this and looked at the final figure, lo and behold – the figure was an almost exact match to the amount I needed! I was now racing against the clock. Time was passing quickly. I needed to be on a plane to Cape Town the following week Thursday for me to attend the English teaching course I needed to do. I told Ryan that I needed to have the money by the end of that weekend. He paid me in full. I prayed I wasn't too late to enroll in the English Teaching course I would need to do before I left for Vietnam. I remember the telephonic conversation with the woman at the English Teaching Center. I told her clearly and insistently, "I have to be on that course!"

She must have thought I was nuts. I must have left quite an impression on her as by the Wednesday afternoon I received confirmation that I was enrolled for the course starting that Saturday. My ticket was booked for Cape Town for Thursday. It was now just a matter of packing up my life and reducing it to a simple travel-sized case. I had managed to reduce my life to a few clothes, Tarot cards, some choice crystals, and my laptop. I have to say, it was probably one of the most liberating feelings in the world. Dropping all my worldly possessions and traveling with the bare minimum, I left Johannesburg with one and a half suitcases and my laptop bag. I was now officially 'homeless', but a roof over my head had been provided for when I arrived in Cape Town. The Universe had my back and was looking after me; and this was a beautiful confirmation that I was doing the right thing. Nothing in the process so far had been a struggle, except for the mini-war! Everything had fallen into place at the right time and everything I needed was given to me at the right time. This Fool was packed and ready to leap!

Before I left, I did have one last conversation with Ryan where he happened to share some very insightful information with me. He explained to me the theory of 'seven'. Oddly enough this was the number of cards I had pulled for myself the week Ryan had left. It was also a number that had come up frequently for me over the months since I had my reading with Leo. Ryan explained that we first deal with fear. Then he explained that we learn to understand death. Before we can move on though, we need to experience a 'war' of sorts. I realized just how accurate this had been when I thought about the previous week that I had with him. He further explained that when the 'war' was over, one needed to go through a period of rest. This is a time where we can restore ourselves to our full power again. He also explained that the likelihood of getting physically ill at this stage was also very high. The very next day that happened to me. I found myself flat on the couch with shockingly low energy levels and a head cold from hell. I also understood the other side of my getting sick. Whenever we go through a lot of emotional upheavals, the body is the last point of release. Ryan explained that after the physical illness is completed, we are then in a position to learn and grow. My Chariot card had been in exactly that position. It is then that we reap the harvest of completion, enlightenment and full understanding in our lives. The last three cards of my reading had summed this up perfectly. The number seven is a significant Soul number. It is the number for the Soul journey and transformation. Ryan had given me some good insight into my journey and I thanked him. He shared one last thing with me -

"Something big is coming, I can't tell you any more than that. But you'll know when it hits, just be ready."

With that, we set to parting ways; he was the one to drop me off at the airport on Thursday morning and as we said our final goodbyes, I felt no sadness at all. We both knew that we were over and that the chances of us ever meeting again were highly unlikely. I knew my decisions over the last few weeks had been correct and that I was journeying as I was meant to. I had closed a chapter in my life and had been more than willing to embrace life off the cliff edge. Packed as lightly as The Fool and with a completely open mind, I stepped onto a plane to Cape Town and off the cliff edge.

5

The Magician's Couch

When I woke up on my first morning in Cape Town, I was stretched out on one of the comfiest couches; rain was falling outside and I had a fluffy companion curled up on my lap. My good friend Dené had offered me a home for the time I would be there. His couch felt like a sanctuary. His home had a peaceful energy to it and a cat named Poppy. I'm a firm believer that animals are very perceptive - particularly cats. I believe that Poppy picked up two things about me: my journey to becoming a High Priestess and that I needed to heal. In the time I spent there, Poppy was always in my space. If she wasn't sleeping on my suitcase, she was on my lap. Some days she would even nap on my laptop. She was very comforting to have around. It was here in this space that I would have some very 'bizarre' experiences. Dené's space was where I learned to understand the 'magic' of the Magician and the art of manifesting. The Magician is pure action. The creator! His connection with the Divine and mastery of the elements proves his infinite power. He is a reminder that we should never limit ourselves because we are limitless. It was during my time in Cape Town that I learned that anything is possible.

My first week there was mostly consumed by my English teaching course. I had nothing scheduled for the second week and it was during this time that the Magician started to make his appearance. I recall a very distinct conversation with Dené where I got to witness and understand that he resonated highly with the Magician energy. We were chatting about our life's purposes and our gifts. We quickly discovered how similar we were. Dené summed it up perfectly: "I am you and you are me. We are one and the same." With me being a High Priestess and Dené being a Magician, this compatibility made perfect sense. More and more Magician energy emerged from the friends I was surrounded by at this time. This included Danny as well. I did a reading for Danny in that second week and sitting in the middle of his spread was the Magician card! What intrigued me was that the High Priestess was sitting off to the left of the Magician. Each Magician I encountered taught me a different lesson; each one broadening my level of wisdom and understanding. How this knowledge and wisdom was passed on varied from Magician to Magician. Some taught me through music and some through writing. Others taught me through bizarre, mind-bending conversations that seemed to just lay everything out for me in crystal clear clarity. Dené and I would have many a conversation about all these aspects of Magician magic. This included conversations with Danny as well another good friend, Les. The amount of wisdom that flowed so naturally from these three was so intense. The joke would become that I was stuck on the couch with the Magician sharing wisdom with me. Les was the first to re-spark the idea of the Collective Consciousness for me. It was something I had not thought about in years; not since my enlightening conversations with Jadie years earlier. Les shared some profound wisdom with me -

"You're not one with yourself if you're not one with everyone else."

This instantly made me think about how aligned I was with myself. Aligning was easy and being in alignment made living intuitively easy.

I know very specific aspects contributed to this alignment: my eating habits, living space, lack of attachments and my yoga practice that had become more consistent upon arriving in Cape Town. It then dawned on me that my entire journey up to that point had consisted of manifesting with the help of the Collective Consciousness. Everything I needed had been given to me. I realize I had never gone without. Someone would always step in to assist where I needed it. I also began to 'see' where I had stepped onto the path of others to do the same. I came to believe this alignment with the Collective was due to the high vibration level I was functioning on at that time. This included being 'in-tune' with everything – including being able to see my path so clearly from an intuitive perspective. This higher vibration wasn't just me, it seemed that everyone else around me was vibrating at the same level too. It consisted of a network of friends, family and strangers. Whether it was wisdom I needed or assistance in the material world, my needs were always being met. What amplified this insight for me was a very 'bizarre' experience I had with Dené and Les. It was another rainy day in Cape Town and Dené had lent me a book to browse through. It was a book on crystals and their properties. The Fire Agate page seemed to catch my attention. After reading through the properties for it, I thought to myself, "Wow I definitely would not mind having a Fire Agate in my life." I did not share this thought with anyone, however, and I soon forgot about it. A couple of days later, Les came to visit me and he had brought me a gift. It was a box with three crystals in it: two Clear Quartz points and a Fire Agate! With the sheer synchronicity of how everything had unfolded, I could not doubt the concept of a Collective Consciousness. I took a moment to then consider the lower vibrational aspect of the Collective. I understood that you possibly did not need to be 'vibing high' in order to be connected. You could still connect no matter what, but what you connect with is a frequency that aligns to yours. This would become a concept I would only fully understand over the years that followed.

I also found that I was excelling in all my projects for the English Teaching course I was doing. I was clear and focussed, and easily taking in the concepts I was learning. I then learned about the ability to share energy and how this shared energy can help you achieve just about anything. I was having another sleepless night, due to the amount of work required in the course; I was absorbing the content easily, but trust me, it's still a lot of work! Danny, who was still sitting on other side of the world from me, was around to chat to and I could feel his high vibrational energy, even with all that distance between us. It felt as if he was making things easier to get done. He was in a flow with his work and this flow seemed to reach out and connect with me. In true lemniscates[2] style, an infinite energy flow developed between us. It was an energy flow that spanned across oceans and thousands of miles. As a result, I inadvertently learned that there is unlimited energy that we all have access to, if we so choose. It is all about the frequency, and if you can catch someone else on the same vibe, you too can create an infinity loop of energy - just don't forget to ground when you're done or you could risk burnout! You don't need to hang onto all that energy though, there's always plenty more where that comes from. This experience with shared energy and the sheer infinity of it, I understood was a key aspect to Magician magic; which when used correctly and constructively, will never run out. I worked through the night with complete focus and finished everything I needed to.

Later that week, I had an experience that allowed me a much deeper understanding of the Magician. More importantly, I understood the purpose of the Magician energy and how it tied in with the High Priestess as well as the conservations that I had with Jadie over the years. Dené, who is a phenomenal trance DJ, was mixing music with Les as we enjoyed a chilled out evening at Dené's. We had smoked a joint and the trance music they were mixing and playing began affecting my third eye. I found my mind wandering off, as it does when I go into full intuitive mode. Suddenly everything made clear sense. It was at that moment that I understood the importance of the Magician - not just on my path but for the world as a whole. I realized that the world had all but snuffed out the core purpose of most Magicians walking the earth. This was the purpose of creation. They had been forced into boxes of conformity. The world had taken advantage of their seemingly infinite supply of energy and good-natured personalities for all the wrong reasons. As a result, the Magician had become very misunderstood and they have become a dying breed. My understanding is that this is why the world is in such turmoil at this time. We have disconnected ourselves from our own natural magic because the world has told us, "That does not fit in our box," or worse still: "That's not real!" The insight was further extended by the realization that these Magicians are starting to take their power back from the system that has enslaved them for so long. Magicians worldwide are reigniting their inner fires and stepping back into their creative selves. If Magicians can learn to guide themselves while harnessing the compatible High Priestess energy, they would once again find their natural gifts flourishing. In turn, the world will be able to recover its balance once more. One of the core lessons the High Priestess teaches us is to recognize our unrealized potential and how to tap into it. She holds the many secrets of life. These are secrets she is willing to share with the Magician. All one needs to do is listen.

Thus, as a High Priestess, all I needed to do was listen: listen to my own higher self; listen to my intuition. As these thoughts were rapidly moving through my mind when I was suddenly pulled back into reality as the three of us heard an odd noise. Out of the corner of my eye, I suddenly saw what looked like a winged shadow. The shadow seemed to 'shoot' into the corner above me and disappear. I looked at Dené and Les and by the looks on their faces, I knew they had seen it too. At the time, I suspected it was angelic energy of some sort and it felt very protective. Not entirely sure of what to make of what I had seen, I chose to store the experience for later. With my current state of flow, I was sure to have some insight soon enough on what had happened.

This was not the last time something bizarre occurred around Dené and Les. An evening a couple of weeks later, I was sitting outside with Dené, Les and a few other Magician energies. Dené came walking over to me from the inside. It looked like he was listening to some good beats. As he got closer I could hear music playing. I could make out the distinct sound of a baseline. I asked him what he was playing, assuming he had music playing on his phone. He smiled and carried on. However, when he stopped, the music stopped. I asked him what the hell had just happened? I knew without question that I had heard the music and that the music was coming from Dené. He simply shook his head and said, "I don't know." He had somehow created music out of thin air! 'Bizarre' was an understatement. Neither of us had understood what had just happened. That same night I encountered a Medicine Man who worked with a few different types of medicines. In particular, he worked with Lysergic Acid Diethylamide (commonly known as LSD or Acid). This is a highly misunderstood medicine and when used with the right intention and great respect, it has amazing benefits. The Medicine Man enlightened me. He explained how LSD works on a spiritual level, how it assists us on our journeys to transformation and enlightenment as well as many other insights. He offered me some and I took the moment to share with him my journey so far. I also told him about the mushroom micro-dosing I had done in Johannesburg as well as other times I had used plant medicine. He emphasized the need to use these plants and medicines correctly and with great respect; that they were put on this Earth to be utilized responsibly. I walked away from that conversation with a deeper understanding and respect and a far more open mind about hallucinogenic and plant medicine. This powerful open share around the medicinal uses of LSD would come into play later in my path as a trip to the future.

My time in Cape Town was coming to an end, plans to leave for Vietnam were being finalized with Ollie and his girlfriend Tracy and that feeling of being in the flow was intense. I did notice tension between Ollie and Tracy and noted that Dené had seen it as well.

"Looks a bit tense there. You going to manage living with them in a new country?" Dené enquired.

"I think I'll manage, I'm in such a good space right now. If it does get too intense I'll head out on my own. I'll be fine no matter what," I replied with certainty. Little did I know I would soon have my first lesson in the importance of sacred space and how the impact of energies within my living environment would have a massive effect on me. This would become a lesson I would repeat a few times; but where I was at the time, I did not feel anything could move me from my flow and alignment.

Shortly before departing Cape Town, I received what I believe was the confirmation of that mysterious energy we had experienced a few nights previously. I was having a conversation with my dad's younger sister, Bev. She expressed that she had a strange question to ask me. It involved a dream about needing to speak to her father (my paternal Grandfather) which had never happened to her before. For about two weeks she felt unable to communicate with him. She then asked me if this had anything to do with my leaving South Africa. She explained, that for the first time since losing her dad, she had a deep need to connect with him. At the same time, I kept coming into her mind during the day. As I listened to her, I got an incredibly 'good' feeling. For me, it was like he was going to be looking after me on my new journey and

Bev was the confirmation that I was looking for. I knew I was going to be okay. My Grandfather would be acting as a guide and I knew that he had been a very protective and loving man when on Earth. It felt right that he would do something like that, especially on a life-changing journey. I believed it was my Grandfather that had appeared in Dené's room that night. I had spoken to my father about him and I learned that he was incredibly protective of his family. The more I chatted to my dad about him, the more I could see that he resonated with the Magician energy. Instinctively, I could feel where a good portion of my natural gifts had come from - most specifically with my gift of healing.

My last couple of days in Cape Town were spent in a positive head-space as I marveled over all the vast and unexpected knowledge I had gained. My flight to Vietnam would be the first time I would ever leave South Africa. I had no fear or worry, though. The wisdom I had been given was immense and everything I needed was provided for. I was ready to tackle the next stage of my journey. My faith was high, I felt strong and my path was clear. I stepped onto a plane to Hanoi, Vietnam and smack bang into my Shadow Self.

6

The Shadow Rises

When one is 'flying high' on the energy of being in alignment, it is crucial that they remember to keep one foot on the ground at all times. This ensures that if one is knocked out of alignment, the blow does not send them catapulting back towards the earth at breakneck speed. Instead, they should be able to keep a firm footing as they work towards restoring equilibrium once more.

Ollie, Tracy and I arrived a day and half later in the city of Hanoi. I stepped off the plane tired, but in full alignment and with a deep sense of excitement for what could possibly lay ahead. Ollie and Tracy however, stepped off exhausted and feeling stressed out. The tension between them had not subsided much since leaving. Every decision I made in my first few days there was intuitive. This included my decision to head to the city of Da Nang as soon as I could. Something about Da Nang called to me. It was all about timing. I had found myself what seemed to be a nice little job teaching English at a kindergarten. I had also been offered a bed to sleep on for a change. The three of us had moved in to stay with a mutual friend of Ollie and Tracy for the first month and a half. Their friend had kindly offered to share her room and bed with me - something I was more than grateful to receive. This was short-lived, however. The three of them had gone out for lunch together in those first few days. When they returned, I was told that the "friend" needed her space and it would be better if I slept on the couch. I suddenly felt like a bit of an outcast. The welcoming energy I had arrived to was pulled out from under me and my alignment began slipping.

Unable to find a solid footing, things began to spiral downwards from there. I could not make heads or tails of why I was struggling to find alignment again. Why was I feeling so depressed? At the time I believed it was just the stress of being in a new country, not having much of a support structure from the friends I had traveled with and the lack of sleep from adjusting to a new time zone. Factors I had not taken into consideration, was the difficulty of being a vegan in a country like Vietnam - where that kind of lifestyle is not a part of the culture; I also did not realize that the continuous days of overcast weather were not in fact cloudy days, but a layer of pollution that hung over the city of Hanoi frequently. As my diet, exercise and yoga practice dwindled quickly, my misalignment worsened and depression set in. With Ollie and Tracy dealing with their own adjustments and relationship tensions, I began to pull away from them and internalize everything I had going on. Danny was still very much a big part of my life, but with him being thousands of miles away in another country, his long-distance support did not do much to help me. I found a small slither of alignment when I learned that Tarot was greatly popular with the expat community, but no matter how busy my readings were, my alignment was too far out for me to find stability. My originally perceived 'nice' little teaching job had proven to be quite the opposite and I found myself dreading the days I would need to be teaching. Teaching English was pushing me even further out of alignment. Daily, I had found myself struggling to wrap my head around the whole teaching thing. Every day, I came home exhausted after just two hours of teaching. Teaching English was just not my thing. As out of alignment as I was, I was still able to realize that a Spiritual Guide and Teacher is what I was meant to be, not an English teacher. I had this strong urge to just get away from everything and the city of Da Nang still called out to me as strongly as ever.

Initially, the friend we were staying with offered to come to Da Nang with me. We appeared to have developed a bond despite my being relocated to the couch; but I felt a sense of connection with her. This helped to alleviate the depression quite a bit. I had someone I could talk to. We chatted about Da Nang regularly and discussed different options, but we never seemed to get a solid plan sorted out together. She often brought up worries and concerns - most of which seemed to be around me: whether I would go to Da Nang and stay there with her or whether I would leave after a short time. I had been chatting to Danny quite a lot about me flying over to Australia to spend a couple of weeks with him so we could finally meet in person. It was also so we could see where our strange relationship was heading. My new-found friend in Vietnam understood that I was keen to fly to Australia to meet Danny. At the time she appeared to be comfortable about this. Things soon soured one night when I found myself having a conversation with her over dinner. I suddenly felt personally attacked as she questioned me about my intentions. She told me I was living in a bubble. She said she was worried I would go to Australia and just never come back. My friend was questioning my plans and motives. Out of the blue, she asked, "Why did you come to Vietnam?" This question hit me like a ton of bricks. Why had I come to Vietnam? It seemed I had lost my way. My head felt clouded. I struggled to make decisions and be practical about life. I excused myself from the table to reach out to Danny. I needed to clear my head. I needed to have some clear direction again. I told him what had happened over dinner. He asked me what I wanted to do. I told him that I knew I didn't want to teach English. I told him that I wanted to do my work as a Spiritual Guide and Teacher. I was very clear about my mission and knew that I wanted to be what I was meant to be. I also told him that I wanted to be with him. Our love for one another had grown quickly and intensely over the weeks. I found there were only two things in life I was certain about. My purpose, and being with him. He listened to everything and then told me to go and sort out a plane ticket to Australia, which he would pay for. We agreed that I would come across and spend three months with him and we could see where life took us from there. I felt like I had some direction again and my stresses seemed to settle.

My new friend was annoyed, to say the least, that I had changed my plans. I tried to explain to her that it was her constant indecision and the questions she fired at me a few nights back, which helped me make my decision. It felt like a pointless conversation, as she spoke over me and would not listen to what I had to say. Yet again I found myself stepping back into a submissive role instead of standing my ground. As much as I had some clear direction again, my inner fire was dimmed and my alignment was far off. Fortunately, the courage to stay on track with my new direction did stay with me. Perhaps my friend's wishy-washy plans were exactly what I needed to get myself back onto my path. If one is not clear on the direction of the path, the Universe will nudge them. As much as I was correct on my path regarding my purpose as a Guide and Teacher, my clouded judgment had not allowed me to see that my other decision was a not a path-based one, but rather a source of escape. I would need to tumble down a bit further before this would become clear.

My plan was to resign from my English teaching job in a few weeks' time and then head to Da Nang for a bit to see why this city called to me so much. From there I would fly out to Australia. I went to see the travel agent that handled all my flight bookings a couple of days later.

She booked my ticket to Da Nang and my ticket to Australia. She did warn me though, that it was a good idea to do my visa application for Australia quite soon as they could be fairly sticky and the process could take a while. I shared the good news with Danny and told him that everything was booked. He was delighted. I now needed to do my visa application, which I started shortly after that. As I filled the application in, I got to the question of how I planned to support my stay while there. I hit a brick wall. I had been working with only cash for the last few weeks and essentially my bank account was empty. The Australian authorities would not grant me my visa in this situation. Danny assured me everything would be fine and that he would sponsor my trip there. The authorities should have been happy with that, but something did not sit right within me. The rest of the fate of my application rested with Danny. I found myself constantly feeling anxious about my visa application. I was worried it wouldn't be approved and my worry felt more like a knowing. I pushed this feeling aside and tried to find my alignment again, instead my depression amplified and I found myself feeling a sense of detachment from Danny. In that space, I felt alone, isolated and very insecure. So much was out of my control. My frustration levels soared as I realized I had no control over certain aspects of my immediate future. I kept questioning myself, "Why am I struggling so much? Are these trust issues, I'm having?" I questioned my environmental factors to see if they were perhaps the reason for me feeling so low. Hanoi is one of the most polluted cities in the world. Could that have been affecting my energy levels and bringing me down? Had my depressed state suddenly manifested into the physical? A few days later I woke up with the most intense physical pain. I had never experienced pain like that before. My whole body ached. I was immobilized for an entire day. I spent most of the day passed out from the pain. I also had a full-blown sinus and chest infection, to top the agony of it all. The sinus issue had started the day before. Also, I found myself alone, having to take care of myself, as everyone was out for most of the day. I had to psyche myself up to have enough energy to walk a couple of steps into the kitchen so I could eat something. I had not been this sick in years. Somehow though, by the grace of the Universe I was fine the next day. My anxiety and depression however, continued to spiral as I awaited news on my visa application.

Every sign pointed to Australia. This often happened many times a day. The Universe had spoken so loudly to me in the last couple of months and I believed that this was where I was meant to go next. Was I misunderstanding the signs? Was I reading them backwards? Thus far, the entire process had been a smooth one and I had been given so much and more. I had kept my faith and stood strong in it. Even when times felt uncertain and stressful I had maintained my balance and alignment. The cliffs I had leaped off were many, not just one, so why was I feeling so stressed about this? There was a lot on the line for me. I was essentially giving up my little bit of stability I had created for myself to venture in another direction. Where I went next would determine a lot for me. I was also coming to the tail end of my [3]Saturn Return. This was a big deal for me. It was my Strength card test. One has to learn to master the self and the lessons of the Chariot card as they will be tested by the next card - Strength. I did feel I had succeeded in the lessons of the Chariot and that I had mastered myself. The question was - could I remain strong in that? I did feel like I knew who and what I was. The intuitive work I had been doing had thrived so quickly and beautifully in Vietnam, that I felt I had received clarity on this. Yet I continued to feel so stressed and negative towards the challenge - the challenge of trusting the signs and heading to Australia. Yet something still screamed at me that something was not right. I pushed that to one side and told myself it was just the fear talking and that I needed to find my faith again.

A couple of days later, I had a conversation with Ollie and Tracy that helped to pull me out of the heavy depression. Tracy asked me about my plans, which I shared with them. Ollie then asked me directly if I had anything else to say. The close bond I shared with them made me realize he had picked up on something more. I blurted out the words, "I'm fucking depressed." The can of worms was open and I found myself chatting to them about everything that had happened. I explained to them that I had come to Vietnam because I felt I had work to do there as a Guide and Teacher. This included work on myself as well, but I just did not understand fully what that work was. The Tarot would once again be my guide as I discovered a Tarot Cafe in the heart of Hanoi.

I had never come across the concept of a Tarot Cafe before, but this was apparently something that was hugely popular for the people of Vietnam. Not knowing exactly what I would find, or if the locals at the Cafe even spoke English, I messaged beforehand and within a short time I had a response back from a well-spoken Vietnamese woman. She explained what the cafe was about and that her older sister did most of the readings there. She then mentioned that it was also a space where eager Tarot students could learn to master their craft. To say I was intrigued was an understatement! I had arranged to go and explore this cafe a few days later and see what a reading in Vietnam would be like. I arrived to a semi-full cafe and a group of local readers just as eager to meet me, a foreigner who shared the same craft as them. I was instantly made to feel welcome by a lady named Tú Annh, who I quickly learned was the owner of the cafe and would be doing my reading for me. Before we settled in to her pulling cards for me, I spent some time chatting and answering questions from her and the other readers. I had hundreds of questions as well. It was my first experience with readers from another culture and country. Once done with the millions of questions and realizing just how similar we all were, Tú Annh pulled a single card for me. It was the card of Faith. She explained to me my need to trust my process and that everything would work out as it needed to. The card resonated strongly, particularly because I had been lacking in and questioning my faith quite a lot recently. She asked if I needed her to look into anything else for me, but I felt my eyes drawn instead to a set of cards. Another reader who went by the nickname 'The Joker' caught where I was looking and said, "That set suits you." A mischievous smile spreading across his face. I trusted his judgment and purchased my set of cards. Something about him resonated with me and I knew he needed to read for me next, but the timing was not right. I left the Tarot Cafe feeling far more confident about everything and I had somehow managed to switch off that voice in my head that kept telling me something was wrong.

A few days later, 'The Joker', whose name I had learned was actually Vũ, messaged me to see if I would be interested in doing a reading exchange with him. I knew without question that I needed to go. I met him the next day for coffee and a reading that would sit with me for months to come. Vũ touched on a few things that day, but one very specific aspect stood out for me. "You are happy, but you are also empty on the inside." The word 'empty' hit me hard and I turned my attention inwards for a moment to see why. I had no immediate answer, but I just couldn't shake what he told me. We finished off our coffees and readings, I thanked him and left still feeling the impact of his words. I had only a few days left in Hanoi - I was once again at the tail end of a journey, but this time I felt unsettled and was questioning the emptiness. All I could do was follow the process that was unfolding and see what it would bring to me. I felt a deep longing for home. Not for South Africa, but a longing for sanctuary. It was what I had originally hoped I was heading for. A couple of days later I left Hanoi, for Da Nang, with my few worldly possessions and what little bit of faith I could muster. I once again stepped onto a plane and descended even further down to meet my Shadow head-on as it questioned me on my levels of faith.

7

Questions of Faith

One of the most liberating and fantastical ways to live is to live on pure faith. It can however, also be the most frightening way to live if one is out of alignment and unable to interpret their intuition correctly. Living on pure faith requires a level of trust that words simply cannot depict! In the instance of misalignment, one can often feel out of control, ungrounded and unclear of what direction is correct for them. A side effect of this, is that one's intuition needs to speak a lot louder in order to be heard and this loudness can often be misconstrued as intense feelings of anxiety and depression. In regard to shadow work and living on pure faith, one can find the process therapeutic and growth-filled. That being said, if alignment is out of place, shadow work can be frightening and confusing - it can leave one questioning many things, particularly their faith - and can exacerbate the feelings of anxiety and depression.

My state of mind in Da Nang was such that it is difficult for me to recall the time frame in which the following all happened. On one of those mornings, I woke up questioning what I was even doing in Da Nang. I felt I had lost the plot. In Hanoi, I had left friends behind and I had let go of the little bit of stability I had built there. So I questioned my reasons for coming to Da Nang even though it had felt like the right thing to do at the time - the right thing as I was doing it mostly on 'gut feel' and intuition. The last thing I had wanted was for it to scare the shit out of me. Here too, I again felt out of my comfort zone and was terrified about whether I would have my needs met. But I realized the Universe had not let me down thus far. Perhaps Da Nang was a big test of my faith - faith in myself and my purpose. Faith that I would be looked after. Perhaps Da Nang was the place where I would learn to ask for help where needed. I started to crave stability and structure. I wanted to wake up in a comfortable space with peace of mind that I was going to be 'okay'. Choosing to live life by throwing caution to the wind was a very freeing place to live in, but it was also terrifying at the same time. I had chosen to live life by being the change I wanted to see in the world. I was walking my talk. Through my readings, I had observed how people had become so stuck and stagnant in their routines. I had met numerous clients that had incredible gifts and life purposes. The majority of them were too scared to step out of their comfort zones and live to their full potential. I was doing what I did partly because I wanted to show the world that you're never stuck unless you choose to be. It is only by having faith in yourself that you find the most beautiful way to live. I was struggling with this! I knew that we are all more than capable of achieving great things and that we can all manifest the life we choose to live. So many people settle for mediocrity because it's safer, more comfortable and easier, yet people wake up every day feeling unfulfilled and unsatisfied with life. I knew this to be true not only from my clients but also from my own experiences that had been unfolding. A mediocre life was not what I wanted yet at the same time I craved the perceived stability that a mediocre life could give me - a life where I would know each and every day that I would wake up and have my needs meet; my basic needs of food, water and shelter. I needed to feel stable, but I also did not want to settle back into the comfort of what seemed safer. My challenge was to find the middle ground, the balance - if there even was one?

I reflected on the reading I had with Vũ. He recognized that I was happy with life but empty on the inside. That struck a deep chord within me for two reasons. The first was that what he had said felt right and the second reason was that I did not understand it. How could I feel so full and content on one hand but feel empty at the same time? Perhaps it was from this emptiness that the depression and anxiety had emerged? Was it being thrown so far out of my comfort zone that had done it? Either way, I did not fully understand the emptiness he spoke about. I questioned whether I had truly dealt with everything that had happened in the past few months. The questions went further. Had I let go of the life I had left behind? I had felt so much lighter when I left Ryan. Every time I told someone about my story, however, their instant response was "I'm so sorry to hear that, I hope you're okay." I wondered whether it was wrong that I felt okay? Having had no feelings of loss or regret, I felt more than okay. Perhaps I was missing something? Somehow the world seemed insistent that I feel a certain way - but I didn't. I questioned if I was perhaps blocking out emotions I did not want to face. At the same time, I acknowledged the many unanswered questions I still had. Once again, I felt stuck! A part of me knew I could trust and rely on myself and my faith in the Universe to look after me. I did not question that part at all as my experiences over the months had proven this to be true. At the same time, I felt like I was not seeing or understanding something. Perhaps insight from an outside perspective was what was required? Who would I ask though? What would I ask? In some ways, it only felt like I was scratching the surface of my journey. Yet in other ways, I felt I had come so far. Perhaps I was too scared to look deeper. Was I in denial?

The days that followed, kept me 'swinging' between being okay with everything and huge depressive lows. It was becoming more apparent that the emptiness Vũ had told me about was a part of my depression. I desperately wanted to understand what the root cause was. The lows seemed to hit when I was feeling more out of my comfort zone than usual. Also, I was still waiting to hear about my visa for Australia. Danny had finally got round to finishing his side of my application and it was now a waiting game. A lot of uncertainty surrounded my future. Living intuitively and going with the flow had become quite a challenge for me. Were insecurities sparking my depression, were they a part of the emptiness? It was no easy task having to deal with all this at the same time. My journey was meant to be one of growth. It was me stepping fully into who I am and who I am meant to be. It also related to my place in the world. I was mindful of the fact that to teach and help people globally, it was required that I learn and grow as well. At the same time, I was struggling more and more with homesickness and depression. In other ways, I understood that dealing with these challenges in a simple, practical manner and keeping the self-awareness going would assist in making the process much simpler for me. The lack of security about getting my Australian visa was huge in the equation, however. The thought of staying in Vietnam any longer than I needed to hung heavily over me. As much as Vietnam had been a good experience and had been very kind to me, I was ready to leave. Then I started having anxiety attacks - something I had not had in years. Thoughts of my visa being declined and being stuck in a foreign country were becoming debilitating. At the same time, I realized I had no home to go back to should my visa be declined. This realization only amplified my anxiety. My craving for stability and structure grew daily. I also realized how much I hated the uncertainty that surrounded my life. I felt I had no choice but to trust that everything would work out. I just wanted to sleep my days away until I knew what was happening. The depression had become a daily routine. It was extremely difficult to pull myself out of it as each day passed. I felt incredibly alone.

Everyone else around me was carrying on with life as usual while I sat alone feeling very stuck. I still struggled with finding a specific reason as to why. What I did know was that Da Nang had called my soul. What I did not understand fully was what I was dealing with internally there. I just wanted the feelings to go away. I wanted to bury my head in the proverbial sand and be happy and content. I did not want to deal with depression and anxiety. I did not want to deal with uncertainty and instability. There had been enough of that in my life that I had dealt with already. At another level, I knew that one cannot expect to step out of a stagnant comfort zone and not have any repercussions.

I then met Nga, the owner of the Home Stay I was staying at in Da Nang. We began to spend a lot of time together. Our conversations were spiritually enlightening. She would share knowledge and Buddhist ways with me and I shared my knowledge and Tarot with her. It was a beautiful exchange and my depression and anxiety began to ease a little. When I read her cards for her, she was enthralled with what I had told her. I soon found myself becoming popular with locals and travellers alike. It seemed like everyone wanted a reading from me. My time suddenly had become consumed with readings and for a short time, I enjoyed reading the Tarot again, as I had not done any readings since leaving Hanoi. My low levels of energy, however, prevented me from asking for an exchange of some form. Then the consistent lack of energy exchange started to take its toll on me. There always needs to be an exchange of energy in an encounter, I knew this! Some people had done these energy exchanges with me in the form of dinner or a donation. The majority of the readings, however, had no exchange at all. I started to feel constantly exhausted and the depression slowly gained momentum once more. I began experiencing the full repercussions of this. My old habit of 'people-pleasing' and becoming submissive took hold. I stepped out of my power completely and the fire within burnt low. I had nothing left to give to anyone or myself and I began retreating within.

The eternal optimism of Danny during this time was a help, though. He felt secure in the knowledge that I would get my visa and all would go ahead as planned. This gave me some light at the end of the tunnel. However, the wait for my visa put me back into feeling like I was hanging in limbo and with each passing day, I felt more and more certain that it would not be approved. Was it my depression making me pessimistic or was it my intuitive knowing that it would not happen? I was no longer able to tell the difference between fear and intuition. I then began to feel disconnected from Danny - it felt like he would not understand what I was going through. The constant anxiety I lived with grew with each passing day and I felt more and more disconnected from Danny. This did not help the feeling of isolation at all. To me, we were on two completely different planets at this stage. In a sense we were. This was further reinforced when one day we were chatting via messages and I was deeply upset. He did not pick up a thing - the one person who in all my years was able to read me clearly. I also realized that I was keeping a lot of the anxiety and depression from him. It resulted in me sliding even further back into old habits and internalizing my stuff instead of me being open with him about it. My 'people-pleasing' side did not want to burden him with what was happening, even though I knew that he would give me uphill about keeping this stuff from him. This holding back was amplified by the fact that I did not fully understand what was happening to me. I was desperate to get to the bottom of my anxiety and depression as well as get the wait for the visa over with. All I desperately wanted was to be centred again. To get back into that flow space I was in only a few weeks previously. My solitude in Da Nang was the space that I was given to work through the stuff I needed to. The question was - what was

I meant to be working through? I felt like I was going in circles and just not seeing a way out or forward.

I then began pulling everything apart: myself, my faith, my purpose, my beliefs and teachings, and the strange relationship I had developed with Danny. Everything about our relationship had felt correct, but something was screaming at me that nothing was okay or correct. My flight for Australia, which we had booked over month previously, was due to leave the following week. I had been so convinced when I booked my flights that everything would land in place in time, just as it had done when I left Ryan. I did not have any other plans in place in case my visa was delayed, or worse, declined. This triggered me questioning my connection and relationship with Danny even further. Had I been living in a 'dream world'? Was I avoiding reality? At another level, I knew I would be able to make it back home if the visa was declined. Thereafter I had no clue. I had nothing but the possessions I was travelling with. Perhaps I had thrown a little too much caution to the wind? I started to feel like an irresponsible adult. But everything had happened so smoothly and the doors had opened just as I needed them to. I felt I had messed up completely. My relationship with Ryan had to be ended and I felt comfortable with that knowledge. However, taking myself off to a foreign country, going broke in the process and making impulsive decisions (decisions I believed to be intuitive at the time) were now being questioned by me. I doubted what I had done. The realization that I was more than likely going to land up back in South Africa and not get to Australia at all, was sinking in fast. I was very aware I had nothing to go back to. My life would have to be built up again from nothing. By this time, I had enough money left to buy food for the remainder of my time in Da Nang, as well as to pay for the remainder of my accommodation. Beyond that I had nothing. My faith in living intuitively was lost. I questioned if there was even such a thing. I was faced with a very harsh reality. I felt horribly let down and very disappointed in myself. My faith in my core beliefs was truly lost. I felt miles off from the journey I had started weeks before. Never at any stage during this journey, did the thought occur to me that I would be in this position - broken, sad and completely alone. From one extreme to the other, I felt shattered. They say we create our realities and my reality was harsh. The realization that South Africa was on the cards was a real possibility that I faced now. Somehow, I found the strength and prayed that the Universe would be kind and help me in building my life again. Yet at the same time, I lacked the power of my faith to believe this.

For two days I put myself to bed. It was a space in which I felt catatonic. I never left my room. I either slept or cried. On the evening of the second day, desperate for some external insight, I contacted Leo to ask for a reading. The message was loud and clear, I needed to work on myself. This meant that I had to decide what I wanted to keep in my life and what I was prepared to let go of. Leo expressed how I was undervaluing myself in my work. She said I was selling myself short and thus settling for less. A renewal of respect for my heritage - embracing and loving it - was called for. She also told me that there were big decisions to be made around Danny. This included our relationship, as well as going to Australia. All the answers I needed would come from looking within - I had been looking without. As a result, this blurred the lines and clouded the clarity I might have gotten had I been able to see the situation for what it was. My inner voice had to be heard by me. Leo felt that Danny was pivotal in 'helping' me with stepping into my power. I was just as pivotal for him to step into his full power. Past assisting one another, however, she could only tell me that decisions needed to be made. She advised that a time out was called for urgently for me to go within and cast aside the external factors that I was allowing to influence me. With the pressure of the time constraints I was under, I needed to make the most with what I had. This included owning my power once again, becoming independent, as well as the decision about going to Australia. It all lay with me. The process was about me becoming who I am. Once again I had forgotten how much power I had and realized I had stepped right out of it. Leo said that there was a relationship on the cards for me. The question was for me to decide what I wanted. Perhaps I was merely looking for something better than what I had with Ryan. She also felt that the whole process that was unfolding was actually me transforming into who I was. The flip side of the coin was that the person on the other side (me) was well aware of her worth and her power. This was the purpose of my journey. A purpose, driven by experiences, that would lead me back to finding my true authentic self, clear in who I am and what I wanted. Having gotten lost in my relationship with Ryan, I had forgotten who I was. Now was the time for me to find my true self again, after ten years. I realized I had never actually been fully independent before. It was a co-dependent relationship and I had known nothing else before this time. Leo had left me with some great insight and food for thought. I felt I knew what I needed to do next. A change in scenery was my first step. I decided that if my visa was delayed and I needed to change my flight date, I would spend the remainder of my time in Vietnam in a town called Hoi An. I felt that my time in Da Nang was done and that I would not gain anything further from being there. I also wanted to go where no one knew me or would ask me for a Tarot reading. I needed my sole focus to be on me - this I knew intuitively. I knew that I would be able to ask myself some of the serious questions that I was required to for my growth. I knew it would also facilitate me in finding my fire again. And it would allow me to step back fully onto my path - a path where I could find my balance and self-worth, by not selling myself short. I had not minded doing the readings for free, however, the need for an energy exchange was vital for my wellbeing. It was an important aspect in taking back my power again.

I chose to open up to Danny about my fears and concerns about my visa being delayed. I also told him that I was going to be broke in a few days. Danny lovingly responded, instantly, that I must not worry, that he had me and would look out for me. He assured me I was not alone and that he respected the work and space I needed for myself. Of course, I felt better in the knowledge that I had received support and assistance. I was starting to see a different dynamic to our relationship. I understood that when my energy levels were so low it was almost impossible for him to pick up my feelings properly. It was a rehash, yet again, of everything that I had been through thus far. I was supposed to be flying out to Australia in four days. My visa had still not arrived. Danny and I had no choice but to change my flight date. He was still very optimistic that my visa would come through. I, however, still sat with the anxiety about it. I spent my last few days in Da Nang taking it easy on myself. I spent most of the time on my own, but this time it was for introspection. I did not isolate myself due to depression this time. I left the Home Stay in a better headspace and I felt ready to tackle the next stage. I felt ready to start answering those pivotal questions. I felt like I had been given a second chance to work through my stuff and make sense of it. I needed to use my second chance wisely. A few days later I left for Hoi An.

8

Surviving in Limbo

I arrived in Hoi An broke (Danny's money had not yet cleared) and soaked to the bone from the monsoon rains! The taxis and buses I needed cost way more than I had anticipated and took most of the last bit of money I had. My anxiety was looming! With a map in hand, I anxiously ventured out from my new Home Stay to try and find something to eat with the last bit of cash I had. On the sidewalk I found an elderly woman selling food. I attempted to communicate with her - despite the language barrier - as to how much her cheapest container of food would be. She simply smiled at me and carried on cooking. After a few minutes, she presented me with some food and showed me how much it was. I had less than half of the amount I needed to pay her. I then showed her how much I had. Still smiling, she took what I had and handed me my food and showed me on my way. What a blessing! I continued to receive more blessings as the next day the owners of the Home Stay invited me to lunch and dinner. The Universe seemed to be looking after me once more. I might have been having a hard time spiritually speaking, but the Universe still ensured I was being fed! I had found a roof over my head and I knew that I would have access to my money in a day or two. My focus needed to be kept on the spiritual task at hand: my transformation. I needed to maintain my faith. All my tests had come from the spiritual aspect of my existence. After all, The Fool does not just simply step off the cliff and expect his venture to be without challenge! He will be challenged every time until he becomes what he is meant to be. I was beginning to see that in order to embrace my feminine aspect, restore my self-worth and self-respect, I needed to be as the High Priestess and embrace the darker aspects of myself. Without achieving that, there could be no light. That was my challenge as the Queen of Cups. All of the above tied very strongly into the path I was walking. I felt I was stepping back onto my right path again. Although I would not emerge from this unscathed, I would come out stronger even if I was a little battered and bruised. After all, one of my purposes is to help drive the world forward. This required me to be the change I wanted to see in the world - a world in which people lived without fear and doubt; and they could. People being able to manifest what they needed for themselves and live in full faith. This meant that I needed to start living in the moment. One of the core Buddhist beliefs is that a truly fulfilling life can only be lived while being in the present moment. If we do that, we will stop worrying about the things that are out of our control and only focus on what is in our control. And I needed to live in that moment. It is in this moment right here, right now that we have full knowledge of where we are and what we can or can't do about it. Just for today, be present - now is all you have. All of these understandings occurred to me in an intuitive rush. I could hear my intuition once again! It was so good to hear my inner voice so clearly. My first two days in Hoi An taught me an invaluable lesson. Faith is rooted in learning that it is okay to ask for help when needed. Always trust and have faith that everything will be okay and that everything will work out as needed. Living in faith doesn't mean just sitting around in idleness waiting for stuff to arrive at your door. You need to be proactive, assist the process and open doors to allow the assistance you need to come through. Asking for help is not a sign of weakness. It takes great strength and courage to ask for that help. Now was the time for me to ask the most important questions: who am I, what am I and what did I want?

While doing my English Teaching course in Cape Town, South Africa, I had made friends with another student in my class, Chené, who had since taken up a teaching post in Thailand. From the time we first met, we had found a great number of similarities within our paths. I began chatting with her regularly. My understanding that we need to reach out and connect with others as a vital part of the transformation process, spearheaded this. It was a relief to chat to someone who understood what I was going through. I was also in regular communication with Leo. Our shared High Priestess energy made it ideal for us to chat and I received a lot of support from her. One day Chene happened to share an interesting video with me. A Numerologist had done a general reading which was about December being a Number Three month. December had just started and so it caught my attention. The Numerologist spoke about it being the month to visualize what one wanted and who they wanted to be. This tied in perfectly with the questions I was working through. There was constant rain in Hoi An at this time and on a symbolic level, it was a great sign of things being 'cleared and washed away'. A sign of release! Tracy had reminded me a few days earlier that a new moon was coming up and she mentioned that it was a time for shedding and letting go. The video, the rain and my conversation with Tracy had clarified that you are always where you are meant to be. I knew on a higher level that from here, I could go anywhere I wanted to. It all came down to knowing what you want and being clear about it. The time for building my High Priestess was now. It was also the time to build the life I wanted to live. This would require reflection and meditation to attain it. Keeping the focus on this knowledge in my mind, my questions started to be answered. The first question I worked through was: "Who am I?" This was one question

I struggled with the most. I decided to try and simplify it. I knew I was kind and compassionate with a tendency to love a little too deeply. I also could be both an introvert and an extrovert. Being highly sensitive, I did not always have a filter. My filter had improved over the years, though and I had become more understanding of others. I was highly intuitive, but I did not always listen to it - much to my own detriment at times. I got angry and resentful if I was taken for granted or my good nature was abused. I found it hard to say no and tended to find myself in situations where people were trying to take advantage of me. There was a tendency to be a bit of a doormat. It had always been a challenge that I had worked on. In Vietnam, I had found myself reverting to these old habits often and as a result, I had become very submissive again and was very easy to walk over. This was the root of my depression. When I used to suffer heavy depression, it was when I was a big pushover, felt undervalued and particularly when I was not in alignment with myself. I found that when I stood in my strength, I was more balanced and the depression was far less. It would go away altogether. While reflecting on these aspects of myself, I recalled a situation I had found myself in a few days earlier. Hoi An is well known for its tailor shops. Vast numbers of them line the streets of the small town. The owner of one of these shops had stopped me on a daily walk I was taking and asked if I would be interested in purchasing some custom-made clothes. I felt I had given her a clear "no thank you", as I could not have any more luggage than I already had. Her response was, "Just come and have a look and see where my shop is and if you do want anything you can come back." I found myself agreeing, going into a submissive mode and could not find the strength to say no again. After arriving at her shop, I suddenly found myself picking out styles and material. What had just happened? Without realizing it at the time, I had handed my power over to her so quickly. Instead of just simply standing my ground and being firm on my no, I quietly acquiesced and took a step backwards. The need to learn to resolutely say no and be strong in that was very important for my emotional and spiritual health. When I allowed myself to be submissive and walked over, it was detrimental to me in every way. My energy levels would plummet and depression and anxiety would take over. I would lose all sense of myself and my needs.

With all this reflective work going on, I soon realized that my need for a relationship was a need for a safety blanket of sorts for when I stepped into the submissive role. Someone else could be my strength because I was weak. It was interesting to me that Ryan had never stood up for me in our ten years together. As a result, I was either left in submissive mode or left to sort out any issues on my own. As I was heading into another possible relationship with Danny, I was vitally aware that I did not want to rely on my partner to be the assertive one and that I wanted to be able to stand up for myself. We all want a partner that has our back, but I did not want to be a doormat that needed someone else to be my strength. It was not truly who I was. I found that I still had deep issues around self-worth. I knew that I looked for outside affirmation to make me feel good about myself. After all, I knew I was worthy, as is everyone on this earth, but maintaining that knowing was a challenge. Working backwards, I wanted to pinpoint the origin of my self-worth and submissive issues. My starting point was about who I wanted to be. I wanted to be strong, independent, focused and living my purpose. I am after all a Spiritual Guide and Teacher and this included the High Priestess energy. My goal was to be the best Spiritual Guide and Teacher I could be and live the words I spoke and taught. As I worked through this question, I found that for years I had dispensed wisdom that I had not been following myself. After all, is a teacher not supposed to practice what they teach? Living in truth and honesty, I could be the best version of myself. This would include putting my energy into worthwhile ventures and not waste it on meaningless ones: including relationships with other people. Where and who was I putting my energy into? I wanted to step fully into my power as High Priestess. My experiences with my past relationships triggered the questions. My trust issues were deeply rooted in my experience with Ryan, other relationships and even before that. Ryan would let me down and disappoint me frequently. Many others in my life had done this as well. This exacerbated the trust issues I already had. My intuition was talking to me and telling me something else was not right as well - I often misinterpreted and confused intuitive feelings with trust issues. I felt the overall lesson was to trust my intuition and myself more. If unsure, it would require me to look deeper at whether I was genuinely picking up something or if it was more insecurities coming to the surface. Quiet contemplation would be required before I acted. In that way, the inner voice would not be drowned out by the insecurities. The Vietnamese culture lives in such divine peace. Even when the mind with its thoughts dominates, they seem to have an ability to not allow those thoughts to control them. I found I had developed a lot of respect for this aspect of the Vietnamese people. It was this aspect that I desired to bring into my daily life.

As I reflected on earlier relationships as well, I found that all of them had left me feeling unworthy and with incredibly low self-esteem. I had continually fed my energy into others who were simply just black holes; draining my life force, extinguishing my inner fire. They would leave me feeling inadequate, low and not good enough. I questioned why I kept having these kinds of feelings and relationships. The answer was the realization that I had some serious self-esteem and self-value issues. They were closely linked to my levels of courage and strength and I so desperately sought stability in those aspects of myself. The next question about where I wanted to go was simple to answer: it was without a doubt Australia The answer to how long I wanted to be there, I felt I would only answer when I was in that space. But that nagging voice inside questioned if this was truly where I wanted to be, however. The feelings of anxiety pushed through again. The trust and esteem issues reared their heads as I suddenly found I was terrified to get on a plane to Australia. Terrified to finally meet Danny in person. What if I was not good enough? What if I did not live up to his expectations? Inside I knew it was vital for me to deal with all of this before I could answer any other questions.

I had still not received any news on my visa and my levels of stress were such that I felt I could not stop the depression from setting in again. The rising anxiety amplified everything. Why was I stressing so much about this visa? The feeling that something was not right had been there from the beginning and it still sat with me. I just could not place my finger on what it meant or where it was coming from. What was my issue with this visa? Why did I doubt getting it so much? I found myself sinking lower and lower. Before I knew it, I was waking up in tears and going to sleep in tears. In the back of my mind, I was still aware that I needed to find my strength and independence and to become stronger. I also needed to learn to embrace being in my own space and not always require the company of others. I reminded myself that we are all whole and complete as we are. I reminded myself that we do not need another to fill the space within us. This can only be done for ourselves. After all, if you cannot be happy and content in your own space, how can you be happy and content in the space of another? My independence revolved more around an emotional and mental state than my financial independence. I knew I needed to build myself up. I could not rely on another to bring me happiness and completion. Hard as that was, I had to accept it. The need to sleep the next few days away become so strong as it felt easier to deal with than the loneliness and isolation. I needed to pick myself up and make myself happy, carry on with life, love myself first and to be with me first. Only then could I love another and be with another fully and completely. It felt like the loneliness and depression were slowly destroying me, breaking me apart. It was just so, so hard. Living in the present and going with the flow was the answer, but living in limbo waiting for the visa felt destructive for me. At this stage I did not care if my visa would be approved or not, I just wanted to know. I was sick of hanging. It no longer mattered what the answers were, I just wanted them. Hanging in limbo was a killer. For weeks on end, I had put myself into this position and I was so tired of it that I never wanted to do it to myself ever again. Not knowing where one is going or being able to plan their own life is a massive challenge if you are trying to live in the moment. I felt utterly powerless and out of control. Yet another anxiety loomed.

My visa for Vietnam was expiring soon and I would need to leave Vietnam either way and soon. The question remained of where I was going to. I had no idea! I started to work with my Tarot cards to try and get some further clarity and guidance. I would repeatedly get the same cards. At the same time, Leo was pulling the exact same cards for me as well. These were the Strength card, The High Priestess card, The World card, and the Star card. They constantly frequented my readings. It was an ongoing reminder that I needed to step into my power as High Priestess. My end of my Saturn Return was looming and work needed to be done! A Saturn Return refers to a stage in everyone's life that we all need to go through. It presents a time of great challenge and often results in a great change in one's personal life. It is where one needs to find clarity on who they are, what is important for them and where they want to go next in life. My own Saturn Return was coming to an end and never could I have envisioned myself being at a point of such isolation and depression. I should have been in a way more positive space at this stage. In my last few days in Hoi An it was difficult to drag myself out of bed each day, being among strangers, hating that I did not belong, hating that I did not have any home, friends, or family close by. I wandered alone and lost. I eventually started waking up numb. I had gone into emotional shutdown. I had no light at the end of the tunnel. My life was in turmoil and I was directionless.

A morning or two later I woke up, still numb, with a strong element of not caring. In my haze, I felt I had reached rock bottom and I no longer cared about anything. It was a very dark and lonely place to be. It is said that when one reaches rock bottom, the only way is up. It was in that dark place, alone, with only myself that "something" subtle shifted in me. I had a sense that I began processing things from an altered perspective. It felt like an internal shift was starting to take place. Once again, I pulled some cards to see what was happening. As always, the Strength card came up along with the Tower card. Once again it was about breaking myself down to build myself anew; that transformation that I needed to accomplish. It was interesting that I was at the lowest ebb when this started happening. But then again, this is how authentic change happens. It was the first day in a long while that I had not cried and even though it was so dark, it did not scare me. It almost felt as if the depressed feeling had lifted and at that moment, I found myself in a mind-frame of clarity. I was right in the middle of my transformation. The Dark Night of the Soul! The visa question continued to hover around. Yet somehow, I found a sense of peace in it all. It felt like everything made sense again. In that incredibly dark place, I felt 'plugged in' and in-tune with myself. My intuition spoke loudly and clearly. In the darkness, I had found the light! The light was me! The light was my Soul! I knew I could do this! And I knew I could step out of my transformation on the other side stronger than I had ever been. I was beginning to shift some big issues. I got up each day and moved with the transformation as best I could. I was mourning the aspects of myself I was letting go of for the change to take place. As it progressed, I felt like I could see and understand the bigger picture. I felt that I understood everything on my journey and how it had progressed in the way it had. I also understood the importance of me needing to be in Hoi An for my transformation to occur. It is a very common occurrence for anyone going through a transformation to find themselves alone and at a distance. At another level, I had purposefully cut myself off so I could find me.

Massive realizations started to occur as I worked through the journals I had been keeping along my journey. There was a massive release starting and I began to let go. I contacted Ollie's mom, Liz. She is a woman I have always held in very high regard, especially because of her high levels of wisdom and intuition. Intuitively, I knew I needed to reach out to her. When I had been sick in Hanoi, I had reached out to Liz to help me understand what was happening back then. Liz had told me it was a stage of detachment. A detachment from Ryan. I had felt that what she had shared with me back then was correct. What I did not understand, however, was what exactly I was detaching from. When I had left Ryan, it felt as if it was one of the best decisions I had ever made for myself. I felt no loss or sadness. I told her that it felt like a joyous decision. I told her about the journaling I had been doing. It was interesting that the word 'detachment' had been written a lot in my journals, but I did not understand what the detachment was from. Another word I had used a lot in my journals was 'isolation'. I explained to Liz about the depressive lows I had been going through and that I understood they were times of letting go. This too, involved detachment. My understanding was that I had detached from my comfort zone, Ryan and the relationship; as well as the damage that had been done in the relationship. I continued to verbalize that I had stepped into a state of complete detachment, but that past relationships had left me feeling not good enough and how this had raised big issues of self-worth. I told her I was left feeling far from perfect. I also explained to Liz about the high level of anxiety around my visa application and that I had never dealt with such a big challenge before. How could a simple visa application feel like such a big challenge? I expressed that I had learned that it was around my arriving in Australia and not feeling good enough. She also heard about the very dark space I found myself in and that at another level I understood it to be a part of the process. I opened up about all my insights into living in limbo, issues around control, doors that had opened and closed and my feelings of powerlessness. This included the stop-start process that had made the journey rough and smooth at times. For me, it felt like I needed to share all of this with her. I based this on my intuitive knowing. I knew speaking to Liz was a crucial aspect of my journey. I also knew she would continue to play a large role in my journey.

Liz responded with the following thoughts: the first thing was around my break-up with Ryan. She explained that I had been in a long term relationship with him - a relationship that was tantamount to marriage. She explained that in a relationship like that, there are many layers. As a result, many cords need to be cut. My walking away from the relationship was just the surface level. She further explained that in a relationship, you either have two healthy people or two unhealthy people relating. My relationship with Ryan was an unhealthy one. We were both unhealthy. She used a very apt term to identify this. Liz called it being 'comfortably low'. She explained that in an unhealthy relationship, both partners tend to take on the other person's stuff along with their own. Being a natural caregiver, this resonated strongly with me. I needed to define boundaries going forward. I needed to learn to understand where and how I fitted onto another person's path. The understanding that it was not my place to 'fix' another person was vital and I was only there to assist or be a catalyst in their process. She explained that detachment was not necessarily dealing with something. She said to me, "Do we not need to stand in the face of that fear, to allow it to wash through us and understand it at the deepest level we can? In allowing it to flow, it facilitates us in letting go."

She then went on to explain that I was in a profession where I helped people. Working in that type of field, a practitioner is not able to show weakness as it is often a mask that we wear to do the work that we need to do. She also said that it is the very things we teach, that we need to learn for ourselves. This inspired me to step into my authentic self, as well as to start being comfortable with showing the world my authentic self. I am still human after all. Liz then touched on my anxiety about meeting Danny. Her explanation was that Danny and I had connected on a heart and intellectual level, but not yet on a physical level. She understood that this definitely would be a scary aspect for me. It had been safe for me to love him from a distance, but stepping into the physical made the relationship 'real'. She then asked a question here, "Do you want a relationship? Are you ready for a relationship?"

This question had also been raised in my reading with Leo when I was in Da Nang. Then it came up again with the question of what it is that I wanted. It was then followed by a question regarding me isolating myself. Was I possibly burying my head in the sand? It meant that by doing so, I could ignore everything I needed to work through. This question hit home hard. Honestly? On one level I believed I was trying to bury my head in the sand, ignoring what I needed to do. The repeated depression kept telling me that I needed to face this. As there was no one around to challenge me at the time, I did not dig deeper to look at the questions, nor force myself to deal with myself. Liz told me to trust the process. She explained that I needed to let go of the things out of my control. Her words to me were, "When you let it go, you let it flow."

I knew it was something I needed to do consciously. She told me I needed to step out of my state of limbo so that I could make my breakthrough. It was a breakthrough to get to the other side of my transformation. She then shared with me her memories of when she first met me. She described me as a young woman that was shy, quiet and unsure of herself. Liz recalled how she had watched me over the years, grow and blossom into a strong young woman. She had seen me step into my power. Where I sat now was a clear indication to me that I had back-pedalled into the person she had met all those years ago. I had stepped out of my power completely. I had done this because I was seeking a comfort zone. I wanted something, anything, that was familiar - even if this meant reverting to being comfortably low. What she told me was so incredibly insightful. It raised very real questions as to who I was and who I had become. It also gave me insight into how these aspects fitted into my role as a Spiritual Guide and Teacher in the here and now. I received a clear understanding that in going forward, I needed to be more self-aware. My awareness needed to be particularly focused around my issues of co-dependence. As a caregiver and healer, it is common for us to step into co-dependent roles. I needed to find a way to maintain a healthy balance in the here and now. This was especially required for me to step into my power as a High Priestess. This healthy balance was also pivotal if I was going to go ahead with a relationship with Danny. It was a no-go to move into another unhealthy relationship. When I had started this journey, it was to become a better version of myself. It was important that as a teacher, I needed to first practice what I teach and to never stop learning. The irony is that I have always taught others to live intuitively and to trust the process. I needed to do this as well.

Furthermore, because I was stepping into such a powerful archetype, I could not expect my lessons and challenges to be easy ones. I would be tested on my faith. I would be tested in every way. I had to remain strong in all these aspects. This stage of my journey to becoming a High Priestess was pivotal in my growth. I knew I would never stop being challenged, but my strength in dealing with these challenges was key. I needed to find a way to work through my insecurities, especially while being challenged. Liz's question about whether I was burying my head in the sand, came up again for me. I had written in my journal while in Da Nang that all I wanted to do was bury my head in the proverbial sand and not deal with any of this. Through the lessons, my soul however, had backed me into a corner and was forcing me to deal with it. It was long overdue that I step fully back into my power! Now was the time to find the strength and courage to do so.

After my conversation with Liz, I went out for a walk. I remember sitting down in a little coffee shop. I started to journal once again. What I wrote was profound. I suddenly felt less anxious about my visa as I accepted that the situation was out of my control. It was obvious that holding onto that fear and anxiety was not healthy for me. To fight the battle, I needed to step out of limbo. Then as I sat there writing, I felt something shift. I felt myself letting go. I knew I would be getting on a plane soon, but I did not know where to. I was okay with that because I knew I would be 'looked after'. There was gratitude for the experience I had gone through and for the hardships that I had to face as well. I knew they would only make me stronger. I understood why Vietnam was where I was meant to go to. It is a kind and gentle culture that could supply me with the safe space I had needed. It was a space to process, shift, and release. It was the direction the Universe pointed me in and I trusted and followed that. Although the journey had been long, dark and heavy, it had been one well worth taking. As I sat there and wrote, I let go fully. What I did not realize was that I would be tested again, so quickly, after having let go and having that moment of clarity.

That evening, when I arrived back at the Home Stay, I found an email had arrived. I read the email. I read it again to check I had read correctly. I went ice cold! My visa for Australia had been declined! I was shattered! I sat there for a few moments in what I assume was a state of shock. When I reread about why my visa had been declined, the reality began to grip me. The Australian government had told me, in black and white, that I was required to have complete independence financially before I would be allowed into the country. My visa had also been declined because I had no ties to assets in my home country, South Africa. This threw up the challenge of independence that had been staring me in the face all along. I began to feel lost and confused. Not wanting to get to get caught in a predicament, I chose to head back to South Africa. I needed something familiar, I needed my comfort zones. I contacted a few of my friends, including Nina, who was living in Cape Town. Every one of them gave me full support and assured me that I would be okay. It made me feel a little easier about the situation. Nina, without hesitation though, offered her home to me and I felt a sense of comfort. At least I now had a home to go to. My sense of helplessness eased a little and I began to plan. Step one was that I would be heading back to South Africa. Step two would require me to spend a few days in Johannesburg, seeing clients so I could start to build some stability for myself again. My next stop would be to fly to Cape Town to stay with Nina while I figured out the rest of the plan. Danny was devastated when I called him to tell him the news. He also assured me that I would be okay. I had nowhere near enough money to buy a ticket back home, never mind from Johannesburg to Cape Town. Without hesitation, he offered to help me. Once again, this man was like a Guardian Angel sent to look after me. Finally, I clearly understood the high anxiety around my visa approval. I must have picked up on an intuitive level that it was going to be refused and because I fought against accepting this, I caused myself an enormous amount of anxiety. Now I had no choice but to accept it with grace.

There were no ill feelings about the situation. I understood clearly now why I had sat in limbo for all this time: it was so that I could deal with and face myself from an internal place. I also realized that the levels of anxiety rose hugely when I had to fill in the part of my application where I needed to show how I could support myself independently. How ironic was this? The very thing that I had been trying to do since the beginning of my journey was the importance of my independence. The Australian authorities had pushed a very sensitive button for me. My independence could not be fulfilled until I had stepped fully into my power. A High Priestess only needs 'herself' and must only rely on herself. I was being refocused on my journey to becoming a High Priestess. Now was the time for me to pour myself back into my journey. I had interpreted all the signs connected to Australia the wrong way around. Australia is somewhere I could go to one day, but when the time was right. I had other things I needed to do before that could happen. As much as my heart was broken over the disappointment, I knew other things needed to be done first. I contacted my travel agent in Hanoi to change my flights once more.

For a few days, the Ten of Swords card kept coming into my mind. The card had never come up in any of my previous readings and it intrigued me. After telling this to Leo, she sent me an odd message a little while later.

"You won't believe what just happened. I was working through a Tarot book of mine. I got up from the couch and it fell on the floor. The page it opened up on was the Ten of Swords. There you have it, my friend."

I thanked her, shuffled my deck and pulled a card for myself. There sat the Ten of Swords. It was my rock bottom. The only way I could go from here was up.

The next day, I was heading for the airport in Da Nang to begin my trip back to South Africa. While on my way, I scrolled through some

Facebook feeds. There on the screen was a card. It was the card of Home, posted by Tú Annh, the owner of the Tarot Cafe in Hanoi. I took it as a sign that South Africa was home and that I was heading back to the right place. I had messaged Nga, the owner of the Da Nang Home Stay to let her know I was leaving Vietnam and she suggested we meet for coffee before I left. There was someone she felt I needed to meet before I left. I agreed and met with her about an hour later. Nga and I had formed a beautiful friendship despite my dark times during my stay at her Home Stay. Nga arrived and introduced to me to the man she was with. A man oddly enough from Australia - ohhh, that Universal sense of humor! We chatted for a while, our conversations focusing around philosophy and spirituality. He then told me about a book he had been given: the I Ching Workbook. He said if I ever came across it, I should give it a read as he felt it could be something valuable for me. I then shared the story of my journey with him and what I had been through. He said I was a very inspiring person and that I had a lot of courage to do what I had done. He then wished me well with the next stage of my journey. What he said brought me to tears. Not because it made me sad, but because a stranger saw something in me that I had not been able to see in myself. To top it all, it was something I had been looking for in myself and not seen. It was something that had been within me all along - my strength! As broken as I felt, I had not lost my inner strength. I still had my power. I just needed to bring it to the fore. I had willingly wandered through hell and back. I had gone through my Dark Night of the Soul. It was vital that my transformation continue so that I could become the High Priestess I was meant to be. As I stepped onto the plane, I stepped off the cliff edge once more and braced for the free fall.

9

Goddesses and Cats

My flight back to South Africa included a layover in Hong Kong and then another short one in Ethiopia. By the time I got onto my flight to Ethiopia, I was exhausted. I had not slept in about two days and there was the time zone differences that came into play. The disappointment of my visa being declined, coupled with the last minute travel arrangements back to South Africa; as well as lack of sleep on my first flight, had taken its toll on me. I passed out within minutes of boarding my flight to Ethiopia. I woke up to a kind gentleman, sitting next to me, gently covering me with his coat and moved a seat over so I could be more comfortable. I promptly passed out again, feeling safe and secure. I slept through most of my flight to Ethiopia. When the plane touched down on African soil, something awoke within me. Africa is where I am from. Africa runs through my veins. I could feel the power 'my' continent held for me. I could feel Africa re-empowering me. This was the place that my power originated from, even though it did not feel like 'home'. After finding a coffee shop, I waited for my final flight. While sitting down with a much-needed cup of coffee, a man came and stood right by my table. Recognising his accent, instantly I knew he was from South Africa. Glancing up at him, my eyes were instantly drawn to a tattoo on his right arm. It was a single word: 'gratitude'! Africa was clearly out in full force - sending me messages and giving me stark reminders. Always, remember to give gratitude. As I sat in that coffee shop, I suddenly realized that it was the day I was meant to have married Ryan. It felt like I had come full circle in my detachment from him. What were the chances of me landing back in South Africa on the day I was meant to have gotten married? I reflected on my journey thus far. There was an absolute certainty that everything had worked out as it was meant to. Going to Australia would have been taking the easy way out - the thought suddenly occurred to me and I immediately understood a deeper aspect to my visa being declined. The easy way out is never an option for a High Priestess - no lessons are ever learned by taking this route. For years, I had nurtured resentment to the Universe for sending me "back" to this Earth, even though it was my "choice"! Had I not returned, I would have avoided receiving my gifts and my soul's purpose. I realized as well, that when I chose to stop 'fighting' the Universe and embrace my gifts, I got to see how richly the Universe rewarded me in every way. I had hoped that once I got to Cape Town, I would find the sanctuary I was looking for - this time knowing that it was sanctuary that I sought and not a comfort zone. This was needed for me to build the stability and structure required for the fulfillment of my purpose as High Priestess. I also hoped that I would find "home" there.

My adventure, although not an easy one thus far, had allowed me to stretch my soul as I learned my lessons. It was important for me to acknowledge what the Universe had given me and to remember to give gratitude for this. The importance of knowing where home was, seemed not to matter as much in the moment. What mattered was right here, right now. Moving forward, I still needed to be practical about certain things. I had given some thought to the question of what it was I wanted; and one thing that had been coming to mind frequently was a healing space - a space where I could teach and support others through their journeys. I knew without question that my inner fire would give me the impetus for this dream; so I needed to keep it burning strongly. In many ways, my journey had taken me to the depths of hell and back and I knew I would do it all over again in a heartbeat. After all, a soul stretch was what I had asked for and it was a soul stretch that I got. The ability to see and understand the bigger picture amidst the darkness and chaos meant that my wisdom had grown. This wisdom was what I could share and teach to others in the world, helping to facilitate a global change. I now knew how important it was for people to step out of their stagnant routines, take risks and live life to the full. An important aspect of my journey was that I could be an example of how to do this. I started this journey so I could be an example of how life could be lived. I then considered my hardships and saw the immense value in them. We learn as much from our 'failures' as we do from our successes. Nothing is ever wasted time if we seek the gifts in every experience. Faith is a vital ingredient to have when going through life. Having faith means you know you will always be okay. Heading towards my gate to board my flight to Johannesburg, I looked out of the massive glass windows and was greeted with an exquisite sunrise - bright vivid hues one could only experience in Africa. "I see you Mama Africa, I know you are with me and within me," was my gentle thought as I stepped through the boarding gates. A few hours later I landed in Johannesburg. Stepping back onto my 'home' soil though, something about there did not feel at all like home. I suddenly had the knowing that I would be in for more tests and soon. As much as Africa had given me a warm reception, I knew I was not in the clear with regards to my journey and the challenges I would need to face in order to step fully into my High Priestess archetype. I reminded myself that it was important for me to keep my head about me and keep the focus.

My friend Bianca fetched me from the airport in Johannesburg. She was the first familiar face I had seen since I left Hanoi. She was a welcome sight. I spent the weekend filling her in on my crazy adventure. I shared with her the insights I had received and what I had taken away from my journey. She shared something interesting with me. She told me that for a while now, she had been feeling unhappy in her current relationship. She shared that she was fearful of leaving because she did not know what was on the other side of ending that relationship. It was strange to hear someone telling me a story that was so similar to mine. I shared with her what wisdom I could, based on my own experiences. This would not be last person to share a story similar to mine in the coming days. While I was there, an old friend of mine, JJ contacted me. He made an offer out of the blue. It was an offer to partner with him in an existing business he had. It was a business he did not have much time to build up properly and asked if I would be interested in running it for him. I took this as the Universe giving me an opportunity to establish the stability I so desperately needed. I agreed to accept his offer and we arranged to finalize everything in a couple of weeks. At least some direction was forming for me - or so I believed at the time. It never occurred to me that the Universe was simply testing me and my faith in my purpose and my dream of opening up a healing space. Two days later, I left Bianca to stay with Nikki for the remainder of my time in Johannesburg. I was looking forward to seeing Nikki again, I had not seen her since our conversation months before prior to me ending things with Ryan - that much needed conversation where she had shown me that glimmer of strength inside me. I had several readings lined up for the few days I was there. It was intriguing that almost every client I saw in that week was going through a transformation of some sort; or they were on the brink of one. The feelings and experiences my clients were having were so close to my own, that I could assist them with ease. This revealed a deeper meaning to my journey - I had become better equipped to teach others. The realization that for one to teach and assist others, one first needed to go through these experiences and come out on the other side - a pivotal aspect in many of the Shaman books I had read over the years. My journey, although rough, had a far deeper purpose to it. My journey was not just about myself.

"Home" and where it was, still sat clearly in the back of my mind. Danny put things into perspective for me. I told him that I was tired of living out of suitcases and that the thought of settling down for a while did appeal to me, but not knowing where I wanted to settle or where I was meant to settle, was still a big question. I believed it was a big part of the ups and downs and constant uncertainty that was in my life. Danny said he felt sure that the path would reveal itself to me and that certain things needed to fall into place for me to find the answer. I thanked him for dispensing Universal wisdom to me again and for reinforcing my faith in trusting the process. It did not mean that I still did not feel anxious about it. I accepted his messages and it helped me to feel a little more at ease. It was later that evening when I got back to Nikki's home that I noticed a saying she had on her wall: "Life takes you to unexpected places. Love brings you home." Was this the Universe telling me that South Africa was home? Or was it telling me that home is where love is? I believed that my love, and my heart, were both sitting in Australia. I had hoped that my arrival in Cape Town in a couple of days time would be able to answer that question for me.

Before I left Johannesburg, I visited my friend, Brigitte who owned the healing center. The same friend that had assured me that I was on the right track with leaving Ryan as she shared what she had learned about him and his tendency to be unfaithful. We chatted for a good while as I shared my journey with her. While I was there, I kept getting the feeling that I needed to walk through her store before I left. It felt like something was waiting there for me. Browsing through the store, I picked up a little traveling Buddha and a Hand of Fatima for protection. But the feeling lingered that I was still missing something. I must have walked through her shop a good eight times before I saw it! The I Ching Workbook! It was the book that had been suggested to me just before I left Vietnam by the man that I met at Da Nang airport. I knew why I needed to go into her store and look around. The synchronicities were starting to gain momentum once more. Eager to see what message the book had for me, I opened it up at a random page. It was the page of the Thunder Trigram, also known as Zhen - The Awakening. The book stated that the trigram represented movement and speed and was associated with growth and development. It then went on to describe the individual meanings of the lines that made up the Trigram. The bottom line represented irrepressible strength and the two lines above allowed for growth to occur with little resistance. It explained that the key to the Thunder Trigram was action coupled with understanding, compassion and self-knowledge. It then went on to explain that Zhen was a reminder for us to be aware of our intentions for the actions we take and that it related directly to those who are here to teach and guide others. It gave the reminder to choose one's teachers wisely and to avoid any unnecessary negative people. The Thunder Trigram was a wake-up call to remind one that their teachers are an energetic manifestation of the life they are living and that they themselves are the spark for those manifestations. The passage reminded me clearly of all the manifesting I had done along my journey. It was a reminder that my ability to manifest was still strong. However, it was a reminder that we also manifest what we think! In hindsight, the Thunder Trigram was also forewarning me of where I was heading to next; and that note about being mindful of the teachers we choose and how they are a manifestation of the life we live – was going to become a hard learned lesson in the coming weeks. I left for Cape Town a couple of days later and once again, that need for sanctuary loomed strongly.

I arrived in Cape Town feeling shattered. The few days of back-to-back readings I had done in Johannesburg and the early morning flight had depleted me of energy. I was exhausted! Nina, who had fetched me from the airport, was talking incessantly about everything that had been happening in her life. I tried my best to focus, but I was so tired and my heart was feeling heavy. Something was out of place, but I could not put my finger on it. I asked Nina how long I could stay with her. She said I could stay as long as I needed to. Somehow, this did not bring me much comfort. I had the intense feeling that my stay with her would be short-lived and I did not know why. Then that unsettling feeling amplified! On arrival at Nina's home, I got semi-settled and decided I needed some intense chill-out time. While she was out fetching her daughter, I took the opportunity to smoke a joint and relax on her couch. I had not smoked marijuana in a number of weeks. I allowed the feeling of relaxation to set in and I closed my eyes and let out a deep, settling breath. With Table Mountain sitting behind me, time seemed to rewind itself. Suddenly a rush of scenes from my last visit to Cape Town ran past my eyes. It was a stark reminder of the first time I had been in Cape Town before leaving for Vietnam. Then it hit me! I was back to relearn the lessons I had missed - lessons I had not got right the first time around. Then a crystal clear memory played out before me. It was me receiving a message from Nina the year before - a message about a dream she had about me; a dream where I had arrived at her house with a bunch of suitcases. Feeling rather out of it, I was not entirely sure if I had actually received that message previously. I questioned my sanity for a moment and sat up. As I sat up, I noticed a book on Nina's coffee table. I picked it up without a second thought and opened it up at random. The page I opened had the following headline: "The point of power is in the present moment". Was the Universe trying its hand at humor again? One of the biggest lessons I had been learning was to live in the moment. I read the passage, intrigued to see what it said. The book explained that it did not matter what our past experiences were, starting today - right here, right now - was the moment we could change. The smallest beginnings could make all the difference. We are all made perfect and that is the truth of our being. Everything else is just learned nonsense that we should unlearn, starting right now, in the present moment. I put the book down and burst into tears. The tears felt like a release and had no sadness to them. Then I just sat there and laughed at the absurdness of the Universe and the blatant messages it was sending my way. Tears streamed down my face, I laughed at the madness that was the Universe and how all that madness made complete sense. I sent a photograph of the page to Leo and she responded with the following,

"I think that it is just so insanely apt, with everything that has been going on. In the present moment, it does not matter what you have done. You begin every moment now and if you mess it up then you just begin again in the next now. When we read the Tarot, we are looking for future guidance, but it remains about now. Nothing is set in stone. Not the tomorrows or the next weeks. All we have is right now. I also find it enlightening, in the sense that you are creating tomorrow out of today, even though, things have felt out of your control. You have made things happen as you wanted them to happen, even if you did not understand it. You chose to study an English course and teach it in Vietnam. You said you were going to take your work internationally and you have done all of that - which you controlled. You met this amazing man and you have this beautiful connection. It is a connection completely different from what you had with Ryan and you manifested all of that, in an amazingly short space of time! On top of that, you arrive at a home in Cape Town, find a random book lying on a coffee table, open it at a random page and read what you need to hear."

This had to be the Universe working in synchronicity with me! The last part of her message just made me laugh! She was so accurate and saw the Universal humor in the passage I had just read. Shortly thereafter, Nina returned home and I asked her if she recalled sending me that message about her dream. She said she did remember and searched through her phone to find it for me. Handing me her phone a moment later, I reread the message she had sent over a year ago, "Dreamt of you last night, made me miss you big time! You came to visit me with lots of suitcases. It looked more like you were staying for good with the number of suitcases you had. It was just you, though."

Somehow, Nina had known at a subconscious level, more than a year previously, I would be arriving at her house with all of my possessions. She also knew I would be arriving alone. When the Universe speaks, it speaks loudly! We may not understand the messages at first, but eventually they do come to light and make complete sense - even if they do arrive in bizarre ways. I understood without question why I was back in Cape Town. I saw the entire path I had just walked with complete clarity and how it all fitted together. I also saw just how far back in time the Universe had begun talking to me.

It was not long after my bizarre experience on Nina's couch, that cats started to appear. Cats literally everywhere I went and looked! There was a cat named Venus that lived in Nina's apartment block. She would come and say 'hello' to me daily. I recalled that in a lot of the readings Leo had sent me, her cat was almost always in the picture. I then spent New Year's housesitting for a friend. Her cat Elvis was my companion for the evening. A few days later, another friend of mine sent me a photo of a Tarot deck she had recently purchased for herself. Curled up next to the cards was her cat. I could not ignore the cats any longer. I sent Leo a message asking her what she thought about it. Her first response was that she was certain there was a Goddess in my space. She said it was something she had experienced recently and warned me that if I did not pay attention, the Goddesses could get a little irritated and they tended to bring a lot of upheavals if ignored. She recommended that I chat with an oracle card reader in Johannesburg that worked specifically with Goddesses.

I made contact with the reader shortly afterwards and shared with her my journey and the abundance of cats in my space. She offered to do a Goddess reading for me to see which Goddess had come into my space. She pulled three cards for me. The first represented who had been in my space recently, the second who was currently in my space and the third was who could potentially be coming into my space. The card for Badb represented the past. Also known as The Morrigan from the Celtic pantheon. This, of course, resonated with me strongly considering my father's side of the family and their strong Celtic roots. The card that referred to my current space was a living deity called Amma. She represented the Divine Mother and pure unconditional love. The reader explained that Amma comes in at times of healing. This also resonated with me as I was essentially in a time of healing. She explained that going forward, I needed to work with Amma to heal. The Goddess sitting in my potential future was Hecate. From there I could choose to either work with Hecate or The Morrigan. I instinctively chose The Morrigan as she resonated so strongly with me. I had researched Hecate in my teenage years and she had filled me with huge trepidation, even terror back then. I had perceived Hecate as a dark, foreboding energy not to be messed with. Knowing who was in my space and why, I knew I could work with the two Goddesses to move forward. It did not mean I was not apprehensive, though. I had heeded Leo's warning about Goddesses bringing upheaval into one's life. I would soon come to realize how accurate this statement would be. The reader then shared with me that cats, throughout history, had often played a pivotal role when one was exploring their feminine aspect and needed to step into their power. The abundance of cats around me made complete sense in that context. She shared one more piece of advice with me, she recommended that I watch or listen to some of Amma's [4]kirtan sessions. She felt it would possibly open something up for me. I thanked her for the wisdom and made a note to explore these Goddesses on a deeper level. Following the reader's recommendation to listen to Amma's kirtans, I searched for one that resonated and gave it a listen. Within seconds of listening, I felt an intense anger and hatred toward men, "All they do is use and abuse us! They just constantly take with giving nothing in return!" Shocked by my reaction, I instantly switched off the kirtan and attempted to understand what had just happened. I personally had no reason to think those thoughts, but they had come from somewhere. Not being able to make sense of the experience, I made a note of it in the hopes that some clarity would eventually come about.

A few days into my stay in Cape Town, I received a message from JJ that everything was a go-ahead for the business. He asked me to start working on things as soon as possible, which I did. I was truly looking forward to building up some stability again. Little did I know at the time that everything would backfire so quickly! The end of January arrived and I was meant to receive my first payment. I waited and waited. The payment just never came through. I contacted JJ to ask what was happening. He told me he was still trying to finalize certain things. He told me not to worry, it would be sorted out as soon as he was able to do so. Again, a couple of weeks went by. I heard nothing from him during this time. I asked him about it again and he said he would let me know as soon as he had something. It felt like a door had just been shut in my face. At an intuitive level, I knew this business was not going to happen and that I was never going to be paid. I had invested a lot of my time and energy into his business and it was all for nothing. I had chosen to pursue a perceived form of stability only to find I had wasted my energy. Energy I could have put into growing what I was meant to be doing - working on my purpose and creating a healing space for others. Not prepared to allow this obstacle to bring me down, I began to focus fully on my work. Not long after that, the Universe would test me and my faith once more.

Nina spoke to me a few days later about a business she was starting with her friend, Sue. She had asked if I would like to do some design work for them. Ryan had started a graphic and web design business years before. When his health had gotten bad, I chose to learn what I could about design so I could help him keep his business going. I had learned a fair amount and found that I had a natural flair for layouts and design. I agreed to help Nina, as she had after all given me a roof over my head. I met with Sue soon after that and we discussed everything that would be needed. Sue insisted that I be paid for my work, saying that I could not put in the hours and get nothing in return. I took this as a blessing and accepted her offer. It seemed that one door had closed and another had opened. I noticed that the cats were still lurking.

A couple of weeks into my stay with Nina, she told me about a plant medicine woman in Cape Town who facilitated journeys. She explained that the medicine woman worked with psilocybin mushrooms specifically. Recalling my previous experience with them, taking a journey with them felt correct and I decided to do it. I arrived at the medicine woman's home where she held and facilitated the journeys. It was quite a large and diverse group of people that would be journeying with me that evening. I chose a spot in the far corner of the room and made myself comfortable with a blanket. Everyone got settled and we all had a turn to introduce ourselves. We were then introduced to a group called Watchers, who were there to assist the medicine woman and to help any of us with basic needs. Everything was explained to us as to how the process would work. It was first made very clear that it was not a social setting and that we were not there for recreational purposes. She then explained that we would each have a turn to receive our sacrament, along with the recommendation to sit up for about fifteen to twenty minutes so our medicine could take effect. Not with me! Within minutes of drinking my sacrament, it took effect and I needed to lie down fast! As I did, colors and streams of light began to form in front of my eyes. In all my experiences with hallucinogenic plant medicine, I had never actually 'tripped'. I remember closing my eyes and seeing the face of an old Asian man floating down towards me on a rainbow-colored stream of light. He was gently smiling at me, almost beckoning me, calling to me. I then noticed a bright light behind me, which was odd as the only light in the room was from candles. I even opened my eyes to double-check that I was seeing what I thought I was. Sure enough, it was still just candlelight in the room. I closed my eyes again and the bright light was still there, just off to my right. I understood the light to be a hallucination and asked myself that if the light was just a hallucination, what did it mean? This was how the medicine worked, right? It showed you visions of things you needed to see and know. I intuitively felt the need to turn over and face into the light. Turning over, I faced the light and I slept. Rather my mind and body slept while my soul went for a walkabout.

It would be more than a year later before I would I ever know exactly where my soul went while slept. Each time I 'woke up', I had tears running down my face and I was repeating the words, "I am so broken" to myself. I repeated this over and over again until the words changed to: "It is okay because I am putting myself back together." I then slept again. The second time I also 'woke up' to tears running down my face. This time I checked to see if the tears were there or not. I touched my cheek to find it soaked. The understanding flooded through me that I needed to just simply sit in the corner and cry. I did this until I slept again. When I 'woke up' the third time, I had a stuffy nose from all the crying I had been doing while I slept. The understanding that it was a sign of the anger and frustration I had been feeling with life, along with the suppressed anger I still had towards Ryan, had eventually come to the fore. Immediately, as the realization occurred, the stuffy feeling started to dissipate. I continued to sit up for a while longer and surveyed the room around me. Again the bright, vivid colors and streams of light appeared. I started to pay attention to the Watchers, as well as the other people in the room. At another level, I could feel and understand every single person in that room and what they were dealing with. I picked up all the different energies and instantly understood them. At that moment, a thought occurred to me, "It is quite something to be able to look through the veil and understand the connection to everything."

The image of the traditional High Priestess came to mind. It is said that all the hidden secrets the High Priestess holds, are behind the veil she is often seated in front of. I then had the understanding that all I needed to do was simply pull back the veil and look. Once again, I felt the need to lie down and sleep. When I 'woke up' again, it felt as if I was being handed my gifts once again. Receiving them came with a thought and understanding. I managed to find my pen and paper in the darkness of the room and I wrote the thought down. It was too important to forget: "It feels good to receive my gifts and not be burdened by them." The fire outside began to call to me strongly. I managed to get shakily to my feet. With the help of the Watchers, I made my way across the room. A Watcher by the name of Anne suggested it would probably be a good time to go to the loo. She accompanied me to the bathroom door and I wandered inside and had a seat. As I sat there, I looked straight ahead at the bathroom door, which now seemed to be miles away. I sat there thinking: "It's going to take me ages to get back to that door." I then considered the symbology of the experience and contemplated if the long walk back to the door was indicative of the long journey I had been taking to step into my High Priestess. Reality set back in with the flush of the loo and I took the couple steps back to the bathroom door. Holding my hand once more, the Watcher helped me outside to the fire. As we approached it, in my haze I blurted out to her, "Where the fuck did I just come from?" My mind had been blown away by what had happened while I slept. I knew my soul had gone on a serious walkabout. To where, I did not know, but with the knowledge I brought back each time, it did not matter. Anne's reassuring words of, "Don't try think about it too much, just flow with it." It helped to ground me. As I sat down by the fire, I noticed a man that was not a part of our group. I knew without question that he was not really there, but I also understood that he was there for a reason. He watched me for a few seconds and I watched him. I turned away for a split second and when I looked back, he was gone. I sat by the fire for a while, grabbing for my box of cigarettes. I had taken up smoking within the first few weeks of being with Nina. It was something I had done off and on over the years, but it was something that had never stuck with me. An older woman came and sat down next me. She looked at me and looked at my cigarette and began telling me about how she had quit out fear for her health. She then said, "Cancer is a very real thing, be careful with those!" She then got up and left. Something about what she had said unsettled me and the cigarette began to taste terrible. I began gazing into the fire once more and then it began to stretch out in front of me in a very abnormal way. It was time for me to retreat to my corner again.

I managed to find my way safely back to my corner on my own. Within seconds I was asleep once again. I was woken up by the woman next to me, covering me with my blanket. She saw I was awake and touched my hand gently. She said to me that I had looked "deathly cold" and was amazed that my hands were so warm. These were odd words to use and I questioned if my soul had wandered off a little too far. Was it a near-death experience that I just slept through? I had heard of people experiencing what is known as Ego Death while journeying with plant medicine and questioned if the same had happened to me. I could feel myself coming back to my normal reality, so I got up and went in search for some coffee. I wandered into the kitchen and joined the others at the table. One of the other Watchers, Sara, came in shortly after me and took up a seat next to me. We struck up a conversation and she began sharing her story with me, which was all too familiar to me. She told me how, after many years of being in an unhealthy relationship, she had managed to find the strength to leave. I then gave her a quick recap of the journey I had been on since leaving Ryan. I told her how I had walked out of my ten-year relationship and got onto a plane to Vietnam. I also shared the massive transformation I had gone through while there. She told me that I was very inspiring for her and that when she looked at me, she saw a lion. That statement right there brought me to tears. The reason was that the animal that is associated with the Strength card is the Lion. Once again, a stranger had not only reminded me of my power, but had also seen that power in me. She then shared with me about the gratitude she now felt towards her ex-partner for the lessons he had given her. As difficult as the relationship was, without having that experience with him, she would never have found her power. She had unknowingly given me a key insight into my journey. She also taught me a new aspect of Gratitude. I understood that for me to cut the final cords with Ryan and fully heal, I needed to have gratitude for what my relationship with him had taught me. I thanked her for sharing with me and she left to carry on with her task of being a Watcher. I do hope that this beautiful soul will cross my path again. She had such a profound effect on me and my journey that night. An effect that I have immense gratitude for. The days following my journey seemed to flow quite smoothly, the cats, however, were still about!

10

Finding Sanctuary

The teachers we choose throughout our lifetime can teach us in many ways: through sharing knowledge, leading by example or through our experiences with them. Teachers can come in many shapes and forms, and it is important to remember that not all teachers will teach us through pleasant experiences. In fact, often it's the teachers who challenge us the most that leave the biggest impact on our lives. When we are faced with challenging teachers, however, it is vital to know that we can choose to move on from them at anytime and that we are never stuck with any specific teacher. It's knowing when to move on that can cause us to get caught in situations that really are not for us.

The Thunder Trigram had forewarned me about surrounding myself with unnecessary negative people; and that going forward I needed to choose my teachers more wisely. As is often the case, however, I did not fully understand the message when I first read it. It was almost three months later that the reality of the Trigram's message began to fully come to light. My choice to stay with Nina was proving to be an overstayed welcome. The space was far from the sanctuary I had hoped it would be. The depressive lows started creeping in again. The thought sat with me about how I had experienced a massive spiritual awakening over the past few months. Yet I now felt as if I was sitting with nothing. I constantly pined for Danny and a different life. I would wake up each morning feeling like brick walls surrounded me and would just keep hitting them. I sat with two businesses that seemed to be going nowhere. Life felt pointless and meaningless. I had no reason to get up in the mornings. I felt like I was grasping at straws. I even questioned if I was doing the right things and if I was even on the right track. The Universe had become quiet for me. I was ready to just throw in the towel and be done with this lifetime. I desperately wanted to escape. I once more felt a wave of anger and resentment towards the Universe for bringing me back into this lifetime to help repair the world. I was done, I wanted out! Almost every night I would sit and listen to Nina talk about HER stuff. Living with her had become a huge challenge. She would constantly ask me for my opinions and advice; insisting I give her the direction she sought in life. She even said to me at times: "Come on you're the psychic. You give me the answers?" I found these comments extremely challenging to deal with because they came across to me in a very careless and disrespectful manner. However, I could not bring myself to say anything about it. There was an obligation I felt to help her work through her stuff each night. This was mainly because she had given me a roof over my head and she had helped me in a big way. This sense of 'owing' her began to outweigh the help she had given me. What I really needed was a positive, productive space to work in. There seemed to be no time for me. There seemed to be no time to work on my purpose. All I wanted was to be left alone to do what I wanted and needed to do. I slipped further and further into depression. I would go to bed exhausted every night, feeling as if I had achieved nothing. Every morning I would wake up exhausted and feeling heartbroken. The stress and fear of what the future held for me was overwhelming. Doors had stopped opening for me and I saw no light at the end of the tunnel. Once again I felt miles from my path. To make matters worse, I was being told by Nina to snap out of my 'moods'. She insisted she was doing this for my own good. What she did not fully understand was the extent to which my emotional well-being was being affected. I kept the fact that I was highly depressed and truly struggling to recalibrate my life to myself. I spoke to no one about it for fear of judgment or being told to pull myself together, or even worse, being told it was not all that bad. Consistency and certainty was what I craved. I had moved from needing sanctuary to being desperate for a comfort zone once more.

I then began to get intense feelings that I needed to move out of Nina's space. Each time this feeling would surface, Ollie's mom, Liz would come to mind. I knew I needed to contact her. I also knew I needed to ask her if I could stay with her - my intuition had been screaming this at me for a while. With my energy and self-esteem levels being so low, however, I found it difficult to find the strength and courage to ask. Once more, the challenge of asking for help reared its fierce head. Things with Nina came to a head when I found myself in the middle of an intense dispute between her and Sue. Nina had asked her if they could meet face to face to discuss some concerns she had. Being that they were friends as well, she felt it was necessary to clear the air before the business developed fully. It was also for the sake of their friendship. Sue replied that she was happy to meet, but would only be able to do so the following week. Nina was not happy! Sue then emailed me later that day saying she had no idea what Nina was on about. It felt as if she was trying to pry information from me. I had no intention of getting involved in something that did not concern me. My only role in their business was as a freelance designer - nothing more! I told her that I was not sure what it was about, but I was positive they could sort out whatever the issue was. I mentioned the email to Nina as I felt she had a right to know. This was not a good idea at all! Nina was furious and said she was going to email Sue back about it. I asked her to please not include me in it as it was their issue. Nina, however, ignored my request and emailed her friend, including me in the message. I suddenly found myself in the middle of a friendship battle that had nothing to do with me from the beginning.

I found myself receiving back and forth emails between them over old issues I really did not want to know about. I requested that both of them please take me out of the equation. It was all too overwhelming as I tried fruitlessly to deal with my stuff. I chose to just ignore the emails and delete them as they came in. An email then arrived a couple of days later from Sue, saying she was pulling out of the business. The design work I had been brought on to do was taken away and in a split second, the rug was pulled out from under my feet. Yet another door was shut in my face, and once again, I sat with no clear way of how I was going to build any type of stability for myself. To add to the already unpleasant situation, Nina decided it was the right time to be honest with me about her thoughts on Sue offering to pay me for the design work. She felt that I should have offered to do it for free out of loyalty and friendship to her. Nina told me how she felt that I had just taken and taken and given nothing back. I went ice cold and I could feel the emotional shutdown taking place. She had made me out to be ungrateful for everything she had done for me. As far as I was concerned, this was far from the case. During my time with Nina, I had tried to show my gratitude in any way I could. This included practical aspects of sharing her space, as well as in the form of regular free readings for her and her family as well as allowing her to share her problems with me almost nightly. It was the only way I felt I could repay her for her kindness. It was often to my detriment as I struggled through my day-to-day living. It was clear to me this had all gone unnoticed. intuitive warnings that had started the week before had now come to the fore. I knew I should have just listened and contacted Liz from the beginning. I prayed that it was now not a case of 'too little, too late'. Feeling uncertain, I contacted Liz regardless. Liz contacted me almost instantly - first to check-in to see if I was okay and to let me know that it was not a problem for me to stay with her. It was actually good timing - she needed someone to look after her cat for a few days, as she would be housesitting elsewhere during the coming week. It was like a saving grace for me. From the beginning, my intuition to contact Liz had been accurate. It had become glaringly clear to me that I had overstayed my welcome with Nina and it was time to move on.

Liz was able to fetch me the next day. I hoped the Universe would be putting me into a space where I could start to focus on myself again. I was desperate to find some stability. I was also desperate to start writing the book you are now reading. It had been in the back of my mind for weeks that I needed to start writing. It was now nagging at me persistently. It would have been impossible for me to start writing while staying with Nina. I did not have space or mental clarity to sit and write. I had once again handed a lot of myself over to another person; at my expense. It was time to write my book and share my message! I arrived at Liz's home and could instantly feel the difference in the energy between the two spaces. Liz's space was neutral and calming and of course, it contained a cat! The sweetest little black cat with little white paws. A cat named Spy. It was time for me to understand on a deeper level why the cats were so constantly in my space. I scanned Liz's bookshelf to find a book that could answer this for me. There was a book about spirit animals and opened it up to the page on cats. It explained that when a cat shows up, it means it is a time of self-sufficiency. It is also a time to trust our capabilities. The book spoke about needing to listen to my intuition for guidance and it mentioned it could well be an ancestor trying to communicate with me. It went on to say that it is a time of magic and mystery. I picked up that I also needed to pay attention to signs and omens to guide and direct me. In addition to this, the book stated that something better and more suited would replace all I had released in the form of negative relationships, material possessions, and self-defeating habits. The accuracy of what I read in that book still astounds me! As I sat reading the section about cats I noticed Spy sitting on a chair across from me watching me intently. I felt I finally understood why the cats had been frequenting my space. It was not just an indication of Goddesses hanging around - they had a far deeper meaning. I knew I had to learn to work with The Morrigan and her lessons of rebirth, war, death, and destruction. This would clear the way for the direction and progress I needed to make. My intense reaction to Amma's kirtan, however, still evaded me.

I took a few days to settle down and to catch up with Liz as I had not seen her much since my arrival back in Cape Town. Dené and Les were actively back in my space again and we spent some quality time together. I had not seen much of them either since I had returned to Cape Town. The effect of being around the Magician energy once more, as well as the healing space of Liz's home, seemed to infuse me with lightness and the feeling of living again. Shortly after that, the mushrooms entered my life once more. While visiting Dené one day, he handed me a small bag of them. I had mentioned wanting to micro-dose to him a few days earlier and Universal synchronicity lined up. A few days later, I was given a second bag by a completely different friend who had no knowledge of my wanting to micro-dose. I continued to spend more time with Dené and Les. Being around their energy and Liz's space was incredibly helpful in finding direction in life again. I was also progressing smoothly with my book writing - the original first part of the book you are now reading today. I felt inspired and brought back to life. Once again, I found myself fully engaged in mind-opening conversations and experiences with my Magicians; and just like the first time around, Dené's cat, Poppy was around and in my space too. On one of my first visits there, she had leaped up onto the dining room table where I was sitting. She came and sat right in front of me and looked me dead in the eye. She sat like that for a few minutes, quietly observing me, before settling down to gently indicate she would like to have her ears scratched by me. It was at that moment, with Poppy sitting in front of me, that I understood her importance to my journey when I had been in Cape Town the last time. Not only had she assisted in my healing process, she also represented everything I had read in Liz's Spirit Animal book. I would never have thought that these delicate little balls of fluff would be so important to me and my journey.

My heart still pined for my Danny, however. We had made no further progress on where we were going with our relationship. I sought comfort instead in the knowing that the Universe would put me where I needed to be. I had found a surge of renewal in my faith with myself, as well as with the Universe. I had not felt this much in alignment in months! I had started my yoga practice once more and my eating habits were improving daily. While with Nina, I had tried on multiple occasions to get my yoga practice going, but with complete disregard for me, she always came in and interrupted me with either a mundane conversation or to talk about herself. It felt good to be stepping back into myself. I could feel my inner fire burning once more. My only challenge was the challenge of dealing with the huge distance between myself and Danny. This was something I chatted with Liz about. We looked at everything from as many angles as possible, but it did not seem to help. I still felt very lost and unsure of the situation. Then a strange encounter took place. It was with a friend of Dené and Les' - James. This complete stranger would be the one to give me clarity about my situation with Danny. James was very clearly another Magician energy. I sat next to him on Dené's couch, amused as he attempted fruitlessly to hit on me. My heart still sat in Australia and I had no interest in anyone else - which I was making abundantly clear. Then I started paying attention to what he was saying and more importantly, how he was saying it. He sounded exactly like Danny!

Even odder was that his height and his dislike of cats was identical to Danny as well. James then asked me a question. A question I had been asked before was, "What do you want, Tam?" This question had stemmed right back from Da Nang and was now resurfacing again in Cape Town. I felt I had worked out who I was and who I wanted to be. But with this question being asked once again, it was obvious that I still needed to look at it and continue to work through whatever I needed to find the answer once and for all. What I 'wanted' was Danny! However, with distance being an issue, I knew it was not the right answer. I needed to relook at what I did want. I knew that stability was part of that answer, as well as my purpose and desire to open a healing space for others. To find the rest of the answers, I had to achieve these steps first. The only way I could do this was to step back onto my path and embrace my purpose once more.

Later that evening I chatted with Liz about it. During that conversation, I knew I needed to decide on a plan for myself. I went straight to following what my heart wanted and decided that I would try and save up so that I could fly to Australia and meet Danny. Another part of me, however, said, "No! Vietnam is where you need to go." This country on the other side of the world had been calling me back for some time. But my heart wanted something else. I began feeling as if I was racing against the clock once more. I felt my time in Cape Town was coming to an end. I also knew I could only move from place to place so many times before I ran out of options. South Africa still did not feel like 'home' for me. I was needed elsewhere. For me, this was obvious because of all the doors that had been closed on me since my return. My stay in Cape Town was, in fact, a temporary one. A short pit stop to re-gather and re-calibrate myself. It presented an opportunity to process my journey, so that when I headed back on the next leg of my journey, I would be better equipped to deal with the challenges that arose along the way. It felt so similar to when I had been in Johannesburg - racing against the clock to manifest all that I needed when I first started on my journey. At that time, I had no doubts that I could manifest what I needed to. It had felt like my path was a clear one. This time I did not have that clarity. Then a had a peculiar meeting with an owl.

Dené and Les had asked me to join them on a hike up a section of the Table Mountain range. They told me about a place they had found that had clear quartz growing in abundance. I was intrigued to see this place and could use some grounding outdoors. I knew without question that I would be leaving South Africa soon - to where I did not know, but when the opportunity to collect crystals from my country of birth came up, it felt like an honor. Table Mountain is the Thirteenth Chakra of the planet and I knew that any crystal that came from there would be intensely powerful. We started our hike around mid-morning, but I did not realize when we started, just how challenging the hike would be. Having taken up smoking cigarettes months beforehand, my lungs felt like they were going to explode and an intense nausea set in that had me needing to stop and rest for a while. I sat down to rest under a tree and tried my hardest not to get sick. As I sat there, I recalled a conversation that I had with Liz the night before. We had been discussing ancient cultures and shamanism, in particular Shaman Sickness. She had told me about how shamans that had been called to their path would often get intensely ill beforehand. Our conversation had then moved to the indigenous cultures of North America and their lore on birth totems. Liz had pulled out one of her books on the subject and we soon discovered the owl was mine. I contemplated my conversation from the night before and thought, "I can't possibly be hiking up a mountain in South Africa to meet with a shaman or a Native American teacher." After feeling a little more settled, we continued our hike. The three of us finally arrived at the top of the mountain and the spot where the crystals could be found. As we reached our summit, an owl flew down to land on a rock just above us. He regarded us for a moment and then flew off to land on another rock a little further away from where we were. I was intrigued to say the least. Firstly, because it was the totem I had been told about the evening before, and secondly, because he was out during the day! I decided to get a closer look. He allowed me to get within a couple of steps from him. I sat myself down on the rock just next to his and I sat and watched him. He watched me the entire time I sat there, never moving or taking off. A sense of calm washed over me, I knew that where I was going to next would be pivotal to my journey. I climbed off my rock, leaving the owl in peace and set to gathering some crystals for myself.

When I got home that evening, I told Liz about my encounter with the owl. She pulled a few books from her shelf to have a look at the deeper meaning of the owl. Having identified him as my birth totem, we felt a need to find out what he represented at other levels as well. Every book she looked in gave us the same message: it was time to tap into the intuitive power I held. I needed to watch quietly for signs and omens that would be presenting themselves to me. They would give me the answers I sought. They also stated that I was stepping into a time of deep prophecy; that I would be learning the ability to see and feel events before they happened. It was also the perfect time for me to work on any creative projects I had. I would be finding myself in the right places and at the right times to manifest what I needed for myself. The books also spoke about my fiery passion and that I would be stepping fully into this. Owls appear in dark times to help one navigate their way through it. One book, in particular, spoke about me being able to see and hear what others could not. It spoke about the ability to see the truth in any matter. It explained that I was an old soul with inherent wisdom, that would continue to expand as I grew. I had a finely tuned awareness and sensitivity to others and that my greatest gifts were the ability to see the future and to connect with the spirit world through clairvoyance and clairaudience. The owl represented silent wisdom and healing. Everything she shared with me resonated so strongly, especially with my High Priestess energy. The owl had flown onto my path as a stark reminder of my powerful gifts. He was also a reminder of my need to complete my journey. My journey of stepping fully into my High Priestess power. The reference to me moving into a deep time of prophecy sat strongly with me and our conversations over the next few days came back to this topic regularly as we explored different schools of thought on this subject. We would always come back to the same conclusion - that the world was shifting into something new and ancient prophecies had a lot to do with it. North America and the indigenous culture there came up frequently in these conversations along with the subject of shamanism. A shift was coming, I could feel in my core: and so did Liz.

11

Becoming High Priestess

Quite a few days later after the hike, I had an emotional breakdown with my situation regarding Danny. I simply could not do the long-distance relationship with him any longer. With the lack of surety about me manifesting the money to travel to Australia and Danny not being in a position to come to me, I felt shattered and exhausted. I sat once again with the question of what is it that I really wanted. I was sick and tired of this question. I was at the end of my tether! During that time I saw James again. Once again, he asked me the question, "What do you want, Tam?" I realized I had to make a set decision about Danny and if I truly wanted a relationship or not. My overwhelming feeling was one of sitting in a state of limbo as far as Danny was concerned. I knew it was time step out of limbo, realising that this space was holding me back. I woke up on a Monday morning with my intuition screaming at me. It was time for me to choose what I wanted! My intuition was telling me that I needed to call off the long-distance relationship. I needed to keep my focus on my purpose and my path. My hanging in limbo and the resulting heartache was detracting from that. Danny had come onto my path at the right time and for the right purpose, but this was never meant to be a permanent thing. I knew what I needed to do. With a very heavy heart, I told

Danny I could no longer have a long-distance relationship with him any longer. I told him how I had sat in limbo for so long and that it was long overdue for me to move on. At one level, it was what my heart wanted, but I also knew it was not what I needed. I also had the realisation that I was looking at the relationship as a form of escape; another comfort zone. What I did want and need was to embrace my Divine Feminine independently of the support of another. It was only at this point in my journey that I realized the importance of this independence in the role of a High Priestess. What I needed was a teacher from whom I could receive guidance and support on my journey, not someone that I would allow to keep me from my journey. I also recognized that I kept myself from my journey by 'needing' a relationship. My connection with Danny had become solely emotionally and intellectually based but had no physical aspect to it. Due to a lack of physical intimacy during the past two years in my relationship with Ryan, I had lost an aspect of myself. I realized I had been running away from this aspect. An aspect I was scared to embrace because I felt not worthy enough. It is vitally important to remember that a healthy relationship requires a balance of all aspects of intimacy to be met. This was a part of my relationship with Danny that he was not able to give to me because of the long distance. Finally, I had identified another missing piece on my journey. I found a sense of peace.

I found myself visiting James that evening. Sitting on his couch I noticed a picture of owls that he had upon his wall. These owls were almost identical to the one I had seen on my hike with Dené and Les. This felt like the right place to be sitting in. What I did not realize at the time was that this would be the space where I would put another piece of myself back together. It was also the space where I found the missing piece to my Divine Feminine James gave me a beautiful gift that evening. After two nights in James' space, my intuition kicked back in at a heightened level and my path opened up before me. I felt whole and complete in the moment as the last missing piece had been restored to its rightful place. A massive part of my journey of transformation was completed. In that sacred space, I could acknowledge and heal many of my insecurities. I knew that it was safe for me to let them go and that they were no longer required to be an aspect of myself. Vietnam then began calling to me louder than before and I knew without question where I was meant to go next.

After having my empowering experience with James, I took some time for myself to contemplate my journey fully. I looked at all the aspects, lessons and experiences I had and came to better understand the deeper aspects of the High Priestess and my journey to becoming one. I understood what stepping into my power meant. As authentic beings, we all have a yin and yang aspect. Yin is our compassion, faith and the seat of our power. Yang is our honor, ability to take responsibility and how we create with that power. Stepping into High Priestess power meant that I needed to step into my yin and allow it to rise. Another crucial insight into the yin aspect was that this is where we store our toxic emotions; usually held there by fear, addictions and low self-worth. The power is there, but it is hidden beneath the murky depths of insecurities, traumas and depression. This was my case throughout a good portion of my journey. I had allowed this murkiness to cloud and stunt my power. I had needed to push through my murky depths and rediscover my power. When I had returned to Cape Town, I knew it was to relearn lessons I had been taught previously. But this was not case - the lessons were in fact teachings I had learned as a curious teenager... teachings that would prove crucial to the next stage of my journey. At that time, I had believed that these lessons were ones I had learned when I had stayed with Dené. I also believed that my journey was about me stepping into my High Priestess power. What I did not anticipate was that High Priestess was just the beginning and that by stepping into my power, I would be stepping onto a completely different journey - the journey of a Shaman.

Had I understood as a teenager, that this was what I was destined for, perhaps my path would have been easier. Looking back, I could say for certain that I was well equipped for my true calling back then already – I had everything I needed in order to commit to the Path. Along with this, I was given the tools required to pass any challenge and manage any experience that came my way. What I was lacking however, was the understanding of my calling and how to pursue it. Returning to Cape Town, I was back to relearn what I already knew: lessons and knowledge I had acquired in my youth. The difference was that I was now applying my knowledge, not just taking in the theory. Leaving Ryan and stepping into my transformative journey is where I went from Spiritual theory to practice. Reflecting on my relationship with Ryan, I knew for certain that he was meant to step onto my path. Ryan had brought me many Universal gifts and understandings. We had frequently discussed the global shift and the need for one. Just before I had left him, Ryan had told me, "Something big is coming, it's going change everything. More than that, I can't tell you. You will need to see for yourself." His words had stuck with me since then and I had indeed seen this for myself. I knew that he was meant as a teacher, not as a partner. I had come to understand the same thing with Danny. He was a teacher and a much-needed connection on the Collective. Having learned the hard way that Magicians and High Priestesses will always feel connected, I faced the painful reality that connections are not always meant to be intimate or permanent.

I then considered my experiences upon returning to Cape Town. I had arrived in a state of mid-transformation. Nina had offered her home to me out of genuine compassion - I saw that clearly - however, she was not in a place to offer me what I needed. She was battling her own murky depths and seemed to be drowning in them most days and had set to clinging to me as her way out. What I needed at the time was a mentor who could understand what I was processing. Along with this, I needed a neutral space where I could be left to withdraw into my own mind. I had come to understand that in my times of deep introspection, I had to be selective as to where I placed myself. I could not focus on anything or anyone else but myself during these times. I understood that if I tried to do this in a space that was not conducive, a feeling so similar to depression would set in and I would begin desperately seeking peace, stability and a way out. In my contemplative state, I understood that what my soul was pushing for was for me to surpass the levels of my emotions and thoughts and to seek to truly understand at the level of my soul. In essence, I was journeying within and for a time, I would not actually be present in the 'real world'. A space, if not understood by an outsider, could be horribly misinterpreted. If my focus is forced elsewhere, my depressed state would amplify to the point of shut down. I was gaining a deeper understanding of the experiences I had while in Vietnam -understandings that would be crucial in the coming months and years. Nina carried a fair amount of trauma that she was desperate to be rid of, but was not willing to do the groundwork required to achieve that. I found us in a nightly routine of her consuming a good bottle of wine or two and then unceremoniously unloading her problems onto me. With harsh comments such as, "You're the psychic, you give me the answer," followed by my feelings of obligation to her for helping me out, I had felt as if my soul was being torn in two over that time. Being in mid-transformation, I was in no space to lay down boundaries and neither was I able to see that boundaries were so desperately needed. The bit of journeying I did accomplish whilst with Nina, was my mushroom journey. To be frank, I was out of alignment at the time and I had slept through important parts of my journey. It was not until I had my falling out with Nina and moved into Liz's home that I was able to complete my transformation. It was in

Liz's neutral space that I pushed through to the other side. In that mindful space of contemplation, I understood all that I had learned, as well as where I had slipped and what concepts I needed to better understand or relearn. The pieces of my strange journey eventually came together to form a clear picture. As the picture became clearer, the more I knew that Vietnam was where I was meant to be heading next. At the time, I did not know the how, just that I knew it was correct. Before I could get to that however, I had some lessons to relearn and it was time for me to take on these lessons from my youth and become High Priestess.

My first lesson was that of mind over matter. I have been physically incapable of consuming alcohol for many years due to a Hiatus Hernia that I have. I acquired this in my twenties due to my high-stress corporate career and lifestyle. I was the 'sober' friend for many years. It wasn't until one sunny afternoon with Dené and Les that this all changed. Oddly, it was the same day that I had my first encounter with my Spirit Animal, the owl. Dené sat in front of me at a beach-styled bar and said, "Come on Tam, have a drink with us." I protested as usual and reminded him of the fact that I was physically incapable. His response was, "Mind over matter! Never mind it doesn't matter. It's all in the mind Tam. If you want to have a drink, you can. You just have to believe it."

Dené and his Magician logic! "Alright then, but if I get sick it's on you!" was my ambiguous response as we proceeded to order a tequila shot each. I took a deep breath, exhaled and shot the tequila back. It still tasted just as horrendous as it did in my twenties. It also shot a flame of fire through my solar plexus as it went past the point where my oesophagus and stomach meet - the exact point where my hernia sits. I took a few seconds to see if I would be sick or not, but it seemed Dené's mind over matter theory had worked. "See, it is all in the mind," Dené concluded, while smiling brightly at me and my accomplishment. Mind over matter is a very useful concept, however. Not just for knocking back rough shots of tequila. It is one of the cornerstones of the Magician. Portrayed on the Magician card are his tools which symbolize his sharp mind, deep intuition, groundedness and ability to create. Mind over matter signifies using the sharpness of one's mind in order to obtain complete control of your mental faculties - where what you are thinking and how you are thinking about it is imperative – for as one thinks, they create. This was one of my first understandings as a young Witch. As a young Witch however, I only had the theoretical understanding. My fiery shot of tequila was a taste of the practical side.

The second lesson I needed to relearn came from my experiences with Danny and Ryan. My relationship with both of them had meant to be exchanges on the Collective. Instead, I had misinterpreted both and had pursued intimate relationships with them that were never actually meant to occur. They had both had a profound purpose on my path. The purpose, however, was never a relationship. My relationship with Ryan was meant to be one of teacher and student. My relationship with Danny was meant to be one of support and strength to give me the boost I needed to leave Ryan and step onto my path – just as I had been for a number of clients previously - the clients that brought their ancestors with them to talk to me so I could give them direction to their path Danny and I had been in similar places with our relationships. He was in an unhappy and unhealthy marriage of ten years. We had both needed a nudge. Essentially, we were drawn together in order to encourage strength and healing in each other as we both experienced our individual journeys. I could see with clarity, just how far out the Collective could extend. A soul on the other side of the world sensing what you need, finds synchronistic events in order to give this support and encouragement to you. The magic workings of the Universe! In that moment, I found true gratitude for the gifts Danny and Ryan had given me. However, my lack of full understanding of the Magician-Priestess connection left me spun out and confused in both relationships. It was in closing the door with Danny and having my experience with James that I was able to fully step into my High Priestess and allow my yin to rise. My understanding of toxicity that came with a murky yin aspect, was my third lesson and a lesson I had learned during my time with both Ryan and Danny. I had momentarily found my power and was set to start working on removing the muck that held my power in place. I instead got lost in my presumed relationship with Danny and my that muck never truly lifted. Rather, a spew of further insecurities and unhealthy attachment to Danny had only suppressed my healthy yin power further. This is where I fully understood the importance of authenticity, and I knew this was the other lesson I had to relearn.

In order to step into myself, I needed to become aware of my authentic self. I had over the months asked the question, "Who am I?" In that moment with James, I had finally understood who I was - I was raw authenticity, I was myself. I recalled a term Liz had shared with me - intimacy - into-me-I-see. And see myself I did. Like gazing into a perfect mirror, my soul laid bare, with no shame or guilt. I had no fears or insecurities and understood that authentic love came from within; that loving the Self had nothing to do with ego. In fact, ego was far removed from the Authentic Self and had no place there. Along with the understanding of authenticity was the understanding of honor. When you stand within your authentic self, you see the importance of honoring the self. Having enough respect for the self to give it what it truly needs and deserves without any feelings of guilt or shame. This was me pushing through my murky layers and rediscovering my yin. This was where I became High Priestess - a High Priestess with a new understanding of mind over matter, toxic yin and authenticity and honor. From here, the lesson of faith flowed naturally. Possibly the most recurring lesson of all, my faith had been tested constantly. However, these tests were not about pass or fail; rather they were about attainment and being better each time. Danny was somewhat of a conundrum though. The insecure, fearful aspect of myself - my toxic yin - had wanted him. However, my authentic self had known better. My authentic self knew that Vietnam was where I was meant to be. I had spent roughly two months with Liz by then. In that time I had found myself back on my path, stronger and wiser. I hardly had to look to see the universal signs and messages. My intuitive voice had become clear and the Universe spoke loudly. It was a matter of maintaining my faith and allowing my journey back to Vietnam to unfold as it was meant to. Trusting my intuition to know when and where to act and to follow the signs.

2

The Drunk Magician

12

The Gift

"Opportunities are everywhere!" Waiting for a flight to Johannesburg, I noticed the words on an advert just in front of me. I smiled and thanked the Universe for its perfectly timed message and boarded my flight. I was en route to Johannesburg for the launch of my first book. I knew changes and Vietnam were coming soon. I needed to keep embracing life with an open mind and continue with the flow space I was in. I arrived in Johannesburg a little tired, but with a sense of excitement. Switching my phone off airplane mode and catching up with the world again, I found a request for my book from a Vietnamese gentleman living in the United States. He was recommended to me by a mutual friend. He explained that Vietnam was his home country and that the city of Da Nang was the city his mother was from. He explained that he had not been to Da Nang, but that he hoped to take his family there one day. We chatted for a good bit and I must say that I instantly liked him. There was a genuine kindness to him, a kindness I had felt numerous times while in Vietnam. I took my strange encounter with this kind man as a sign that anything was possible. It left me feeling rather optimistic about things and Vietnam felt that much closer. Receiving a message from Liz shortly after amplified this for me. "Be in the moment," were her words and the moment was a profound one! Walking out of the airport to the parking lot, I pondered on the moment and felt my mind 'stretching' in a sense. I couldn't just feel Vietnam - I could I see myself there and I was doing my work.

An old client of mine, Krissy, had offered to fetch me from the airport. Her message had arrived the night before with synchronistic timing, offering help if I needed. I gratefully accepted her offer as a welcomed relief. The idea of a long Uber ride from the airport to the friend I would be staying with had not sat comfortably with me, particularly when it would be late in the evening. So when the offer was made, I took it as a sign and gladly accepted. However, her being the one to fetch me from the airport was a little more than just 'Universal help'. We were sitting in contemplative silence when Krissy asked, "Tam, how do you use your intuition?" I had started to respond when we realized that we were lost. We had driven up and down what we thought was the right road for a good few minutes. I was sitting with a flat phone battery which did not help, and I could sense Krissy's discomfort with the situation. [5]It was late at night and we were two women lost in a Johannesburg suburb. This would make anyone feel uneasy. Krissy suddenly pointed out a man standing by the side of the road. "Should we ask him if he knows?" The man had appeared out of nowhere and seemed to be just standing there, waiting. It felt correct and so I trusted my intuition. We were both somewhat skeptical about asking a random stranger for directions at this hour of the night; particularly one who seemed to have appeared out of nowhere. We pulled over regardless, wound down the window to a safe level and asked him for directions. Needless to say, he knew exactly where we were going and gave us smooth directions. With directions so simple and precise, we arrived at my friend Wendy's home without any further issue. On the last few minutes of the drive over to Wendy's, I took up my explanation on intuition once more. Choosing to use our strange direction encounter as an example, I had explained that it was about getting the messages, seeing them for what they were and then having faith to follow through with those messages, "We needed direction. A man appeared to give us that. We trusted that asking him was correct and we arrived at our destination."

Krissy laughed as she caught the understanding and the odd way the Universe worked. I left Krissy in good spirits and embraced my beautiful friend Wendy. We then stepped into her home for what would be a truly synchronous visit.

Sitting across from Wendy, I happened to notice the owl pendant she had on. "I'm definitely in the right place," I expressed, as I began to fill Wendy in on my strange encounter with my owl. I recalled my encounter with my Spirit Animal weeks before on the mountain. I then shared about a second sighting I had just before I left for Johannesburg. A second, identical-looking owl, had landed on a tree outside of Liz's home early one evening. He let me get within close proximity before flying off. This set Wendy and I straight into catching up with one another. We shared stories of our recent experiences and the similarities were astounding! From our mutual healing processes, to our journeys with plant medicine, and stepping into our power. Then there was the obvious Spirit Animal. I was sitting across from an empowered Priestess and I knew that empowerment could change the world - that Priestesses, like Wendy, would change the world. We discussed our shared feeling of purpose and I shared the insights I had acquired. In that moment, I noticed a saying on her Kitchen wall. It was a saying I had seen before: Life takes you to unexpected places, love brings you home. Those were words I had seen previously in Johannesburg, while visiting Nikki. I had still been feeling disconnected with where home was for me. I still knew for certain however, that home was not South Africa. Seeing those words for the second time while I was still questioning where home was, was nothing short of serendipitous. It would be months before I would fully understand the true meaning of those words. That saying was a sign, however. Literally and figuratively. I had not been in Johannesburg more than a few hours and already I knew the next stage of my journey had begun and it was now out in full force.

With the conversations I had with Wendy and the massive influx of signs and synchronicities I was encountering in a short space of time, I knew I was on the right track. I had been in that space before and I knew it was correct. My short trip to Johannesburg felt like the completion of a cycle. It brought about a sense of closure, growth and a higher level of understanding. The icing on the Universal cake was my third owl sighting. It was my last night in Johannesburg while having dinner with Leo. Outside in the parking area, we both noticed a man. He seemed to be waiting for something and kept looking at us. He then looked up at the roof and back at us. "Come have a look, there's owls on the roof." We sat for a second in disbelief at what he had just said. Leo was well aware of what had been transpiring on my path, including my owls. We got up to have a look for ourselves and sure enough, sitting on the roof was a pair of owls. Owls that were identical to the two I had already seen. The feeling of everything being in alignment was intense. I saw myself in Vietnam clear as day. "Looks like you're heading to Vietnam my friend," Leo's words were more than confirmation of what I was seeing. My feeling had moved to vision and I knew I would be getting on a plane soon. I returned to Cape Town filled with faith, but I was also beginning to sit on limited time. My journey with Liz as my in-house mentor was coming to an end. Liz was moving and I needed to move as well. As much as Vietnam beckoned me, I had no means of getting there. I was seeing myself there almost daily and it frustrated me as the means to make it happen was not there. I still knew without a doubt that I would be leaving for

Vietnam, and soon. It was the same knowing I had the first time round. It was not something I could dispute.

Trying not to dwell too much on how to get to Vietnam, I found myself passing my days with a Magician that had recently walked onto my path. Jeremy, a rather broken and troubled Magician, but he was also soft and genuine. Our time together was short but enlightening. It was during our time together that he lent me a book on Shamanism. A book that was given with strict instructions to return - especially if I was destined for Vietnam. I never did get the chance to see Jeremy again or return his book. The book however, spoke directly to me. The author of the book expanded on ideas and understandings I had on my mind for years. There were teachings and concepts that I had acquired in my teens, as well as the understandings I had received during my past life regression. He spoke on how the world is on a tipping point and humanity still continues to repeat history to our detriment. We continue to repeat the cycles of intolerance, corrupt power and war. He expressed concern about the destruction of the earth and explained that humanity could soon be obliterated once again if we did not bring about a shift in consciousness. His comparison of the world to be that of a ticking time bomb sat with me strongly. That deep knowing of the shift that was required resonated within me. I knew without question that the ways of the Ancients would be our salvation - much the same as my brother Jadie had expressed so many years before. The author went on to expand on the topic of women and Mother Earth; discussing how the Divine Feminine had become abused and suppressed - thus forcing the world into its current state of imbalance. Having recently stepped into my Yin and knowing how empowering it was, I could not dispute what I was reading. I combined his concepts to my theory on Magicians. How their oppression by society and forced conformity was causing imbalances in the world. It seemed the world was out of balance on both its Yin and Yang. The

Shamanism book landing in my hands was more than synchronicity. Particularly when Liz insisted I watch a specific DVD she had.

"Tam we have got to watch this movie before you leave! I feel it is relevant for you and the things we have been discussing."

It was The Shift, by the late Dr. Wayne Dyer. Looking at the title, it did not take much to convince me. Later that evening, I found my mind being expanded once more. The movie was themed around the feminine and how it had been misused. Once again Yin and the shift were making themselves known. I knew that where I was going next would be an expansion on these two recurring themes. I also knew without question that the shift was one into a Yin-based consciousness - one sustained with compassion and nurtured by acceptance. With little over a week left with Liz, time was running out for me. I knew where I wanted to go. Yet something was not yet in alignment. I felt there was something more I needed to understand. Along with this was the feeling of a new teacher coming onto my path.

My experience with James and stepping into my power was raising questions for me. My questions were around the Eastern concepts of Kundalini awakening and Shakti energy. The feeling of a teacher kept raising itself along with these questions. I felt compelled to contact a friend of mine – Anton, whom I had met through Nina. Anton walked a similar path to mine - one filled with synchronicities and strange, magical happenings. He aptly called it the 'Cookie Trail'. Anton is a Yogi. As such, he has spent a fair amount of time in India studying Yogic practices. We had chatted previously on the subject of Shakti and Divine Feminine energy. I sent him a message expressing my feelings about a teacher, along with the questions I had around Shakti and Kundalini Awakenings. His reply was insightful,

"I am lately often asked about the topic. So in response, asking about a Guru is valid. However, recommending a guide or a teacher is ultimately filled with an immense amount of danger and possible pitfalls. Especially for a woman, for all obvious reasons. In my experience, ego acts at its most deceitful, even subconsciously, on this topic. Tantra is exactly what led Yoga onto the wrong path over the past thousand years as man used the powers of Kundalini for all the wrong reasons."

Everything he was saying was resonating with me. Anton then offered to send me a book he believed would assist me, along with additional information on the word Guru - the Eastern word for a spiritual teacher. The book he sent me was a fascinating read. It expanded on the knowledge and understandings I had already received. His explanation for Guru was immensely helpful as well. He explained that the Guru resides in all of us and that the self is the best teacher. My conversation with Anton had sparked something else for me - it was something that I had raised previously with Liz. One of the biggest factors that had kept me from being in my power, was the fear of me losing my humility and misusing my power. I wanted to make a difference in the world - inspire change on a much larger scale. Could I achieve this without ego getting in the way? As much as I was in my power, this fear would sit just above it for a while still. I knew I had far more wisdom and a higher awareness of my core lessons, yet my lesson with self-worth was still needing some work. Over the months that followed, I came to discover that this was the basis for my fear.

It was Saturday morning and I was meant to be leaving Liz's space on Wednesday. I still did not know where I was going. I knew where I was meant to be going, however. I reached a breaking point with my frustration and breathed into a deep meditative space. I pushed past the fears and doubts and I asked myself the infamous question, "What the hell do you want Tam? It really is time to choose." I had asked myself this question repeatedly for months. To add to this, I had other people asking me the question as well. I knew the next stage of my journey had begun and I needed to take the next step. The next step required me to decide what that step would be. I directed the question at my soul and the immediate response was, "I want to open a healing space in Vietnam. I have souls there I am meant to be working with."

I was not going to dispute the response and sought deeper insights. I messaged Leo and asked her what I felt guided to ask. I then messaged Vũ, the Tarot Reader from Hanoi. The feedback from Leo and Vũ was consistent and clear. A healing space was correct and it came with a higher purpose. It was also noted that I would receive the assistance needed and that it would come without hindrance. Vũ shared an additional insight with me - he warned that I would have an issue with local police later on in Hanoi. However, it would be a matter that could be resolved easily and that I should not worry on it too much. Not stopping my intuitive flow, I messaged someone else: Sue. We had gotten back into contact with each other after she learned I moved out of Nina's space. We had cleared the air between us and both understood what had happened while I had been staying with Nina. Sue had become very kind to me and had often told me to reach out to her if I needed help with anything Her words were ringing in my mind and I knew it was correct to reach out to her. I sent her a message and allowed the Universe to do the rest.

I knew I had one last task to complete. I reached for my Tarot set and drew a single card. The Devil. My intuitive response was a single word: addiction. The topic of addiction had not been present on my path for a number of years. Following a falling out with Jadie years before, I had very little connection to the world of addiction. Yet somehow it felt very prevalent. I stored the Devil detail in the back of my mind and drew myself out of my meditative space. I decided to take a walk to clear my head and burn off some of the excess energy I was carrying. Minutes into my walk I received a call from Sue. With an immense amount of compassion in her voice, "Tam, darling I'll help you. I will send you what you need to get you to Vietnam. You have done so much for me. I'm more than happy to help you."

I stood there on the sidewalk, speechless for a moment. I could not believe what I was hearing. I had done some Tarot sessions with Sue previously, but I never knew the full impact of the gratitude she had for me. To this day, I still have not found the words to express my gratitude towards her. The manner in which she gave was unconditional and filled with compassion. I then knew without question that I was destined for Vietnam. Once again, this country on the other side of the globe was pulling me back. I contacted a travel agent in Hanoi to make arrangements and shortly after that, my visa was ready and my flights were booked. I would be leaving within days. It still astonishes me how fast everything fell into place and how my assisting someone would come back with so much gratitude. I had also just needed to authentically ask for what it was that I truly wanted - then BAM! It all just connected and the Collective Conscious did its magic thing. Who says miracles don't happen?

That Wednesday I moved from Liz to Sue, as I passed my final days in Cape Town. It was over this time that the Serenity Prayer and the Lion kept nudging me. Before I had left for Vietnam previously, I had acquired a Tree of Life bracelet. Over the months that followed, that bracelet came to represent Wisdom for me. Whilst in Hoi An, I added a Buddha bracelet as I learned the lesson of Serenity. I felt drawn to add a representation for Strength; and with the Lion being so prominent in my mind and a main feature on the traditional Strength card, it seemed to be the correct option. The Lion however, was proving to be very elusive! I had searched in almost every shop, crafters stall and market that was within my reach. Elephants however, seemed to be in abundance. Every shop or stall I visited would respond with, "Sorry we don't have a Lion, but we do have Elephants." It was not until my second last day that I finally found my Lion bracelet. It was in a tiny crafters store in the center of Cape Town's city. I had found a Tiger's Eye necklace with the Big Five on it. I asked the woman that managed the store if she would adjust it to my requirements and leave just the Lion. She happily agreed and asked if I was a Leo. I responded that I wasn't, but explained why I wanted the Lion. She understood the meaning, and then explained why she had asked. Leo was her astrological star sign. My Strength bracelet being crafted by a Leo was perfectly fitting. With Lion sitting strong on my wrist, I knew I had everything I needed and I was now ready to travel. Filled with intrigue and excitement, I wondered what Vietnam would have in store for me this time around. Would I be able to achieve success in creating a healing space? What lessons and transformations would ensue this time around? Arriving at Cape Town International Airport for the long twenty-three-hour journey in front of me, I once again stepped onto a plane and into a massive shift.

13

Base

I left Cape Town in mid-winter and arrived to the scorching heat and humidity of Hanoi. I was set to stay with Ollie and Tracy for a couple of days while I looked for a decent hostel in the Old Quarter of Hanoi. I had not seen either of them since I had left Hanoi the first time round. We had a lot of catching up to do. I also found myself fully booked with sessions almost every day. I had not been this busy since I left the crystal shop in Johannesburg. In fact I had never been this busy! Within a few days I had found a semi-quiet hostel with a private room close to one of the main streets in the Old Quarter. The location was ideal and allowed me to explore the Old Quarter more than I had done the last time I was in Hanoi. I stepped out into the nighttime humidity of the Old Quarter, completely open to feeling the energy and allowed my intuition to guide my steps. I had been walking for only a few minutes when a rather attractive Israeli man called out to me. He was saying something about a drink promotion for a bar he was standing in front of. I simply smiled and carried on walking. Something about the bar seemed to catch my attention however, and I felt a pull towards it. Still figuring my way around, I happened to walk past the same bar a second time. I recognized it as being the same one because the same drink promotion was being shouted at me

- this time by a rather loud Canadian-sounding guy. I was not quite done with my explorations however, and I walked on somewhat amused, but most certainly curious about this bar. This time I made a mental note of the location as I had the intention of returning there later. Something in the intuition suggested it was a good idea.

Taking in the sights, sounds and smells of Hanoi's Old Quarter, I was captivated. Something about the energy intrigued me. It was a magic energy of sorts, but I could not quite place the type of magic that surrounded me. I felt far more in-tune with Hanoi than I had during my first time there. When I had stepped out into the streets earlier that evening, I had set the intention to connect. Not fully understanding the connection, I allowed it to remain open in order to fully understand. Finally done with my explorations, I decided to head back to the bar from earlier. I snuck in before anyone else could shout that damned promotion at me again and took a seat at the bar. I ordered a drink from the friendly Vietnamese bartender and took in my surroundings. It was very much what one would term a *dive bar*, but the energy in there was identical to what I felt on the streets. The energy was more intense however, and felt very welcoming.

I had not been there more than a few minutes when one of the other promoters came up to me. "Good grief, what promotion did these guys have for me now?" was my amused thought. In an accent which I could not quite place as British or Irish, I was offered to join a group of people he was sitting with. A fiery ginger from London, he introduced himself to me as Greg. He resonated on the same frequency as the energy in the bar and his smile was genuine. I took him up on the offer and was soon being introduced to a large group. There was a natural flow through the place and I found myself enjoying a number of enlightening conversations that flowed naturally through the group. When it came time for the bar to close, I chose to join a small group at another place around the corner. Walking out, I looked for the name of the bar. A London Underground-styled sign greeted me with the words Base Bar. I felt a bizarre tug on my Solar Plexus and knew I would be back. I soon found myself in a small bar with a smaller group of people. Again, there was that natural flow. The group I was with seemed to be mostly people that worked at Base. This included Greg whom I had met earlier, as well as the owner of Base. She was a captivating Vietnamese woman, whose warm, genuine smile seemed to exude magic. She was introduced to me as Lily. I realized I was sitting next to the loud Canadian from earlier, who introduced himself as Joe. I took to Joe and his peculiar offbeat energy instantly. I was then introduced to Matt, a rather inebriated youngster from the Southern State of South Carolina. He was like a rebel with a cause and looked like a whole heap of trouble, but in an oddly genuine way. Matt felt like pure authenticity. He was who he was. And owned it! I was also briefly introduced to one of the bartenders of the bar we were in. Chris or "The Benz" as everyone called him. He had an affectionate smile and welcoming energy and I could not help but like him. He joked about serving degenerates at rough hours and handed Matt his drink. "Yeah, yeah don't give me that shit. We're all degenerates at heart, Benz," was Matt's good-natured response. I looked at this group of new energies. Took them all in and felt cords extending from my Solar Plexus to reach out to these Souls. Making a solid connection, the sensation felt strange. I felt safe, secure and for the first time, I felt at home. Entranced by the enlightening and light-hearted conversation for a few hours, I eventually returned to my hostel at the ridiculous hour of pre-dawn. Closing my eyes for a much needed sleep, I knew I could not dispute the pull towards these people and Base.

I was in Hanoi for just over a week before I headed down to the city of Da Nang. I had pre-planned two separate trips to the coastal city. My fond love for it nudging me to consider making it my home while in Vietnam. However, I needed to establish if that was where I was meant to be. Could I establish a healing space there? I already knew the viability of Hanoi. Yet I had struggled quite severely with my physical health there previously. The high level of pollution and the strange intensity of its energy made living in Hanoi a challenge. I was no stranger to the chaos of city living, having grown up in Johannesburg. Hanoi however, was something completely different. I much preferred Da Nang over Hanoi for numerous reasons. However, I was not sure if Da Nang was where I was needed. My first month in Vietnam would involve a bit of 'backwards and forwards' between Hanoi and Da Nang to work it out. My first trip to Da Nang though, was rather short-lived. I had arranged to stay at Nga's Homestay once more. I had maintained contact with her over the months since leaving Vietnam and we had grown a lovely friendship over that time. Shortly after arriving, she introduced me to a youngster from the Ukraine. We did not have much in common, but when he began discussing Sa Pa with me, my interest peaked. I had heard of Sa Pa before and seen pictures of its vivid green, terraced rice fields. I had yet to see it for myself. Something about Sa Pa seemed correct and I chose to shorten my time in Da Nang and head back north.

Sa Pa is a town in the Hoàng Liên Son Mountains of north west Vietnam, a well-known trekking base that overlooks the terraced rice fields of the Muong Hoa Valley. Hill tribes, such as the Hmong, Tay and Dao, make up much of the town's local population. It was here that I discovered shamanism in the East. It had never occurred to me to research shamanic roots in the East, much like I had never considered researching Tarot in Vietnam the year before either. I spent one night in a local Hmong Homestay. Here they shared their history, traditions and systems with me and the other guests they had. It was during one of the conversations that our hosts mentioned they had shamans in the village. It took a few seconds for my conscious mind to comprehend what I had just heard. Then my curious nature took over and a flurry of questions ensued. This was the first time I had an opportunity to speak to a different culture about their shamanic roots. Prior to that, I had only interactions with African and Western traditional healers. A few of them had often asked me to come and train under them, but that inner voice would always say, "That's not your path." I learned that the Hmong villages consisted of at least one shaman - a chosen one who underwent a transformation of sorts. They explained that while most were male, a female shaman was not unheard of. It was then explained that once a shaman has gone through their transformation, they begin speaking a different language - a language the local people do not fully understand. This is said to be what distinguishes the shaman from the rest of the village. Their shamans are healers for ailments of any kind. This includes physical, mental and spiritual dis-eases. They are renowned for the ability of prophecy, as well as being consulted to connect with the Spirit realm. That link between what I had read in the Shamanism book and what I had discovered in Sa Pa was staring me in the face. I suddenly found myself recalling my mushroom journey; a very specific part of it. As the mushrooms had started to take effect, I recalled seeing an Asian man floating towards me on a stream of rainbow-colored light. This time however, I recognized the face as being that of a Vietnamese man. A very well-known national hero in fact. It was like watching puzzle blocks falling into place as I assessed the symbology of the journey I was re-seeing. I knew in that moment that Vietnam had presented itself to me back then already. It took five months to understand this part of my mushroom journey. It was no coincidence that the Vietnamese culture had Shamanism at its roots. It was also no coincidence that I was there and seeking to create a healing space. This was where the insights stopped.

I returned to Hanoi and spent a few days there before heading back to Da Nang. I spent my evenings at Base, as had become custom for me - engaging in enlightening conversations. It was during this time that I met two more members of the peculiar Base group. Tôm and li Kai rui. Tôm was a two-meter tall hooligan from the supposed 'rough' city of Luton, England and li Kai rui, an almost just as tall hooligan from the frosty cold state of Minnesota, USA. They were the perfect picture of mischief and a feeling of authenticity radiated from them. That connection from my Solar Plexus reached out to them and I knew they were also just as significant as the rest of this strange group. Tôm and li Kai rui were out on a bar hop for the night. Tôm, asked if I would care to join their mini 'pub crawl' and my curiosity got the better of me. I wanted to know more about these peculiar characters and why they seemed to resonate with me so strongly. Thank goodness for that shot of tequila and Dene's lesson on mind over matter weeks before. These boys could drink! I quickly learned I was running with the big dogs. I managed to keep pace however, and was privy to very deep and insightful conversations. This group were without question, highly enlightened souls. It was also safe to say they behaved like degenerates. Yet this is what gave them their authentic quality - they were who they were. I still however, felt I was missing something about them. The night before I left for Da Nang, I was chatting with Joe. He was telling me about his life back home. It was very apparent he was no stranger to nature. From what I was hearing I got the feeling that he felt very at home in nature. 'Shaman' keep repeating in the back of my mind to the point where I could not ignore it. "What do you know about shamanism?" I enquired seemingly out of nowhere. Joe's response threw me for second when he replied with "Peru, Amazon and, oh yeah, Ayahuasca." He then gave me a somewhat peculiar smile and walked off. Was my intuition messing with me or was Joe a shaman and either did not know it or he knew very well to test some theories before imparting wisdom? This group from Base had left me wondering who the hell they were and what they were all about. I left for Da Nang shortly after, this time feeling discontent about leaving Hanoi. Almost as if I was leaving home.

My second trip to Da Nang was proving to be very uneventful. I was beginning to feel stagnant and Hanoi pulled at me constantly. After mulling over where it was I actually wanted to be settled, Hanoi just seemed to dominate. Even the health factors became minor adjustments that I would just need to make. Hanoi was pulling me in - and quickly. I hit a point with that old restless feeling and I knew without question that I was meant to be in Hanoi. I had work to do there and a part of me knew lessons were there to be learned and understood. In that moment, I made the decision to return to Hanoi and without hesitation, I booked myself a bus ticket. I would be arriving the next morning at the splendid hour of five AM and would not be able to check into my hostel until ten. Nevertheless, it was happening. I just did not know if I had chosen Hanoi, or if Hanoi had chosen me. All I knew was that it felt perfectly correct. I also knew I would be in for an interesting challenge. How much strength would I need to make it in the city of Hanoi, without losing my health? Physically, mentally and spiritually. Through the Collective, I had manifested myself to Vietnam; trusting my intuition all the way. Would I be able to manifest my healing space? Just how far could I take the whole mind over matter concept? Then there were my questions around Shamanism, the peculiar souls at Base and why the ancestors had brought me here. These were my ponderings and contemplations over the fourteen-hour sleepless bus trip back up to Hanoi.

I did indeed arrive at the ridiculous hour of five AM. I had not anticipated the sleepless journey, however. My hostel was kind enough to let me store my luggage there until check-in, but check-in would need to wait. Where does one go at five AM in Hanoi to pass the time? Base Bar would have been ideal, but I knew it would be closed already. The only other options were the infamous "Beer Corner" or the bar I went to on my first night at Base - Pirates Den was a rather shady-looking bar hidden away on the first floor above a motorbike repair shop. As I had suspected, it was still open and filled with the usual late night degenerates that probably should have stumbled home already. I had only met the guys that worked there a few times in passing. The "Benz" was working along with a few of the other bartenders I had met. Two of them were trying to see who could get a lemon quarter into the mouth of a customer. A customer who had passed out in the corner and was snoring on their couch, mouth wide open. If nothing else, at least I would be guaranteed some entertainment to help keep me awake. Pirates Den, as offbeat as it was, had a magic to it as well. It was another place I felt rather at home in. Its energy was somewhat different to that of Base, but it was a space I felt comfortable and safe in. By eight AM however, exhaustion got the better of me. I returned to my hostel in the hopes that, if I dozed off in their reception area, they would let me check in a bit earlier.

14

Initiation Training

Within my first week of having chosen to live in Hanoi, I found myself in a steady routine. I also had a follow-up reading with Vũ. My reading was optimistic and showed I was on track. He made mention that things may slow down a bit over the coming month of August; which at the time, had just begun. He advised that this was common and that I should not be concerned. He did mention however, that if I got ill, I was to contact him as he would have a solution for me. Vũ then went on to give deeper insights into the month of August. He explained that the seventh month of the Lunar calendar is said to be when the spirit and ancestral realms walk the earthly plane - a time when ancestors are allowed to be as close as they possibly can and loved ones can connect with the other side. The month of the Hungry Ghost, as it is known in most Asian countries, is a time when one simply lays low. No big decisions should be made and one should be wary of wandering souls. With my steady routine however, I soon put all thoughts of wandering souls and hungry ghosts aside.

To add to my routine, I had chosen to take on a couple of English teaching classes in order to build stability quickly. Stability that included getting my own space - something I had not had in over a year. Not since I had left Ryan. I was beginning to feel very done with suitcase living and craved my own sanctuary. My decision to take on teaching English however, was a fear-based one. As much as I was incredibly busy, I still had my doubts. Doubts of being able to rely solely on my work. I knew intuitively that it was not the right decision, particularly when my Strength bracelet broke and left pieces of itself on the streets of Hanoi. It happened on the way to teach my first class. While holding onto the back rail of my scooter taxi, I felt something cold land in my hand. I looked to see pieces of my bracelet and I knew instantly that something was not correct. I knew that in taking on the classes, I was handing over my power to fear. I pushed the thought aside and carried on with my routine.

As the days passed, I was drawn to carry a specific crystal with me. I had been having some peculiar experiences at Base and I wanted deeper insights. I had a piece of polished kyanite with me. I had acquired it a few years back when it's multitude of blue tones had caught my eye. I had worked with it since then to help enhance my intuition. My experiences over those nights when I carried it with me, were profound. The knowledge and wisdom I acquired was intense. A good portion of the insights were repetitions of lessons and teachings I already had - teachings I had come across as a curious teenager and the ones I had relearned prior to returning. The number of teachers that passed through and frequented Base was exponential. By teachers I'm not referring to English Teachers that one finds so commonly in the city. I'm talking about Spiritual Teachers. Mentors from all walks of life. Base was proving to be a very enlightening space indeed. If it was not me finding a teacher with lessons, it was me doing the teaching. I almost never found myself sitting alone. Base seemed to attract high level souls and I often found myself in transformative or highly synchronistic conversations. An interaction with a very young Vietnamese woman named Jasmine, was one in particular that stands out. She seemed to appear out of nowhere and offered her hand to me, "Hey I'm Jasmine. Can I sit here?" indicating the seat next to me. "I think you would understand the meaning of life and I would like to share it with you."

Nothing about what she said sounded crazy or delusional; particularly considering the types of conversations and experiences I had been having. She sat down, and the energy that emanated from her would possibly be best described in vivid colours.

"Live! Freely! But keep your head about you. Life is about doing what you want, but remembering your respect and responsibilities."

She then patted me on the leg, smiled and stood up to disappear into the crowd. The ancient Wiccan law of 'harm none, do as you will' came to mind. It had been one of the first teachings I had gained as a teenager. As long as one had no ill intentions, it did not matter what they did. It was a teaching that had become a core philosophy of mine. Jasmine's explanation however, seemed to come with a deeper sense of freedom.

With kyanite in hand, I had found myself encountering Matt more around Base. I also met one more important member of the peculiar Base group: Zain. Zain and Matt had been best friends almost since meeting one another. Soul brothers for sure, their bond ran deep. The more I got to know Matt however, the quicker a fondness and love grew for him. He was so genuinely authentic, that it was easy to love him. He seemed to have his life together, but he looked lost at the same time. I would catch him staring off into space, looking like he had the world's issues on his shoulders. He was rather guarded and would not open up to just anyone. I recall one of our first conversations. I had asked him about a tattoo he had on his hand. Something about the tattoo felt symbolic and made me curious. He gave a very short reply and indicated it was a personal thing. However, as our friendship progressed, the more open he became. I never once felt uncomfortable in Matt's space. On some nights after Base had closed, he would walk me back to my hostel and stay the night. There was no awkwardness at all. Often, we both had plans for the day and we would part ways after morning coffee. During the days of carrying my kyanite however, there was a day where neither of us had plans. We opted for a chilled day that started with coffee, a joint and a deep conversation.

We sat drinking cups of coffee and smoking joints as we chatted for hours on varying subjects. I learnt much about Matt that day and he about me. I learned about his Cherokee roots, his passion for working with trees and nature and that he was another broken, yet highly gifted Magician. I showed him a copy of my book that I had with me and offered to lend it to him. I felt the insights I shared may help him find some direction. He said he would think about it and maybe borrow it later down the line. "Sure, when you're ready," I replied and placed the book back on my shelf. Only for it to fall straight back off again. I picked it up and gave it to Matt. "I think you're ready to take it now," I said jokingly. We had chatted a fair amount about synchronicities and spiritual experiences that morning. Matt seemed very new to the world of Spirituality. He had experienced a few altered states of mind and moments of connection while sober. Yet, like with most Magician energies I had encountered, he struggled to reach that space in a sober state. Matt began sharing the meaning of his tattoo with me. He explained that it was a replica of a compass. He had been on a two month-long trek through the Appalachian Mountains in North Carolina, USA. For two months his only concerns were shelter and food. He explained that it was the most connected he had ever felt. The compass was a reminder of where that connection came from - a reminder of where True North was. That understanding of humanity needing to re-connect with the Earth leapt to mind and I knew that returning to the ways of the Ancients was correct. I took the opportunity to ask him about one other tattoo he had, "Why the Lion? That's my country's animal. It's an odd tattoo for an American to have," I questioned.

"I don't know. I've just always been drawn to them." He explained that the tattoo had a few meanings, but mainly it represented courage. He then explained his third tattoo. A tattoo of three letters - SBS. He explained it was a tattoo that was shared with a few people. It had started as a joke and was meant to mean "Stop Being Sober". However, the group that shared the tattoo began to see other meanings to it as well. "Start Being Sober", "Start Being Smart" and "Stop Being Stupid". The tattoo had become a representation for whatever was appropriate in the moment. Matt then went on to share intriguing information about Base. I had been sharing my bizarre experiences there and he instantly understood what I was sharing. He explained that Lily was an interesting lady. She was, in fact, very gifted! She had the ability to look through the veil and sense people's vibes. She also knew how to create space. She had built something special with Base. He added that the people who worked there helped to hold the space. He shared that he had built a family with the people there; that Base was home for him. Base suddenly made a lot more sense. Lily and most of the people that worked there were Magicians. I had stumbled across a Magician bar. Who would have thought!

That night at Base, I was more mindful than ever. Now knowing the space I was sitting in, I was paying attention on all levels. I once again had my kyanite with me and once again, I had a number of profound experiences. The first was when I noticed the letters D.M.T written on the back wall of Base. DMT or Dimethyltryptamine is a psychoactive substance that is found naturally in plants and animals. It is also commonly produced in humans. Known as the Spirit Molecule, DMT is an active ingredient in the well known Ayahuasca. It can also appear in a smokeable form known as Changa. The first time I had an opportunity to experience it was with James. He had been given Changa by a friend and offered for me to try. My soul had leaped at the opportunity, but my fears talked me down and I declined. I asked Joe about the DMT being written on the wall and was told there was a rumor that it would be around Hanoi in the coming weeks. As always, he spoke with a strange twinkle in his eye. I then turned to find myself sitting next to a rather attractive man. He struck up a conversation with me and I soon learned he was a US Marine. I had never had the opportunity to speak with someone who had experienced war first hand, aside from my dad who never divulged very much. With war being a dominant subject on my path, I felt pulled to ask some questions, "War is a concept that I struggled with. It makes no practical sense and yet we seem to keep repeating it."

I asked him why he would go to war in the first place. He explained that he did not agree specifically with the idea of war or killing. However, the concept of brotherhood, taking a bullet for another soul and loyalty were strong enough reasons for him. He shared how deep the connection was between soldiers, "You have no one else out there. You have to trust and rely on one another. We're able to read one another without needing to say anything. The connection between me and my brothers is a special bond."

He then paused for a second, looking like he was reflecting back on something, "Can you name one person that you, without hesitating, would take a bullet for?" he questioned out of the blue. Without hesitating I pointed to Matt behind the bar and said, "You see that guy over there? I'd take a bullet for him. In fact, I know a few people here that I would do that for."

I surprised myself at my response. Yet I knew what I had said was the truth. Strangely, this Marine was so at peace for someone who had experienced war first hand. I have had the conversation of a coming war with numerous people. The Shamanism book and my past life regression had amplified this idea for me. I could not help feeling that with the shift, there was the strong possibility of war. Then I understood it! We were already at war - with one another and with ourselves. I knew that aspects such as brotherhood and loyalty would be imperative for the shift. Along with this, we needed to find our connection again; the connection with the self and the connection with the Collective. I then knew what it was that we were shifting away from - the war against ourselves.

The night progressed and I found myself at Pirates Den. Yet another space run by Magicians. It was in watching and paying attention that I saw them - their playful energetic interactions with one another; the enlightening level of the conversations; and the sheer magic vibe that was being weaved before my eyes. They were creating the space in which they were working. There were four of them behind the bar that night. It was like watching magic happen as they set the tone and flow in the place. There was not a bad vibe in the room. Everyone was connected as much as they were all separate. A man sat down next to me and said, "I'm sorry there is just something about your vibe. Do you mind if I sit here? I really want to know who you are."

He had noticed me earlier on in Base and each time he had seen me I looked genuinely happy. This seemed to strike him as being very out of the ordinary. He then questioned me about it. "You're either permanently on drugs, genuinely happy or you've mastered social engagement so well, that you can disguise your true feelings."

This one threw me off for a second, but then I knew without question that I was genuinely happy. I realized in that moment, how far I had come in just a few months. I was in complete alignment with myself and had discovered authentic inner peace and self-love. "Yes, I am genuinely happy," I replied. Well, this seemed to cement a friendship with this guy, "Then I definitely want to hang around you more often." This brought the understanding of how much people lacked authentic connection and how inauthentic social engagements could be. It was no wonder that finding authenticity felt rare. I then understood that we attract the things we want most for ourselves. The connection within the Collective is expansive, yet many do not know how to plug-in or even realise that the connection is there. The secret to plugging in, is that you connect through yourself.

My final experience for that night was my encounter with Cat. A rather crazed, off the wall character from a small town in the middle of nowhere, Australia. Cat was like a walking canvas of spiritual symbology. If ever one was looking for a sign, Cat was it. The artwork on his body struck chords all over the place - from the full moon cycle tattooed on his neck to the pictorial image of Shakti along his back. A bit of a conversation flowed between us, but Cat seemed to be in a rather messy state. It was almost as if he was stuck between states of consciousness. In that moment, a thought occurred to me. Sometimes the Magician back-pedals and reverts to Fool energy. They back-pedal to either willingly relearn the lessons of the Fool or because they have overstepped the boundaries and pushed it too far. This leads them to blindly wander the world - directionless. It seemed Cat was on a tipping point with this. Sitting in the group was another familiar face, li Kai rui. He had been watching my encounter with Cat and out of nowhere proclaimed, "What the hell, you two are identical. Like a weird set of twins from different parents."

Cat happened to be a Sagittarian as well. Born the day after me to be exact. Yet this was not enough to explain li Kai rui's strange proclamation. I asked him what he based his logic on, and he explained that we looked the same. Not physical looks - it was something else that he couldn't quite explain. Cat for sure was Magician, so I could see the connection link. Cat was also the most lost Magician I had come across. He had stepped far out of reality and possibly did not know how to find a way back. If Cat was a twin of any sort, he would have been a representation of my Shadow. He was like an understanding of what could go wrong on one's path if they did not keep their head about them. Jasmine's words rang in my ears and I felt I had obtained more than enough insights for one evening. I returned to my hostel where I contemplated on what had transpired over the last few days. I noted how much Magician energy I had been around and I knew an inner shift was coming. Nothing could have prepared me for the transformation I was heading towards.

15

The Goddess Rises

It was ten in the morning and it was time to go home. I had been up since the previous morning. I had seen clients, taught an English class and then spent the remainder of the night at a trance party that Ollie had thrown. I was now at the after party with the hot Hanoi summer sun beating down on me. I was starting to feel off center. I asked a friend of mine, Sid, if she would order me a taxi; my phone having died hours earlier. She asked where I was going and I gave her my address. "You're staying in the Old Quarter?" she asked with great surprise.

"It's temporary until I find a more permanent place. Which should hopefully be soon. I'm quite over the hostel life!"

I was also quite over the day and was relieved to put my head on a pillow a while later. Sid had reminded me of something I had needed to do, however. I was at a turning point where I needed to either extend my hostel living or find a more settled option. The area of Long Biên had been mentioned to me frequently, but I had yet to find anything that resonated. While contemplating my living arrangements, I mindlessly scrolled through Facebook when an advert caught my attention:

"Room for rent in Long Biên." I read through the post and the place sounded ideal. There were no photos however, but something prompted me to make an inquiry. The synchronicity of Long Biên was too much to ignore. Directly beneath the rental post was another post that caught my attention: "The dark Goddess rises to take the throne. The King will be removed." It was a reference to a solar eclipse that was due the next evening. The same night as the New Moon, hence the dark Goddess reference. With all the synchronicities I had been seeing around the shift and Yin, the words resonated strongly. I thought back to my conversations with Liz about the shift into a Yin-based consciousness. I contemplated the war of humanity and I noted just how important a shift was for all. As my thoughts progressed however, I began to feel feverishly unwell.

I was meant to be teaching an English class that night, but by late afternoon I had to cancel. My throat was on fire and a high fever had set in. By that evening I knew I had to cancel my upcoming appointments for the next couple of days. I was not okay!

That night I ran a high fever and had frightful dreams that made no sense. I had moments where I was not sure if I was awake or asleep and by the next morning I was completely delirious. My body was in extreme agony and my voice was gone. I slipped in and out of consciousness throughout that day. When I was awake I could barely make the few steps to the toilet. This made for messy work when my period set in that afternoon. This added to my physical agony and weakened me further. I remember thinking, "If I'm going to die, I'm fine with that, but please let it be less painfully!" As the day progressed into evening, my fever had set in once more and I found that feeling of delirium setting in again. It was in the midst of this delirious fever that I experienced a massive shift. The awakenings and understandings I was having I can only explain as Universal insights and teachings. I found my mind racing through ideas and concepts - understanding them all at once. It was as if everything I had come to learn and know over the last couple of months and years were falling into place. It was there that I knew I was destined for more than just High Priestess. That was not the level I was striving for, that was just a stepping stone. In the early hours of the morning, I lay in feverish pain, listening to the teachings of Universe. By dawn I had taken all I could and out of exhaustion, I slept.

When I woke again, it was mid-morning and I knew I had a choice to make. I could either continue to lay there or I could use what I had learned and start healing. At the time I did not understand fully what was happening. I did have the understanding that I needed to heal myself, however. I also knew that if I chose to continue laying there, I would not step foot outside that room again. I lay in bed for a moment, pushing past the delirious feeling that was setting in. With sheer mind over matter, I got up and managed a shower. By the time I was done however, I was beyond exhausted. I desperately just wanted to lie down and sleep. I knew that I could not. If I went back to sleep, the fever would set in again and I would be back to square one. I sat for a moment, gathering myself and my strength. I finally rose to stand by my doorway and looked at the three flights of stairs I would need to walk down. I reminded myself of the much needed nutrients I required and stepped out my door. Getting down those stairs was a nightmare I hope I never have to relive again. I sobbed the entire way down. Clinging desperately to the railing in case I passed out and fell. Every step was excruciating. The walk down the long corridor that connected the stairs with the front entrance, was a complete blur. When I stepped outside into the afternoon sun, I had to sit down. A walk that should have taken a minute had felt more like ten. Collecting myself, I managed the last stretch to where I was heading. Relying on my Kitchen Witch healing knowledge, I acquired what I needed. This included a smoothie - a quick and simple way to get the nutrients I needed. I opted to think ahead and ordered myself a couple - each with specific nutrients and healing properties. I knew what my body needed in order to heal. I sat and sipped on one of them and instantly felt sick. I used the remainder of my strength and hauled it back to my room. This was not going to be an easy battle.

A couple of hours later, exhausted from my outing, I could not hold the fever off any longer. The delirium set in once again and then the ancestral and spirit realms stepped in to teach me. I learned of the connection between all things and the need to honor the ways of the Ancients. A return to our roots was needed if we were to find true connection. I pushed myself past my fever in order to learn more. The understanding of a shift not just into a Yin-based consciousness, but a shift into another dimension was already taking place. Many key souls had been placed upon the Earth to assist in facilitating this transition. Too many were far off from where they needed to be. This is where I needed to come in. "You must teach and guide!" I could hear the words clear as day. I then pushed further to understand more deeply, but the exhaustion set in and I could not hold sleep off any longer.

When I woke the following morning, I found my energy levels had improved, but I was far from healed. It was later that day that Matt messaged me. In all my transformative, madness I had not stopped to consider messaging anyone to ask for assistance. Matt offered to come around with some things for me and asked if I needed anything specific. I took the opportunity to acquire what I knew my body needed; grateful I did not need to tackle the stairs again. He arrived a little while later, like a saving grace, but as I sipped my fresh juice, Matt seemed troubled, "Tam I know you're not feeling so great, but I really don't know who else to talk to. I feel like I can trust you."

Matt shared with me that he had been on a Valium bender over the last few days. Valium, along with a number of other high schedule pharmaceuticals, are easily available over the counter in most SE Asian countries and is surprisingly very cheap as well; making them highly accessible and dangerous.

"I don't know why I keep using the stuff, I don't even like it. I got it because I've had trouble sleeping. I've been having a recurring nightmare about something that happened a few years back."

Matt began to divulge some very intimate details of his past to me. Details of his life with using and dealing drugs. Matt had seen and experienced some heavy stuff. I felt no judgment towards what he was telling me, however. Instead, I felt empathy and compassion.

"You are not a bad person, Matt. I don't think you could ever intentionally hurt someone."

I could see he still felt quite distressed, so I let him chill out in my space for a couple of hours. He spent the time chatting to me and tending to any need that I had until he left. After he left, I contemplated on what Matt had shared with me and how I had felt towards him. What followed was an additional Universal insight. Just because people do bad things, it does not mean they are bad people. At the authentic core, no one is bad. Later that evening, I received a message from the lady that had posted about the place in Long Biên. I had yet to see it with being so ill. However, within two days I would need to either move or stay. I took a risk and took the place without seeing it and I was set to move in two days' time. I hoped I would be feeling stronger by then.

Two days later, I woke up early to give myself time to finalize my move and check out of the hostel. That morning was quite the struggle. It was a process of packing a bit here, sitting down for a moment there; and wanting to pass out through most of it. I was on day six of being ill, but I was recovering. I finished packing and pushed my bags down the stairs. I would deal with any breakages or damage another time. There was just no way I was carrying those bags! My taxi eventually arrived and drove me across the bridge to the area of Long Biên. I had never actually been to that side of the city before. It looked very traditional and not a single Westerner was to be seen. The taxi dropped me off somewhere in the vicinity of my new home and drove off. I was left to carry my heavy suitcases around the neighborhood while I tried to find my new home. I was walking up a large road when I spotted another Western woman. She looked at me curiously and then called out, "Tam, is that you?" It was the woman I had been chatting to about the place. Thank the Universe! She helped me carry my stuff around the corner and showed me to the house. I put my stuff down inside and about passed out on the couch. "Are you okay?" she asked concerned.

"Yeah, I'm just not quite right yet. I'm doing better, but I'm still feeling quite ill."

I relaxed out on the couch for a good hour, before I felt okay enough to get up the single flight of stairs. I chucked my stuff in a corner and passed out. I was ill for a total of nine days with what seemed to have been a severe throat infection and all over body meltdown. To add to this, was my New Moon shed. For nine days I bled. I have never bled for nine days, nor have I had any form of irregular period for years prior to those nine days. Neither have I had an experience like that since. I did however, understand the symbolic representation of shedding old layers in order to create space for the new.

I had lived out of suitcases for over a year. Feeling fully healed, I unpacked my life. I then looked around and knew I was home. I took the opportunity to pull myself a Tarot card. With everything that had transpired over the previous, weeks it seemed an appropriate time. I drew The Hermit and my initial insight was that I was to be as the Hermit. Looking back, I realized that I had slightly misinterpreted this card. The Hermit was correct, but not in the 'hermiting' sense. What I had experienced over those nine days was Shaman Sickness and initiation. I had transitioned from High Priestess to Shaman. I had been given many insights and valuable information over the weeks leading up to me falling ill. Then when my illness struck, it was in my altered states of delirium that I heard and understood my Universal teachers. When I sensed I had a teacher coming more than a month prior, I did not anticipate being flattened and shown the workings of the Universe and everything in-between. I recall pulling out the Shaman book I still had with me and began to reread sections that were of importance to help tie up the loose ends. I knew I was moving into a new phase. Not just in a physical sense, but on a much higher level.

I was reveling in the comfort of having my own space. In solitude you are able to re-orientate yourself; which was something I really needed after being ill for nine days. For the first time in many years I set up an altar for myself and created a sanctuary. A few days later I earned myself the title of 'Witch'. I was at Base with Matt and li Kai rui and happened to have my cards with me, "Who wants to pull a card?" I asked in a joking manner. My friends at Base had a rough idea of what work I did. It was only after letting li Kai Rui draw a card that he decided I was in fact a Witch. "I always knew there was something off with you Tam," he joked. He had drawn The Devil card which was accurate for him at the time. He was facing his own inner demons; I could see it. He joked about the card, but we both knew it meant something to him - that it had given him a much-needed insight. Matt drew a card as well, enjoying the joke about me being a Witch. He drew the Ace of Pentacles and I gave him a quick interpretation. He seemed to light up, like it was confirmation that life could actually work out alright. li Kai rui then asked if it was possible to get the same card again. I said it could happen and gave him the set again to pull another card. His next card was insignificant, but Matt pulled the Ace once again. This answered li Kai rui's question. "Yeah, she's a witch!" shouted li Kai rui with mock accusation. I did not mind the mock accusations at all. In fact, I found it rather intriguing that my friends saw that aspect of me and were completely comfortable with it. It was this group that allowed me space to be the Solitary Witch I always was. It soon became custom that if someone was not feeling well or had landed themselves a black eye or a broken heart, I was there giving out healing remedies and Witchy advice. I had not felt that fulfilled since my time at the Metaphysics Academy more than ten years prior to that.

As I progressed with my first month in my new home, my friendship with Matt became stronger. We were spending a large amount of time together and had gotten to know one another on a deep level. We would spend a few hours talking about whatever thought was occurring at the time. We would however, always come back to the same conversations about the way the world was and how change was desperately needed. Our conversations resonated so strongly with everything that had been occurring on my path. Matt got it! He got it for sure. He knew and understood what I knew and understood. The world needed to go back to living in harmony with itself. The shift was needed now more than ever. We also talked a fair bit on borders, visas and the ways and systems of the world. We shared how we both struggled with the complexities and difficulties of them. Matt knew about my declined visa for Australia and how much it had broken me. Such a simple thing as getting on a plane to meet someone was made impossible by the decision of another. As much as Matt and I were from very different upbringings and cultures, we clicked like we had been friends for lifetimes.

Having gotten to know me well, Matt presented me with a gift one day. "I've got a present for you. When are you coming by Base again?" It was a message from Matt that instantly made me curious. What present could he possibly have for me? Matt, sweet as pie, did not quite strike me as the type to know much about gifts and women. He was adamant however, that I would love it. Curiosity got the better of me and I was in a taxi to Base later that evening. "So where is this impressive gift?" I asked with a hint of good natured sarcasm. "Wait! Give me a sec. It's here somewhere, I had it earlier." After a couple minutes of turning the backside of the bar upside down, he handed me a book. Maybe he was not so bad at gift giving after all. The book was titled 'The Wisdom of the Enneagram - The Complete Guide to Psychological and Spiritual Growth'. I had heard about the Enneagram system a couple of years before. A friend of mine had introduced me to the basic principles and it was a system that had caught my attention. A system based in human psychology, the Enneagram is unique in that it links the spiritual aspect of a person's psyche to their psychological wellbeing. This link is very rarely considered in psychotherapy, yet I knew it to be crucial for true healing. It was one of the links I had made when my interest in Psychology had peaked as a teenager. I had struggled to find decent information on the Enneagram, however, and it soon fell to the back of my mind. Sitting with the rather large book in front of me, I was intrigued, excited and really wanted to leave so I go could home and read. "It's one of the best gifts I've gotten. Thank you!" I exclaimed.

"See I told you, you would like it," he grinned with a rather pleased look on his face. Clearly, Matt had being paying attention to most of our conversations. It was also clear that for someone very new to ideas around Spirituality and spiritual experiences, Matt was very advanced. An old soul indeed. It seemed for him that it was a matter of already knowing, it was just putting the knowing into practice.

It was during this time that I began to passively look for a location for my healing space. I had been putting out feelers and was considering my options. li Kai rui had caught wind that I was looking and happened to have an open space. It was a space I had been to before. At night it ran as a bar and was owned by a bubbly Vietnamese woman named Ashy. I had met her and her manager, Trang, a couple of days before that. They both spoke impeccable English and bubbled with life and curiosity; yet both had seen and experienced so much already. I took to them instantly. Ashy was letting li Kai rui use the space during the day and he was now offering to share the space with me. On the intuitive level the space felt correct, but something felt misaligned - which I could not put my finger on. I told him I would think about it and get back to him in a few days' time. A couple of days later, I was chatting to Matt about the space. Where I sat at the time, I was almost a stone's throw away from Ashy's bar. As I talked to Matt, the more I felt a pull towards the place. Matt and I chatted in depth about the space I was wanting and where I could go with it. I mentioned wanting to eventually open a full healing centre in Hanoi. I had the knowledge and experience to start on a small scale and build it up. Matt seemed to be highly intrigued with everything I was saying about crystals and therapies, even my jokes about teaching magic and witchy ways. "I would love to learn from you," He suddenly expressed out of nowhere.

"What do you mean?" Like an apprentice of sorts? You would seriously want to learn everything I know about crystals, magic and Tarot?" I questioned.

"Yeah, why not? You seem to know what you're doing and I trust you. So yes, if you opened a healing space I'd like to help you out with it."

I was somewhat stunned. Matt had previously expressed his level of respect for me, but I would never have considered being his mentor.

"Alright then, you can be my apprentice. Your first lesson is how to make my coffee," I joked as we continued to chat about a potential space of healing and mystery.

I declined li Kai rui's offer not long after that, however. I just did not feel in alignment with him as much as I did with Matt. The pull towards Ashy's space I did not dispute at all! I knew it to be correct, it was just a matter of knowing clearly what I wanted and then manifesting it.

16

No Strings Attached

I had been in Vietnam for almost three months and I was needing to renew my visa. I was referred to a travel agent and met with her to chat about options. I wanted to be able to remain in Hanoi both legally and correctly for the long term. The idea of having to renew visas every three months sounded rather impractical, yet the cost for a one year visa was rather pricey. The agent assured me though, that once I had it, I would not need to worry about my visa for a year. The practicality and cost saving in the long run seemed to outweigh the initial large outlay for the visa. I was also not quite in the position to pay that amount for my upcoming visa. "It is okay, you can pay me when you have the money," the agent assured me. I felt a knot tighten in my stomach and something did not sit well with me. I ignored it and dismissed it as just me being paranoid. I agreed and she set to arranging my new visa. She assured me there was nothing else I would need to do from there, other than fly to Thailand for a few hours and then return to Vietnam on my new visa. I duly did so a few days later, returning with my one year visa in hand. This would become a strong lesson in listening to my intuition when my visa decision came back to bite me a few months later.

It was a few days after my visa run and Matt was round for a visit. He seemed troubled and mentioned he was growing tired of working bar shifts. He was looking for a change, but was not sure what. He felt sure that I had something to do with it. He was very sure I had come onto his path to teach him. He went on to say he felt ready to work through his old issues and become something more. He also felt ready to start dealing with his addictions. He knew his drinking had become out of control and he wanted to shift. He then mentioned he needed to move as well. Before I had even stopped to think about what I was saying, I was saying it,

" You can stay with me till you sort yourself out. Don't make it too permanent, but take what time you need."

I had been in situations where I was stuck and others had helped me. I was well within a position to help him as well. Looking at what he was needing, I knew where and how I could assist without placing a burden on myself. It looked like a huge weight was off his shoulders. I had noticed the last few times he seemed to be bothered about something. Now I understood. Matt had spoken to me a few times about his past, his relationships and a lot of his trauma. Matt had mentioned a few times that he wanted my help. So we came to an agreement that he would stay in my space. I would assist him from a mentor perspective to work through his past and his addictions. Included in the agreement was that I would teach him everything I knew with regards to Spirituality. I assured Matt that I would give him a space without expectations or conditions, just that it was temporary and that he had to be prepared to do the work. With our agreement in place, Matt was set to move into my space a little over a week from then.

It was about two days later that Matt came over to visit me again. We chatted till the earlier hours, as was often the custom with us. It was late so I offered for Matt to spend the night. I joked and said he may as well get used to sleeping here if he's moving in for a bit. We both fell asleep pretty quickly and I slept right through till morning. I woke and found Matt looking a little a confused and unsettled.

"I saw something in your room last night." he said.

"What do you mean? Like a ghost?" I joked.

"No not quite. A spirit of some kind, yes. It was female in form, but it did not seem good or bad. She was just floating there, facing me at the bottom of your bed. I swear I saw something standing next to you as well, but I can't be sure. I'm a little freaked out right now."

"It's okay. I have a lot of protection on my space. I also don't tolerate nonsense from the spirit realm and the bad ones are not allowed," I assured him. Something about what he was explaining made me think about Yin and the Goddesses that had come into my space. Had another Goddess stepped in to poke about in something? We both felt a little unsettled by the experience. Looking back now at the events that followed, I know that something Yin-based was in my room that night. I also know that it had a hand in what transpired shortly after.

It was eight the following morning and I was woken to the sound of my phone ringing. "Tam, Oi!" It was Matt, from the sounds of it a rather drunk Matt. "Come play pool!"

"You do know it's eight in the morning, right? Where on earth are we going to play at this hour?" I questioned, while trying to make sense of what was happening.

"I'm at Rock Store, they have a pool table upstairs. Come on Tam!" Matt has this strange knack for convincing me to do odd things. Like going to play pool at eight in the morning on a Thursday. I arrived half an hour later, ordered some coffee for the both of us and joined my rather intoxicated friend upstairs. Matt and I had been challenging each other to a game of pool for a few weeks. We had never actually played against each other before, however both of us were pretty convinced we were better than the other. I proceeded to annihilate Matt and after beating him five times out of six, he insisted we play pool somewhere else. Clearly the table was the issue. We got a taxi over to a small local pool hall in Long Biên, not far from my place. We got as far as eating some breakfast and then Matt was done for the day. It can be a problem when you are starting your day and your friend is now finishing theirs from the night before. "You are ridiculous right," I told him jokingly.

"I know, I 'm a terrible friend, but you know what? I will be the best, worst friend you will ever have." It took me a few seconds to catch what he had actually said.

"I think you may be right on that," I joked as I got up to get him functional so we could head back my place. We stopped past his friend's motorbike shop that was down the road. I had met Nhất a few times. He was very well-spoken and around my age. He was down to earth and as genuine a person as you could hope to find. Nhất gave Matt a bit of good-natured uphill for being drunk at ridiculous hours, wished me good luck and I willingly allowed Matt to ride us home. When I say I trusted Matt, I meant it. I knew it was okay to get on the bike with him. I knew it on a higher level. The average person would have told me I was mad!

We arrived back at my place and Matt flopped himself down on my bed straight away. "Ugh I'm still super drunk," he complained.

"Sleep it off, you'll feel horrendous later, but it's okay. We both know you will manage," I teased.

"You're a terrible friend, Tam," he said with mock hurt. I sat down on my bed next to him and told him to stop being so sensitive and that I loved him anyway. Then Matt looked at me in a way he had never done before. Matt had sometimes joked about us sleeping together, but that was as far as that went. Up to that point we had the bond of best friends and neither of us had shown any interest. "Do you want to have sex Tam?"

"What?! I think you're a little too drunk for that, Matt," I laughed. "I really don't see that going well."

"Oh come on Tam, it'll just be this once. So if it is terrible, which I know it won't be, you don't have to do it again."

I cannot tell you what possessed me but, "Alright fine! But no attachments Matt, I mean it!" I said in semi mock frustration. If only I had known what I was in for. Matt was far from what I expected. In fact he exceeded my expectations. Don't worry, I won't go all 'Fifty Shades Of Matt' on you here. However, our one time went to Friends with Benefits quickly. We discussed what was happening and how we wanted to work things with him moving in. Neither of us wanted a relationship, but a friend with benefits was definitely alright. Matt was still set to move in with me as agreed. There was just a slightly different dynamic now. Matt and I seemed to fall into a very natural routine with each other. He had not quite moved into my space as yet, but we were together every day. Matt and I were like two teenagers having a secret love affair. It took about two weeks before our friends started to notice. We took this as a private joke and wanted to see how long we could keep up the act. We lasted nearly the first month. Our friends were rather persistent in their accusations, though. That's the trouble with having enlightened friends. They just know that they know what they know. Matt was soon introduced to Ollie and Tracy and my other South African friends living in Hanoi. I seemed to have two main groups of friends at the time. My friends from Base, who were from an array of foreign countries as well as a host of Vietnamese locals; then there were my South African friends. Thus began the strange integration of two very different worlds for me. The one symbolised my roots and what had moulded me into who I was, while the other symbolised where I had done my most intense spiritual learning, healing and growth.

Our first month was smooth, had natural flow and Matt seemed to be learning as much as he could from me. I gifted him a set of my Tarot cards and he took to them quickly. By the middle of that month he had finished working at Base and for the first time I got to know sober Matt. For almost two weeks he did not touch a drink. Matt's health seemed to swing around and I realised just what an impact his lifestyle had had on him. From previous conversations, I already knew Matt's history with substances and addiction. I had come to learn a few things around addiction over the years. One of them is that abuse comes in when one is unable to achieve the same altered states of mind and connection that comes with using the substance. Addicts find themselves constantly chasing the same high, never being able to achieve it fully, or to keep it a permanent state of mind. This altered state of mind is often not much different to the state of mind where shamans and healers, including myself, work. A highly connected space that includes connection with the self, others and higher realms. With us however, we have the training and understanding that one cannot stay in that mind state. It would surely lead to madness and psychosis. One would never again be able to correctly distinguish between reality and altered state; hence souls risk getting lost in the world of substance abuse - forever chasing that state of mind. The reality is that one can achieve that state without the substance. When Matt went trekking for two months, he had seen and experienced that for himself. Those two months were the first time he had connection without substance. Every addict has their drug of choice - their quick and reliable access gateway to the other side. For Matt this started out as Opioids. How he got there was not the way you would think.

In the world of mind-altering substances, we have two main categories, Stimulants and Opioids. Stimulants consist of substances such as Cocaine, Amphetamines and Psychedelics like LSD and MDMA. Opioids consist of substances like Heroin, Barbiturates, Opium of course and scheduled painkillers such as Morphine. The stimulant Methamphetamine is otherwise known as Meth or Speed, and in South Africa as Tik. The name depends on how the finished product hits the streets and is used. A highly illegal street drug that has become a massive problem worldwide, it is also the same drug found in the well known pharmaceutical, Desoxyn, which is used to treat ADHD. We then have something called D-amphetamine, the main active substance found in the commonly prescribed, Adderall - again prescribed for the treatment of ADHD. Methamphetamine and D-amphetamine are essentially the same thing. As with many youngsters during the ADHD hype of the nineties and two-thousands, Matt was diagnosed with ADHD and prescribed Concerta. From there he was moved to other variations of the same chemical and was finally settled on Adderall - a prescribed pharmaceutical that became the cause for a pre-teen to not be able to feel anything except disconnected. A child at that age is only starting to navigate their emotions and feelings. When you introduce a central nervous stimulant like Adderall, the child's brain begins to develop differently. Chemical reactions do not function naturally as they should. Hence, we have a run of teens and adults who cut themselves just so they can feel; along with a group who seek connection through substance abuse. This was the case for Matt when he discovered the high of painkillers and felt what he had been missing: connection. His first experience with getting high on Opioids cracked open the gates to the world of substance abuse. What put him in front of the gates was Amphetamines. Matt put it perfectly one day:

"We've been raised on substances. It's what we know. It's how most of us learnt to connect, we don't know how to connect any other way."

From Opioids he found Alcohol. This was a different type of connection, something more social. In his mid-teens he found Barbiturates and substances like Valium. It was here that his use for Opioids went from allowing him to feel, to numbing the pain of life as he experienced a run of hard knocks. This presented the flip side of substance abuse - the side that does not want to feel anything; that can lead to things like severe depression and suicidal tendencies. Alcohol became his point of connection instead. When Matt drank however, his capacity to put away the spirits was frighteningly impressive. In the time that I had known him, I don't believe I could recall a single sober day. He openly spoke about being an alcoholic and knew he had addictive problems. "I just really love drinking. I don't know how else to put it," was his response when I would ask him about it. Hence my surprise at his two week sobriety when he first moved into my space.

Matt's sober space did not last too long however, when he learned that Lily was closing Base. This news devastated Matt. Base had been home for Matt for nearly three years. He had built a family around the space. Lily had broken the news to him while they were out. As things worked out, I was not able to join them that day. Within a couple of hours of Matt leaving however, an uneasy feeling set in. It was as if something or someone was nudging me. Then what felt like anxiety started to kick in. It was around eight PM and I had not heard from Matt much. I pushed the worrying aside and found ways to distract myself. As it began approaching midnight, I grew exhausted and could not wait up any longer. I tried calling Matt one last time, to no avail and went to sleep. I recall having vivid dreams and waking nightmares. I woke with start at around two AM with the words, "He needs to go home," in my mind and an incredibly anxious feeling gnawing at my gut! Something felt very wrong. Matt was still not home, I had not heard anything from him and then panic set in. I saw Lily was still online and messaged her to asked if she knew where Matt was. She messaged back that he had passed out in Base. I asked her if it was possible to wake him up and send him back to my place. She said they had all tried but he was properly passed out and very drunk. My anxiety heightened. I ordered myself a taxi to the Old Quarter and arrived at around three to find Base very much closed. Matt was passed out cold with no shoes, no wallet, and no jacket. It took me more than five minutes to get him to wake up. He was so out of it, he barely knew where he was. When he finally got his head right and started looking for his possessions, he seemed to get really angry. In the time that I had known Matt I had seen his temper come out only a couple of times. It took a lot to trigger Matt, but once that trigger was pulled, he was like a straight shot and quick with his fists. It was not specifically that he was looking for fights either, Matt is actually incredibly gentle. However, if you happened to push the right button, you will know about it. I watched his anger increase and then he lost his cool completely. Picking up an empty shot glass off the table, he hurled it at the wall in front of him. He threw it with such force that a large piece bounced off and just missed my face.

"Shit, Tam, I am so sorry. I did not mean for that to go anywhere near you!"

He was looking at me very concerned, checking to make sure he had not hit me by mistake. "It's alright, you missed me," I gave a short answer, feeling rather frustrated with the way the evening had progressed. I wanted to go home and be done with the night.

After the incident at Base, old habits began to set in. Matt's days of sobriety were over and he was back to drinking consistently and daily. I could see Matt down-spiralling back to square one, yet I did not know what to do. My feelings for him at that stage were deep and I was struggling to see the boundaries. I once again found myself experiencing the dark aspect of addiction and my old patterns of dealing with addiction had re-surfaced. Jadie's journey with addiction had spanned more than twenty years by that time. For a good portion of that journey, I walked in a co-dependent cycle with him. Included in that cycle were threats of last chances and me desperate to fix my brother. This was until our falling out and I gave no more chances. Jadie and I had since then made amends, but kept very little contact. When Matt began his path of self destruction, my old habits with Jadie took over. The more I dealt with Matt's destruction, the more I engaged his Shadow aspects. In our first two months, I knew all about Matt's Shadow and its capabilities. I also learned that Authentic Matt was connected to me in a way I still do not fully understand. In those two months, I established that our core aspects were almost perfectly in alignment; that we matched to the point of being able to generate pure energy. With Matt's downward spiral however, the energies had become murky and my healthy connection with my Yin, became toxic.

17

Ancestors At My Door

The more I engaged with Matt's Shadow, the more out of alignment I grew. This increased my anxiety and depression soon settled in. It was mid-December and we were both feeling very low. "I think we need a change of scenery," was Matt's random suggestion early that morning. I believe he had grown tired of my down mood. I did not know what to do about it either. I did not even understand where it was coming from. My work had also dropped right down to a couple of sessions a month. Something was not right. Perhaps a change of scenery was what we both needed. We settled on a short trip out to Cat Ba Island. The story of Cat Ba is that three women were said to have floated ashore on the three main beaches of the Island. As a tribute to these women the Island was named Cat Ba (Women Island). It was here that Matt first witnessed what being out of alignment could do to me. Matt and I arrived to a very rainy island. Being early winter, the weather was not ideal. We went out that evening for some dinner and happened to find some very tasty rice wine. A traditional rice liquor that comes in varying flavors, the stuff is deadly potent and strangely very pleasant to drink. I sat there and utilized some mind over matter to drink a few shots with Matt. I then watched as authentic Matt stepped out and his Shadow stepped in.

With the passing moments, my anxiety levels increased and the realization that being with Matt was detrimental to me, my health and my stability. I remember sitting there thinking, "This is not okay. None of this is okay." Then I heard that voice again, "He needs to go home."

Waking up the next morning, my anxiety had kicked into overdrive and I broke down. I felt myself slipping into an all familiar catatonic-like state. I don't recall much of the day from there. Being somewhat stronger than I had been, I managed to pull myself out of my state by the next morning. I do not recall much from that day other than just the consistent words, "He needs to go home."

Matt felt it was a good idea to get out of our room for a bit. I agreed and we took a drive out into the jungles of Cat Ba. Here I went with my intuition and opened up to Matt. I explained to him that I felt as if people that came into my life took what they needed and left. He asked if I felt he was doing the same and my response was that I did not know. I did not know because I did not truly understand his intentions with me. I asked him outright what his intentions were.

"I don't know, Tam. I know when we started I had no real intentions, it was strictly just friendship. Now I don't know what I want. I know I don't want to hurt you."

We needed to make some decisions. We had both become stagnant and a change was needed. I also knew it was time to find my healing space.

"I need to improve my work. I should not be this quiet. I need a space to work from. I know this is part of it. I can't do it alone, though. Matt we've spoken about us working together before - you learning from me. Maybe we can look for a space together?"

It fitted and felt in alignment as I made Matt the offer. I knew he needed a healthier space and something more productive to do with his time. We arrived back in Hanoi just before New Year's Eve and set to finding a space we could use. We ideally wanted something that was available during the day. Matt understood that his drinking needed to get under control and that working during the day would limit his cravings to drink. We chatted to a few of our local friends but came up short. Then Matt suggested,

"What about Ashy's? I'm sure she would let us use the space. She did let li Kai rui use it a while back."

li Kai rui had stopped using the space three months prior; shortly after I had declined his offer. This time, however, Ashy's space felt fully in alignment. We set a plan to head to the Old Quarter later that day to meet up with Ashy.

We met up with Ashy later that evening. As always, she had this warm welcoming air about her. I loved being in her space. Her bar, although small, had that same magical feel to it that Base had. There was also something very powerful about Ashy and her family. I felt that their ancestry ran deep and they carried the ways of the Ancients. I had met a few of her relatives during my time there. None of them spoke much English, yet all of them had this magic to them. We chatted to Ashy about possibly using her space during the day. Ashy was more than enthusiastic about the idea. We agreed on a small rental fee and the hours that we could have the space. Matt looked at me with concern when she mentioned the rental amount. "Faith! Do you trust me?" I asked him in a hushed tone.

"Yes! I trust you." was his quick reply.

"Then we've got this," I assured him. I knew the space was right and I knew we would have enough for our rental. Signs within Ashy's that aided my reassurance was the two cats that were permanent residents within the space and a massive painting of a Raven on the back wall - a bird that is strongly associated with The Morrigan. I had to trust that this was correct. The cats had continued to frequent my space upon arriving in Hanoi months before; as always they were everywhere to be seen - constant reminders of the lessons they taught.

The next morning, Matt was up earlier and very restless. "I'm going out for a bit. I'll be back later," he said as he picked up his keys.

"Alright," I answered, rather confused as to where he would be heading so early. He was back about an hour later, with the correct amount of money required for the rent. "What? How? Where did you go?" I asked in confusion.

"I sold one of my bikes to Nhật. I don't know why I didn't think of it before. Good timing I guess."

Matt had clearly been paying attention to my lessons on manifesting. Within less than twenty-four hours he had arranged the amount needed and we were set to start planning the opening of our healing space - a space that became known as Mystics. For the first time in weeks, things felt like they were in alignment again. We were quiet at first, but things soon picked up and flow happened. Then the Ancestors came knocking, very loudly!

They choose a prime time to come visit as well. It was a Blue Moon, literally. Plus a total lunar eclipse. You could say my Luna-tic was a bit eclipsed that day. We arrived as normal and began setting up for the day. Then things were not normal anymore. I sat down on the couch as Matt asked me a question. "It doesn't matter. None of it matters," was all I said and then I was gone. I was consciously aware of everything going on around me, yet was unable to communicate on that level. I was sitting between worlds, but something about being there was not fully correct. I was not in the correct alignment to be there. What should have been a simple communication with the Ancestors turned into a nightmarish experience. It was an experience that took me more than two years to fully process and understand. I was physically sick, I had severe body shakes and I was seeing and talking to people that were not there. Some of them were friends, some of them I did not know at all. I struggled to find where reality was. I recall laying in the upstairs section of Mystics, racked with body shakes that left my body feeling like I had been beaten by something solid. I was nauseous and felt like I was running a fever. I swung in and out of consciousness and when I slept, I had vivid dreams. Matt kept insisting that he take me home, but something told me I had to stay. I recall having a conversation with li Kai rui. I had to ask him a few days later if the conversation had actually taken place. I recall him asking if I was alright. I managed that I was not feeling well.

"Yeah, you don't look so good, Tam. Maybe you need to just get sick. You know sometimes we just need to get the bad stuff out and then we feel better."

What he was saying was making sense, but it was like he was talking to me on another level. Like we were not sitting in the Earthly realm. We were elsewhere and we were talking soul to soul. He was not talking about me being physically ill. As the day progressed into early evening and Mystics shifted into Ashy's bar, I have a recollection of seeing Sid. She appeared in front of me seemingly out of nowhere. "You okay babe?" I heard the question, but cannot tell you if I replied. She looked at me concerned for a moment and then went to chat to Matt. Even at the distance and above the music that was playing, I could hear every word. She was asking if I was alright. Matt was explaining that I get like this sometimes. That he did not quite understand it or know what to do. He explained that he had tried to take me home a few times, but I had insisted on staying. A few moments later, Matt was there telling me it was time to go home. It was not authentic Matt however, it was his Shadow and it was annoyed and frustrated.

"I don't really want to go home right now Tam. I want to hang out for a bit. I can take you home if you want or I can get you a taxi. You decide."

I was still struggling to string sentences together and the body shakes were still pretty extreme. I knew I would not be okay with a taxi. I knew Matt needed to take me and I knew he was not meant to go out that night. His Shadow grew angry and he snapped at me, "God dammit Tam! Get your shit together. I don't know what you want. I don't know what I am meant to do."

His rush of angry energy set the body shakes off again, this time with full force. I have a blurred recollection of somehow getting onto the back of his bike and holding on as best I could past the shakes. I could feel Matt's rage in his driving. This added to the shakes and the intensity of the situation. By the time he had me home, I was in a state I had never experienced before. I went upstairs and do not recall much past Matt telling me he was going out and he would be back later. I passed out shortly after and dreamt the same vivid dreams. I woke up with a fright and reached for my phone. It was on charge at the bottom of my bed. It suddenly rang in my hand and I saw Matt was calling.

"I don't want to talk to him." I told myself.

"You need to talk to him, he needs to go home," it was that voice again.

A message then come through from Matt, "Tam please talk to me." I ignored it and put my phone down by my pillow, passed out as the shakes set in again. I woke up again with a fright. This time my phone was ringing, except it was not by my pillow where I had left it. It was still on charge at the bottom of my bed. Everything that I had just experienced had not actually happened. Then I looked to see that it was Matt calling, that same thought of not wanting to talk to him was there. Was I dreaming future events? I chose to answer my phone this time.

"Hey, I'm sorry for shouting at you. That was not okay. I'll be home in a bit I promise."

I did not know what was happening. I did not know how to process the day that I had just experienced. When Sid came to see me the next day to check on me, I had a breakdown, "I think I lost my mind yesterday." I tried as best I could to explain what had happened. At the time, I believed I had experienced a psychotic break; when in fact I had experienced an intense encounter with the Ancestors. That was on a Wednesday. By Friday, Vũ's warning, months earlier, of an encounter with local police came to fruition. I arrived home to find the local police at my door with a letter stating that I needed to report to Immigration on the following Monday.

A very unsettling feeling set in when I was handed that letter. I knew something was very wrong as much as Matt assured me that he had no bad feelings about it. The letter was in Vietnamese, so I messaged a few local friends to ask them to translate it for me. All of them assured me it was nothing serious, just a check-in with Immigration. I still felt very unsettled. I contacted Vũ as well to ask for his insights.

"You will be okay. Just speak to them honestly and tell them you are here doing healing work. Explain about the work you do and your gifts. Also, you must take a friend with you. I think Matt is the right person, but I don't know, maybe I'm wrong."

He hesitated with the last part about Matt. It was almost as if he knew it to be correct, but an insight was missing that he did not quite understand. I listened to everything Vũ was telling me and did the complete opposite.

18

Deported

Matt dropped me off at the Immigration offices the following Monday morning and insisted that I would be okay on my own. He felt it better that he was not there. I went up to Reception, handed them my letter and was soon being escorted to a small room with two other foreigners. One was French and the other sounded American. The American was called to sit at a table with three Immigration officers and asked for his passport. When he told them he had not brought it with, things in the room got tense quickly and my anxiety heightened. This definitely wasn't going to go well for me. I was moved to another room with the French man before I could see the end result with the American. We were escorted into a bigger room with a large meeting room table. As we sat down, more foreigners were escorted in. Two officers sat down in front of me and asked for my passport, which I duly handed over. I was then asked a series of questions:

"What are you doing in Vietnam? Are you working? Are you liking it here?"

I answered all their questions, trying to stay calm and centred all while failing to mention my healing work and gifts. When they asked me about the company that had sponsored me, the 'calm and collect' flew out the window. I had no idea what they meant and asked them to explain what was happening. They explained I was sponsored by a company in Saigon and that I should be there and not in Hanoi. Full-on panic began to set in. As much as I tried to explain that I did not know any company in Saigon and that I had no idea about this apparent sponsorship, they would not hear me. The conversation then escalated to the fact that I had committed an Immigration offense and that I was to pay a fine and leave Vietnam. I stared at them, bewildered, like a deer in the headlights. The only thing I could say was, "You're deporting me?" I could not hold back the tears as I pleaded with them to reconsider the deportation. They said they would speak to their supervisor and I was then handed a page in Vietnamese. I was shown which offense I had committed and told to sign. My passport was then taken away and I was told they would contact me in a few days. They explained that I would need to come back to pay my fine and finish the process. I would then need to leave the following week. I essentially had less than two weeks to figure things out.

I arrived back at Mystics in a state. Matt took one look at me and knew something was very wrong. All I could manage was, "I'm being deported." My frugal attempt at stopping smoking was short lived as I shakily reached for Matt's cigarettes and lit one. I had been suffering with a four-month-long chest infection. Living in the Hanoi pollution, riding in the traffic every day and my habit of smoking cigarettes that I had picked while living with Nina, all added to the problem. However, with the morning I had just endured, this was not an ideal time to quit smoking; regardless of how bad my chest was. My mind was racing. I had never felt so lost. Matt trying to maintain his calm, said, "It'll be okay, we have time." I knew differently, though. I had the sinking feeling that I did not have time and that things were probably going to get very bad, very quickly. In the midst of all of our chaos, a South African woman named Christine had come into Mystics with her son. She had come in previously with another friend of hers and we had chatted for a long while. I had liked Christine from the moment I met her. For some reason it felt right to share with her what was happening to me. She was horrified to hear my story and suggested I chat to the South African embassy. In my fog of panic, I had not even considered that. Without hesitating, I caught a taxi straight there. Stepping out of the elevator, I was greeted with my home country's flag and warm African colours. I stepped over what felt like a threshold to stand on South African soil. Tears filled my eyes quickly as a sense of safety washed over me. This was short lived, however, when the Vietnamese receptionist called upon another Vietnamese woman to come and talk to me. I explained to her what had happened, to which she quietly listened. I ended with, "Is there anything the embassy can do for me?"

Her response was "No, there isn't anything the embassy can do. This is between you and Vietnamese Immigration. We cannot help you." There is nothing like standing next to your country's flag, being told by a foreign person that your own country can do nothing to help you. She then contacted the travel agent who had done my visa in the first place and told her she was to sort things out for me. In that moment, I felt the full force of the Vietnamese Ancestors. I believed I had upset someone, somewhere along the line. This was not between me and Vietnamese Immigration. This was between me and the Ancestors. All I knew was that lines had been crossed and the Ancestors were not happy. I felt my African Ancestors turn their back on me and my Celtic side did not feel pleased either. There was another energy there as well: "He needs to go home."

I returned to Mystics to fill Matt in on what had happened and then headed down to meet with my travel agent; to whom I had still owed money. I had found this situation to be strange and stressful. No matter what I did to manifest, I was just not able to pay her the full amount. Then all this arrived. She greeted me with a very nervous smile and offered for me to have a seat. She made me some tea and explained what had actually happened. In order for her to have gotten my one year visa, it needed to be sponsored by a company. The visa she recommended was a work-based visa; which was not what I had wanted at all. I was not looking to be employed. As required with this visa, she found a company to sponsor me. The catch? It was a company based in Saigon. To add to this, it was a ghost company and did not actually exist - except on paper. This is where Immigration had flagged me. I was registered as living in Hanoi, but yet I was meant to be working for a company in Saigon. I was already four months in on my visa. No wonder the flag. The agent called to speak to Immigration to find out more details. It seemed they had reconsidered the deportation, but I still had to leave Vietnam. "When would I be allowed to come back?" I asked. She said something in Vietnamese to the Immigration Officer she was speaking to. "You cannot come back," was all she said and then carried on talking to the officer on the phone. "What does that mean?" I could not comprehend what she was telling me. I was not allowed to come back ever again? What about my life here? I had built a family for myself. Mystics had just started to flourish and Matt and I seemed to be working things out. Within split seconds my entire life was being ripped away from me.

"There is nothing I can do?" I asked in desperation.

"I am sorry Tam, there is nothing anyone can do. I am sorry this happened to you."

A big part of me wanted to lay into her and tell her where she could put her sorrow. Instead, I opted for the passive route and left. As I was walking out the door, she called out to me, "Tam Oi! Please you don't need to pay me the rest of the money you owe. It is the least I can do for you." Before my anger grew any stronger, I said nothing in reply and headed back to Mystics. I sent Liz a message on my way back there. I felt the need to fill her in on what had happened. Something was going on and it was more than just being kicked out of Vietnam. Liz replied that she agreed there was more going on than just Immigration stuff. She suggested that I try to stay as grounded as possible and see how things unfolded. I returned to Mystics and once again updated Matt. We decided to close for the rest of the day and head home to figure out what I could do. We contacted Nhất who was in Sa Pa at the time. He said he would be back in two days' time and would hear the full story then.

To add to my pressure of time, Tết holiday was fast approaching. This is Vietnam's New Year. For two weeks, everyone goes back to their hometowns to celebrate the New Year with various festivities and traditions. Being mostly populated by people who are originally from outside Hanoi, the city apparently becomes like a ghost town for these two weeks. It is estimated that around seventy-five percent of locals living in Hanoi are not actually from there – this is just to give you an idea of how quiet the city could potentially get. This also means that departments like Immigration are closed so that staff can go home. I was about two weeks away from Tết starting when I went to see Immigration. Time was not on my side! I needed to have this resolved before Tết, otherwise I would need to wait those two weeks out before anything could be done. The first week was a bit of a blur. All I could think of was how I could get out of this one and the fact that I had not followed anything Vũ had said. Matt was meant to come with me that day, I knew it for certain. I was also meant to speak honestly about who I was and why I was really in Vietnam. My fear of being judged for speaking on higher levels had got the better of me instead. Sometimes stepping out of the broom closet as a Witch is scary. More often than not, however, not stepping out is far more detrimental.

Nhât arrived back from Sa Pa and was able to hear what had happened. "Hang on one moment. I need to make a call," he was on the phone for a good few minutes. He was speaking to someone in Vietnamese. I caught my name and the words Nam Phi, which is Vietnamese for South Africa. I knew whoever he was talking to, he was talking to them about me. The conversation energy seemed a bit intense and official. He clearly knew someone that could help me. It seemed this someone owed him a favor as well. He assured me if anyone could help me it would be this man. He gave me the details of a man named Zee and an address for a hostel not too far from Mystics. It was a hostel I had been to before. One of the options I had considered when I first arrived was possibly doing Social Media work as opposed to teaching. Doing that kind of work in another country had the potential to be exciting and perhaps I could learn a few new things. The man Nhât had sent me to I had been to see already, but it was for Social Media work. He had seemed very keen on me working with him, but something had not felt in alignment and I landed up declining. Although he did make me a very nice offer, it felt like one of those too good to be true offers. Now I was back again, needing this man's help. I could feel his judging looks and I knew the exact assumptions he was making. He assumed I had attempted to bypass the laws and get the cheap visa. I had now been caught out. Another foreigner there to try cheat the system. I found myself mustering what dignity I could, "Actually no, Zee. That is not the case at all. Let me explain to you my side of the story."

I proceeded to explain how I had gone with a very expensive visa. The visa I was given however, was not clearly explained to me. I went on to explain that breaking Vietnamese laws was not my intention at all. In fact, it was the last thing I wanted to do. I was looking at being in Vietnam for the long term and I believed I had opted for the best way to do that. I could see his energy soften as he realised he had been incorrect with his assumptions, "I understand what has happened." He explained the full process of the visa I had been given. He explained in detail the offense I had accidentally committed and that he understood it was not an intentional thing. He said he would call and speak to a family member who was at the head of Immigration somewhere. He said he would contact me later that day and let me know what he could do for me. He then told me not to talk to anyone at Immigration until he had spoken to me. This left me in a predicament when Immigration called me later that afternoon and I had no idea if I was meant to be answering the phone or not. To be safe, I followed Zee's instructions and did not answer. I got a message from Zee later that evening, telling me to come and see him the next morning.

I arrived the next morning with very mixed feelings and Zee looked troubled. He said he was able to help me, I would still need to leave Vietnam, however. They had already canceled my current visa, so I would need to let the process play out. Once I had left, he would be able to submit an application for a visa on my behalf. He said I should decide where I wanted to go as I would still need to leave Vietnam the following week. He recommended Thailand for me, saying that there was very little in Laos and that Cambodia was not suitable for me - saying that it was too dark a place for someone like me. He told me to have a decision by the morning as I would need to have a booked flight in order to carry on with my current process. He did make mention that the fine I had to pay was surprisingly small. The amount had struck me as well. I had been in a room with a number of other people being questioned for the same thing. I was hearing fines of up to $2000. Mine worked out to about $50 in total. The feel of the Ancestors having a hand in things lingered strongly. Zee said I would be gone roughly eleven days and then I would be able to return without an issue. I felt more at ease about things and took Immigration's call when it came again.

Figuring out what I was going to do in Thailand for eleven days and how I was going to afford this unexpected expense, I remained grounded enough to reach within for answers. I contacted Sue and explained the situation and asked if she was able to assist.

"Gosh love! You have got yourself into quite the predicament over there. Are you going to be alright?"

She was concerned about me and my situation. She was able to send what I needed and wished me luck. The Ancestors were still looming and felt unhappy, though. I contacted Liz and explained what energy I had been picking up. I then asked if she would do an offering on my behalf. I felt it needed to be done on African soil. She happily agreed and shared what she would be doing and when. I then contacted my Aunt Coll. I knew she held an incredibly strong link to our Celtic ancestors. I explained everything that had happened and that it felt as if I had upset some Ancestors. She offered to do something for me on that side. She also gave me some rather strange advice, "Don't stress too much. Just think of it as an adventure!" My Aunt Coll - the woman is like walking wisdom. Her light-hearted laugh and change in perspective is, what I believe, eased me the most. The Spirits and Ancestors were clearly plotting something and I was at their whim. I felt I had one last thing left to do. I contacted my friend Chené, whom I had met previously while on my English Teacher training course. We had maintained pretty consistent contact, but at that point, I had not spoken to her in months. She was the only person I knew who had a good knowledge of Thailand and would be able to point me in the right direction. I contacted her and explained my situation and that I was looking for a place to stay in Bangkok while I waited for my new visa. Chené had offered for me to stay with her while my visa was sorted out. Between these three ladies, Sue, Chené and my Aunt Coll, I felt a sense of comfort and stability. I knew I would be okay. It was just eleven days and I would be back to carry on with life. I finished my process and was down to my last evening in Hanoi when things with Matt and his Shadow came to a head.

With everything that had transpired since I had lost my mind in Mystics two weeks prior, I found myself exhausted. I had slept very little since the start of my Immigration process and I had been severely ill. When my last day arrived, I was desperate for a decent night's sleep. I asked Matt if he would get me a Valium from the pharmacy. It all came to a head when I asked him for the Valium.

"Just be careful with it Tam. I know what that stuff can be like."

I had spoken to Matt about my run with painkillers and the unconscious addiction I had with them for a few years. Yes, unconscious addiction is a real thing. I would always have a headache, or some reason to take them. I did not actually understand that the pills I was taking were highly addictive and that I did not need them at all. Once I had shed a light on it, I had dropped the habit straight away. My relationship with addiction has always been one of avoidance. I did not ever want to be an addict. So when Matt gave me the Valium with such a strong warning, something felt off. Then I saw it - there was one missing.

"I just didn't know how to handle everything. I'm just not coping in general. Everything that has been happening... I'm just not managing okay!" he snapped. And then I snapped.

"Well it seems we have a situation of the pot calling the kettle black here. You sit there and give me shit about taking something I have never actually taken before. You make assumptions and presume me weak!"

I ended with a rather expressive run of expletives. This was not how I had wanted to spend my last evening. The mood in my space was somber and some very harsh realities glared me in the face. For the very first time in my life I actually understood addiction - what it really looked like; and saw it for the Devil it truly was. My own Devil then came to ask me some questions. I found myself pulling back my addiction layer that was hidden beneath the insecurities and fears I was working through. Perhaps they were still there because the addiction had been supporting them. I began to question my own use of substances and my intentions behind it. Cigarettes is where it began. I had never had an issue with cigarettes. Over the years I had smoked on and off, but I never took it on as a habit. Then when I started smoking while staying with Nina, this changed. She was also an experience of living with addiction. Within three months of being in Hanoi, I developed a severe chest infection. I suffered with it for four months and yet I struggled to stop. "When did I become so weak?" I questioned myself. I found myself living with addiction once again - mine and Matt's. I believed I understood the meaning of his Lion tattoo even more. It was now a reminder of how one can lose their strength for standing against the necessity of addiction. Mine, lost in a box of cigarettes, and then an unhealthy relationship as my co-dependent nature returned. In that moment, I understood the lengths one would go to in order to have that next fix. I felt the desperation behind it, the lust and desire. The need for instant gratification.

Matt and I kept a bit of space that evening and I took the opportunity to work through the Enneagram book he had gifted me months before. I had not worked with it much since we became more than just friends.

However, in the last couple of weeks, I had been drawn to work with it. Opening the Enneagram book to where it first explains the personality types, I began working through the layers of myself. Each personality type I seemed to have was either imbalanced or healthy – all except for the number eight, where I had nothing at all. I put the book aside for a moment and drew myself a card. I was asking specifically why I had to leave Vietnam. I pulled the all too familiar Chariot card. The self mastery lesson yet again! I put the card down, picked up the book and turned the page. "The healthy eight is self mastering". The Universe seemed to have a strange time for humour. Then a 'number' of things occurred to me. I was living at number eight and Mystics was at number eight. Then I caught the punch line. In Vietnamese, my name means eight. My first time round in Vietnam the number seven was prominent, now it seemed it was the eight. At least I knew I was making some kind of progress. I did one last thing before I went to sleep. I knew I needed to 'come clean' with Matt in some way. I needed to find a way to tell him what had been happening, but in a way he would hear me. I was leaving for just over a week the next day. I was beyond anxious as I would be leaving Matt to run Mystics on his own. Everything about it unsettled me. I chose to flush the Valium and sat down to write him a letter. I finally climbed into bed to find Matt still awake. We chatted for a while, settling the air a bit. Yet I still felt very unsettled. I was struggling very hard with the reality of having to leave my home for eleven days over an ill-advised visa. I also had the unsettling feeling I was in for an experience of some kind. I could feel the Ancestors afoot and knew things could possibly get very heavy. The next morning I handed Matt my letter and gave him some space.

"Matt,

Addiction is an ugly demon. I have seen that personally for myself. I don't just mean yours. I am talking about mine as well. I have never had a big issue with addiction and I do mean that genuinely. I never had an issue admitting my pharmaceutical addiction and stopping was actually incredibly easy. The same with any substance in fact. I have never craved anything before until I picked up a box of cigarettes roughly a year ago. It is also almost a year since my mushroom journey. It was done exactly on the New Year (Têt) and of course Full Moon. I am missing parts of my journey because I was not clean enough to 'see'. I was also very out of alignment with myself. Two unhealthy changes and you have read my book, so you know where I was at, mentally and spiritually. Not in a good space! So I have to be clean in a sense, especially with the work that I do. How can I heal if I am unhealthy? There are a lot of lost souls here, highly gifted ones! I know and respect the boundary of fixing others, I'm talking past that. The World is very messed up and there are souls here that can rectify that. I am a teacher and guide. I cannot expect to live an unhealthy lifestyle and then be allowed to work on such a high level. I know you understand about vibrations and I hope at least some of this makes sense so far.

I have never understood addiction on the level I do now. I believe I actually have empathy for Jadie for the first time. I don't believe I have ever actually experienced addiction before, but I do get it now. It starts with the 'bullshit'! The mindless things we tell ourselves to need it. It is never a want, it is a need. I understand that. I have seen and felt it, but I have also seen the sober side. No matter what, life is going to challenge you. You cannot hide behind your addictions or allow them to become what makes life better.

I need to find my boundaries again. Co-dependency is an adverse reaction to being an empath. Especially an unhealthy one. I am not making a decision about us yet, but boundaries have been trampled on and I need to take some power back. I do love unconditionally, it's in my nature. I cannot change you and would never try. That is not my place. Those are your demons to face. I can only guide."

I then carried on to write about how his lack of communication was not okay. Matt had not been present throughout the process with Immigration. He had drunk his way through a good portion of it and then the Valiums. I expressed to him how the situation with my visa had been hellish and how I had needed him. That it was not the time to be looking for answers at the bottom of a bottle; or that it was not okay to just switch off and numb himself because he did not know how else to cope. I asked him to open up and have a conversation with me. It was wanted and needed. When we got to Mystics he opened up, "Everything you wrote does make sense. Yes, I did step on your boundaries and I know I should have been more present. I just don't know how cope with stuff like this. I love you Tam, but a relationship is not what I want right now. I don't think it's what I need either. I know I need to focus on myself and heal."

"Should things not work out for some reason and I cannot get back into Vietnam, my biggest loss in all of this, would be you. I can only respect what you are saying though, and that is probably the healthiest decision you have made a in while," I was gutted in all honestly, but I had to agree with him. A relationship was not healthy for him at that time.

I spent my last few hours in Hanoi at Mystics. Matt once again had other things to do and once again was not present. He was, however, meant to be due back later to take me to the airport. I found myself spending the afternoon with Tôm instead. Tôm noted Matt's absence within a short while of being there. "Where's Matt?" he inquired.

"He has some things to sort out. He's with Nhât, but said he'd be back in time to take me to the airport." Tôm looked rather skeptical and openly expressed his concerns about me and my relationship with Matt. I explained that it was over between us, as of that morning.

"I see... well it seems Matt still has his capacity for self-sabotage in place." Tôm explained that when Matt could not deal with something, or when life got too much, he would hit self-destruct mode. It generally was not a pretty sight. Matt and Tôm had been friends since meeting in Ha Giang three years earlier. Tôm adored and loved Matt like a little brother. I could never dispute his love for him. I did fully understand his disapproval of Matt's behavior and decisions, though.

Our conversation shifted from Matt to far deeper things - as was standard for Tôm and I. We did not stick around the day to day conversations for very long before we moved onto conversations around magic, Magicians and the mystery of cats. Our conversations had begun soon after I had settled in Hanoi. Tôm and I were still getting to know each other and his curiosity had asked me out for a date for one evening not long after settling in Hanoi. Throughout that night I had established that Tôm was 'switched on' and clued in. After a run of deep, enlightening conversations, I had no doubt that Tôm, was a Magician. Our conversations on the night of our date had flowed to the point that our discussions prompted me to explain my theory on Magicians. He seemed to grasp the theory quickly and it resonated with him. Tôm was indeed a Magician, another one who knew he was destined for something, but could never quite explain it or understand it. He was also another Magician that seemed to do his best 'work' when not sober. Not knowing how to connect in a sober state, he was also somewhat unaware that he was doing any work to begin with. Tôm was more high level than he understood. It's funny sometimes with Magicians - I'll feel a pull towards them, but I won't understand what it is, not until they let their guard down and drop their societal masks. This is when I can see them clearly. Magicians can be pretty crafty at disguising themselves sometimes - even unknowingly. I've found over the years that many Magicians have been hiding themselves due to societal 'punishment' for being different. This also explained the attraction factor. Because we're such good matches, what with being one and the same - Magicians and High Priestesses will always have some form of attraction to one another. Often there's a bit of confusion between men and women though, when connection gets confused with physical attraction. Not all of us are meant for one another in an intimate relationship sense, although the misinterpretation happens. This is usually where hearts unintentionally get broken. That night on our date, however, Tôm knew I was not meant as a partner, but as a teacher. Since then, our conversations had gravitated towards the ways of the Ancients, the shift and Magicians.

My last afternoon in Hanoi rolled on at a steady pace and my anxiety with Matt grew.

"I'm concerned about leaving Matt here on his own to run Mystics," I expressed out of the blue to Tôm.

"I don't blame you. Look, Zain and I will be around. We will keep an eye on him for you."

I still did not feel very settled. Matt then called at the last minute, "Hey Tam, is it possible you could get a taxi rather? I just don't think I will make it back in time." This time my boundaries stepped in, "No Matt, that is NOT okay. I'll see you in half an hour as promised. I won't let you drop me on this one."

After a bit of attempted protesting, he said he would see me in a bit and hung up. He arrived with enough time for a rushed goodbye with Tôm and hurried me onto the bike. I could see he was frustrated. Thankfully riding is something that helps Matt clear his head. By the time we got to the airport he was in a better space. We ate a really bad airport dinner and a final attempt at clearing the air was made. I felt somewhat settled as I walked him to the exit to say goodbye.

"I'll see you Tam."

"I'll see you Matt."

I hugged him and then he kissed me. By then it was just a natural response to kiss him back. He looked a bit unsure of himself, said goodbye once more and walked away. When he turned around to smile at me one last time, my heart skipped the proverbial beat and I could not dispute that I loved him.

I spent a rather uneventful layover in Bangkok airport before flying out the next morning to the city of Hat Yai, where Chené was living. The unsettled feeling had stalked me through the night, but as the day progressed, I allowed my Aunt's words to take over and I felt lighter. I finally arrived at Chené's apartment block early that afternoon and was greeted with the same warm smile I have always remembered her having, "It's good to see you my friend. I just wish it were under better circumstances. I do feel I need to tell you this - I think you may be here more than eleven days. I know that is not what you want to hear right now, but I feel I need to tell you."

My lighter feeling suddenly felt heavy again. She said she felt unsure of how long it would be, but thought it best if I looked at fourteen or fifteen days. My heart sank somewhat as the truth in her words hit me. I knew she was not wrong. I just hoped she was not too far off from her estimation. Despite the uneasy start, I soon found myself comfortably settled into her cosy studio apartment and the catch up conversation started flowing. We chatted for a good while, catching up on the months we had missed out with one another. I was settled and comfortable in Chené's space, yet I also had that unsettling feeling while sitting there. I did my best to push the uneasiness aside and chose to focus on this strange mini adventure the Universe had sent my way. Chené told me of a few things we could do. She was still working a few hours a week, but we could certainly make the most of my time there, no matter how long or short it was.

My first few days went smoothly. I was doing some sightseeing, and just general shenanigans with my friend. Matt seemed to be managing things alright with Mystics and I was still set to come back within the eleven day time frame. I knew that Tết had begun and that Immigration was closed. Zee assured me that my application would be processed as soon as Immigration was open again. A few days in and I believed all was in order. Then Matt started slipping. He was struggling with managing Mystics on his own and he was struggling with his own stuff. Something told me to check in with Tôm. I asked him how Matt was doing and I learned that he had been on a bender pretty much since I had left. It was not just drinking either. Matt had asked Tôm for Valium earlier that day. He had said he was on a come-down from MDMA and was struggling. Well I was furious. I had known something would happen. I had known that Matt would not keep himself together. It seemed Tôm was more than right and that Matt was on a path of self-destruction.

19

Stepping Into Shaman

I went on to spend nearly a month in Thailand. Torn between embracing the unexpected adventure, another massive transformation and Matt's self-destruction. I had been in Thailand roughly a week and sadly, I was missing Matt's birthday. I spoke with Matt in the morning. I wished him a happy birthday and asked if he was at Mystics yet. He told me that he had just arrived, but that he did not feel well. He told me that he did not want to see anyone on his birthday. The next thing I knew he was closing Mystics for the day and apparently heading out for a ride and then probably back home for a quiet night. Something was very wrong. I felt panic set in as I franticly tried to call him. He kept declining my calls and messaged me: "Chill, everything is good!" Everything was not good! Up till that point Matt had been far from responsible. He had consistently opened Mystics up late and closed early. This was also not the first day he had just not bothered to open up at all. His abuse of substances had gone to the extreme and I felt helpless. I cannot express that kind of panic to you. I was sitting in the country next door, literally only a short plane trip away and yet I could do nothing! Helpless does not even begin to describe it. It was like watching him fall off the cliff edge and I could do nothing to catch him. All I could do was wait for the impact at the bottom.

When I had not heard from Matt by the next day, I was beside myself. Matt could take his benders to the far limits and often a concern of mine was that one day he would kill himself. That thought sat so heavily with me and just heightened as I struggled to track him down. I messaged a number of people that day in desperation. It was a mutual friend of ours that happened to be moving into my share house later that month that tracked him down. Not before I did, however. I had been experiencing a constant nagging since Matt had ended things with me. I kept sensing his ex-girlfriend, Sheryl. Matt had broken contact with her previously after a bad break-up. A good portion of their relationship had been narcissistic and toxic; along with addictive tendencies and behavior from both of them. When he ended things with me, my intuition very clearly told me Sheryl would be in the picture. That morning her energy felt intense. She had something to do with this. Matt had given me his Facebook login details months before to help him with something. Before I knew what I was doing, I was logging in and looking at what I knew I was going to find. A conversation between Matt and Sheryl. My anger began to boil. These were probably some of the hardest messages to read. Things he had been saying to me, he was saying to her. I felt played! I knew where the messages were heading next, but I continued to read. I still did not know where Matt was. From the messages I had established that they had met at Mystics and then headed to my place. It did not require much other than common sense to work out what had happened. Something possessed me to call Sheryl from Matt's Facebook. I still did not know for sure where he was. She, unfortunately, was the last person with him. I somehow refrained from shouting, in fact I don't recall raising my voice at all, "Sheryl? It's Tam. Where is Matt?"

A very confused and now embarrassed Sheryl stuttered out that she had left my place that morning and that was where she had seen him last. I then asked the very blunt, obvious question. Her tone was now highly embarrassed as she answered yes.

"Out of common decadency and respect for another woman, do not do that again. And do not ever step foot inside my house again."

It was moments later that I got a call from our mutual friend Dee. He was at my place and was with Matt. He said he was fine, just that he was looking a little unwell. Well, that was that. My anger reached a breaking point and I asked to talk to Matt. There was no talking, I can assure you. Just my sheer rage and frustration with Matt. I was floored and shattered. He had already negatively impacted Mystics and I was desperate to get back and repair the damage. Now this! Never mind the self-destruction and substance abuse. I had never felt that helpless or out of control in my own life before.

After raging at Matt, I went out for a walk to cool my head and arrived back to find that Chené was home. She had been out teaching a lesson when all of this had transpired. She took one look at my face and knew something was not right. I recounted my events from earlier with her, trying my hardest to keep my anger under control. It was the next day that I noticed I had developed an angry looking rash on the back of my hands and wrists. It was more prominent on my left hand. Little did I know at the time that this angry rash was actually burn marks. It was not until a couple of days later when it started to blister and change colour that I realised what it was and what I had done. In the heat of the moment with Matt I had somehow summoned up a massive surge of energy. Not knowing it was there to begin with, the energy simply sat in my hands, waiting to be used. It needed to go somewhere and I believe it burned up on my hands. I had literally burned my hands with the energy of excessive anger. It took a good month before my hands were fully healed. Shortly after burning my hands, my transformation began to kick in. I could feel it starting as a mild anxiety and as the days progressed, it grew. I did my utmost to keep it under control. I did not want to experience a transformation in Chené's space, knowing how intense they could be. As I ignored my transformation, the spirits pushed and I fought to keep the feeling of depression at bay.

Aside from my frustration with Matt, was my increased frustration at waiting on my visa. Tết was over and Immigration was back at work; yet my application had not been processed. It was in my third week that my despair turned to full on depression. I knew I could not give up. I had been chatting to Vũ about everything. He had been checking the cards for me at random. Before I had left, he had told me that I would be okay; that it would be difficult, but I would get my visa. He also mentioned Immigration needing to meet three times first before a decision could be reached. I believed all of this would happen before I had left Hanoi. When it did not materialize, I despaired but carried hope. It was in my third week that Vũ mentioned a spell he had found. He believed it would work and said he would help me from his side. I trusted Vũ and I trusted his ability to cast magic. Something told me to reach out to Tồm, Matt and Liz as well. I told each of them what I was doing and asked them to help manifest me back home. The instructions from Vũ were simple: write down my intention as specifically as I could, including dates, and that I would need a crystal as an offering. He explained that this was to be wrapped up in the paper with my intention and I was to then go and ask a deity for help and a blessing. From there I was to throw the complete parcel into moving water, preferably the ocean. Vũ's words to me were, "The closer to the Ocean, the quicker it will work. Don't worry about finding the water. A woman will guide you there."

When I had arrived in Thailand, Chené had taken me to see an exquisite temple that stood atop a hill. It had three levels and three deities to choose from. I knew this was the correct place and knew instantly which deity to approach - Kuan Yin or Lady Buddha as she is known in Vietnam. As for the water, the ocean was a good hour's drive away and I was not going to ask Chené to make that drive so I could throw some paper and crystals into it. I knew there was somewhere else we could go. Then I recalled a waterfall that her and I had been told of a few days prior. It was not far from the temple. Intuitively, I knew this was where we needed to go. Chené was a bit skeptical, particularly when we had been given a rough direction and told to follow the road.

"Trust yourself, sweetheart, you've got this." I assured Chené. Vũ's words about a woman guiding me came to mind and I knew Chené would find the place. I set my intention and chose my crystal. I had intuitively packed a Sugilite with me when I left Hanoi. Now I knew why I had. Sugilite is only mined in South Africa and is seen as a precious mineral. It felt a good exchange with the spirits. Chené and I then headed to the temple where she let me go off to speak to Kuan Yin on my own.

I entered the place that held Kuan Yin's statue. I walked around to set my space, ringing the bells that lined the walls. I then arrived back at the foot of Kuan Yin, and out of respect I knelt and asked for her blessing. In my years of performing rituals and working with deities and spirits, Kuan Yin is by far my most powerful experience. I felt myself being filled with raw love and compassion. I allowed myself to feel how loved I actually was. I allowed myself to be consumed by it; to feel it fully. I breathed it in deeply and exhaled gratitude. I have never been one to publicly display my feelings. Yet there I was, on my knees, weeping openly. All while being filled up with pure unconditional love and compassion. The love and compassion that I had for myself and the love and compassion that flowed, unhindered, from my family too, as they worked to get me home. Something in me shifted that day as I understood my full capacity to be compassionate and unconditional. I sat with Kuan Yin for a moment longer, before continuing on with my ritual. I met up with Chené and we headed out to find the waterfall. I could sense Chené's unease as she rode in the direction of where the waterfall was meant to be. I assured her once more to trust her judgment and follow her gut. Within ten minutes we had arrived and found ourselves in a spectacular setting. I knew I was in the right place. I then stepped out into the water and noticed a cluster of spiders. I had been haunted by dreams of spiders for years. I had then started dating Ryan and taken up smoking marijuana and they stopped. Over the years that followed, I had come to understand that the spider had come to me as a child as a representation of my power - chasing me down so that I would embrace it. The spider had come to represent my Yin and my ability to weave into reality anything I wanted. As much as I still had a rather irrational fear of them, I had over the years come to understand the spider and the role she plays in weaving the webs of life and magic. I cast my intention out into the water, said a final incantation and gave a blessing. I felt charged and knew the manifestation had worked. I was aiming for some tight dates, though. I wanted to be back in Hanoi that weekend. The weekend came and I had heard nothing new. My faith dwindled and the upcoming full moon got intense. As mentioned, I can be quite difficult to be around or understand when I am going through transformations or in heavy processing stages. I had also come to understand that the moon amplified this. This was the first full moon I chose to try to do things differently. I could tell Chené was struggling with me in her space. I was struggling to process my transformation and being in another highly sensitive person's space was not particularly fair or healthy.

"I'm checking myself into a hostel just down the street. I know I can be a nightmare to be around at full moon. I think this is better for both of us. I will be back tomorrow, I promise!"

She seemed to understand, but also looked rather concerned. I assured her once more that I would be okay and left. Ten minutes later I was checked in and sitting in my new, albeit temporary space.

There I was, in a hotel room in the city of Hat Yai, Thailand. Room number eight on the fifth floor to face myself and my challenges. Black cats decorated the bathroom towels, a butterfly adorned the chair I was seated on and the cutest little owl flowerpot sat on the desk in front of me. The light above me had a mosaic design, reflecting the love between the Sun and the Moon. How the hell did I land up in THIS hotel room? I knew I was in for a night of transformation, downloading and processing. I had been through quite the journey already and up till that point I had not really had a chance to stop and assimilate all that had transpired. This was now my space to do just that. It was here that I understood myself, the Moon and how we flowed with one another. I started to find forgiveness for Matt and most importantly, I came to understand that I was in Thailand for an internal shift. I spent the rest of that night, well into the early hours of the morning, working through and making sense of everything. It was then that I felt I understood whose voice I had been hearing - the voice that kept insisting Matt needed to return home. Matt had spoken to me a fair amount about his home in South Carolina and his family. He had often spoken about his maternal grandfather and the tree nursery he had started and grown years ago. Whenever he spoke about his grandfather, I would feel a sense of connection to this gentle energy. His grandfather was a Magician for sure and a natural with the ways of Mother Nature. I cannot tell you how I came to understand that voice was his grandfather's, just that I knew it was correct. I felt I also understood what his grandfather had meant about Matt needing to go home. I arrived back at Chené's apartment the next morning, feeling far more in alignment.

The rest of the weekend came and went and I was heading into my fourth week of being in Thailand. I was at my wits end with Zee and Immigration. I felt like I was being given the run around and not getting any actual, solid answers. I finally received a message from Zee with some actual progress. It was a picture of an official document. "You are being processed," was his message. My Vietnamese had improved and I made sense of the document he had sent me. This was the application for my visa. Zee had not yet even applied for my visa. I was furious and did not understand at all what was happening. I contacted Lily, who used to own Base, to ask if she could make sense of it for me. She contacted me a while later and explained that my process was complicated and had been delayed. Immigration had an issue with the fact that I had not answered my phone when they had called during the first week of my passport being taken away; something I had done under Zee's advisement. I was about ready to throw in the towel. I messaged Liz and Leo as I felt there was something I was not seeing. There was a reason I was still in Thailand, as frustrating as that was. Leo offered to look at my Astrology chart and pull some cards for me. She messaged me a few hours later with some very helpful insights. The insights I received were that I was in fact being hit in my astrological house of governments, foreign travel and home. She had looked at a few aspects of my chart and astrologically speaking, everything that had happened was in alignment with my chart. She then forecasted a bit for me and indicated that in three months I would have similar issues, but that they would be less severe. Things would finally begin to settle towards the end of October that year. By my next solar return (birthday), I would know where I wanted to be and what I wanted from life. She pulled a few cards as well. All of them aligning perfectly. Then she asked the direction question of why I was in Thailand and she sent me a picture of the Magician card. "It is time to step into your power as shaman," were her words. I had not spoken to Leo much over the last few months and not mentioned anything to her about shamanism or my experiences. She then told me that I would be going back to Hanoi, she could not see when, but that it would happen.

I shared these insights with Liz and soon I found us discussing, once again, the shift and rise of a Yin-based consciousness. I shared with her all that I had been witnessing on my side of the world. How I had witnessed women trying to step into their power but were not quite getting it right. I made mention of a Goddess Empowerment workshop that was going to be held at Mystics later that month. I told her how the organizer and I had been asked by a man if he could join. I was very familiar with this man, he had been around Mystics a few times: Reid - he was a very interesting soul! Every time I had encountered him, our conversations were pure enlightenment. The organizer of the workshop, Lee-Anne, ran it past the ladies that were attending and there were no real objections except for one. The lady who objected was known around Hanoi as a prominent speaker on women's rights. She argued that it was a Goddess-based workshop and that it did not allow space for men. I expressed to Liz how mortified I had felt at the apparent reality of where women were on their paths. We were desperate to step into our power; to feel empowered. For centuries women had suffered oppression across many cultures. We were now figuring out our power and how to use it. For some, it went to the extreme and I saw women of arrogance; some abusing power as men had done for centuries. Women were trying to rise, but as men. They did not fully understand their power. Many however, were able to feel it, but that power was sitting underneath toxic layers; hence the power they used was toxic. Both Leo and Liz advised that when I returned to Hanoi, I would be fully in my power. I was Shaman and needed to step into that. Liz then added that clearly there were big things transpiring in the world and me being firmly in my power in a healthy way was needed. Before retiring for the evening, I sat reflecting on the souls I had come to call my family. I recalled the feeling of compassion I had felt from them and I longed for home. The words: "Life takes you to unexpected places, love brings you home," rang in my mind and I finally understood the meaning. Sometimes we find home in unexpected places and that is where we find authentic love. Receiving a message from Joe in that moment saying he missed me, was my confirmation.

I woke the next day and my faith was down to a tiny spark. "I don't think this visa is ever coming," I expressed in exasperation. "Don't talk like that," was Chené's instant response.

"Please don't ask me to be quiet, please I need to get this out. I am so used to not being allowed to speak my truth; please just give me that," I replied.

She gave me space and allowed me to speak freely. In doing so, it seemed to open something up for her as well and she began to speak freely about things that had been troubling her on higher levels. We consoled one another and were starting to feel better when my phone rang:

"Hello? Yes Tam you can come back to Hanoi. I have your visa," it was Zee and I was floored at what I was hearing. I recall needing to sit down for a moment as I took in what I was hearing. I was going home! I made quick arrangements to get myself back as soon as possible and was set to arrive the next evening. I would be traveling up to Bangkok that night by bus and would then fly out to Hanoi the next afternoon.

My bus trip up to Bangkok was uneventful and I read a book to pass the time at the airport the next day. Matt and I were chatting a bit, he was saying how happy he was that I was coming back. He then asked me about my visa and how much I had paid for it. He was asking about the one that had previously been revoked; the one my travel agent had arranged. I asked him why he wanted to know as I was getting a bad feeling.

"I'm going to get that money back for you," was his response.

"Are you mad? That is not your place!" I could feel Matt's Shadow was still very much around. I argued with him for a good few minutes. He then finally gave in after I told him to stop pushing me. I had shown him what I had done to my hands a few weeks earlier when I had inadvertently burnt them. In a little way, it was to put a bit of fear into him, but mostly so he could see the potential consequences of misdirected energy. The conversation then shifted to the money situation back in Hanoi. Matt was not able to fetch me from the airport so I would need to take a taxi. I was running very low on funds by that time. Having spent way more than eleven days in Thailand had left me in a rather broke situation. Matt had not exactly run Mystics to his best ability either. I learned that he had lost money, spent recklessly and that essentially there was very little money. I knew I was going to have a very big mess to clean up when I got back. I just hoped that I could salvage Mystics.

I arrived back in the early evening. I had agreed to meet Matt at Mystics and he would then take me home from there. When I arrived, I found Tôm, Joe and Matt waiting for me. I was beyond happy to see my family. It had been nearly a full month since I had left. We all caught up for a bit and then I was just too tired to stay any longer and Matt I headed out. Before I left, Tôm whispered to me to try not to kill Matt. I laughed and said I would try. In all seriousness though, it took a lot for me to not lose my cool with Matt. My first few days back were rough. The raw wound of what Matt had done was still fresh. He was also still staying in my space. I understood that Matt was trying to get 'clean' and was attempting recovery. The agreement was that he could stay in my space while he sorted something else out, as long as he stayed sober.

I had Mystics turned around and running smoothly within my first week back. On my first day back I cleansed and cleaned the space, top to bottom. The energy in there was heavy, dark and dirty. It had not helped that while I was away there was a massive water problem which resulted in the place being flooded regularly with dirty water from the restaurant next door. It had been sorted out just before I returned. When Matt had told me that he was essentially dealing with shitty water almost daily, I joked that it was a karma thing. In a sense however, I suspected that either the ancestors or Goddesses had a hand in that one. By the time I was halfway through with my first day, Mystics felt lighter and more welcoming. It did not take long for things to start flowing again.

"If you had just kept your head about you and ran Mystics as normal, we would be okay right now. Do you see that?" I asked Matt a few days in. He seemed to be doing alright, but he was fighting his Shadow heavily. I could tell he had a lot of uncertainty going on. It did not help that I swung between being okay with everything to being triggered and angry once more. It took me about two weeks to finally be okay around him, without getting short or angry at small things. Then I was given a gift.

20

Trip to the Future

My first two to three weeks back in Hanoi were just plain bizarre, yet perfectly in alignment. It began with my first session with a client soon after returning. Mel seemed like your regular expat. She had been in Hanoi for a while and was teaching English. I asked her a couple of standard questions and then began her Energy Healing session. It was about halfway through, that she began to look like she was having convulsions. This was not something I had experienced before. In sessions I usually worked with binaural frequencies. Along with the healing benefits, they allow those in session to rest undisturbed. I immediately assumed that it may have been the frequencies having too much of an effect. I gave her a bit of a gentle shake and called to her to see how responsive she was. I had no response and opened one of her eyes to check her pupil. It was fully dilated, almost glassy and unresponsive. Then she opened her eyes fully and looked at me. "You alright Mel?" I asked concerned.

"Yes, sorry I should have warned you upfront. I get body shakes when I'm processing. I've had them since my shamanic training.

Suddenly my experience during that full Moon in Mystics, weeks before, made a lot more sense. The Universe really needed to find better ways to communicate things! You know, maybe schedule me for a massive transformation so I can be prepared? Perhaps provide a simple pamphlet outlining what is actually happening? It was a relief to finally have some sense of the experience I had endured weeks before. We then began to have a new soul frequenting Mystics. Luke was in Hanoi traveling through. He had stumbled across our space one morning and then seemed to make it his home and became a daily visitor. I was then introduced to Hilary. Hilary had known the Base group for years, but had been out of Hanoi for a while. Hilary had an amazing energy about her and I connected with her almost instantly. She had been into Mystics a few times and we had chatted a fair bit. She then came in one day with something peculiar to share, "I dreamt about you last night."

"Um, alright have a seat. Let's chat," was my confused and now very curious response. She proceeded to explain that she had a lucid dream where I had come over to read her cards. She explained I stayed the night and from there, the dream just got strange. She explained how she had heard a strange noise and went into her kitchen to find a group of South Africans in there - having a party! Well, that sounded about right for us South Africans. They offered for her to join them, but she was not feeling in a party mood and decided to go back to bed; only to hear another noise outside. Here she saw animals of various types, from different countries, all getting along. Standing with these animals were Vietnamese men who said to her in perfect English, "See, we can all get along." She then went back to bed only to hear the noise of someone rattling a lock. This was where she realized she was lucid dreaming and woke herself up. As she sat talking to me, I just kept reflecting on the shift and the move into a Yin-based consciousness. I knew her dream was prophetic and that it indicated the direction we needed to go in. It now become very clear that South Africa and Africa had something pivotal to do with it.

My bizarre experiences continued as the planned Goddess workshop happened. It was being hosted by Lee-Anne, an incredibly gifted healer and Goddess in her own right. Matt and I had met her the year before at an outdoor festival and had hit it off well. I was curious to see what would come from this workshop. The presence of Yin and its rise had been the biggest constant on my path next to shamanism and the shift. When Lee-Anne had spoken about it the first time, I just knew it was correct and that Mystics' space was right. Lee-Anne came in the day before to finalize everything and we got to chatting on deep things pretty quickly. The topic soon shifted to all the Western teachers that were coming over to the East. We then looked at it on a higher level. We saw how the West was coming to the East to teach, but the subject was not English. It was Spirituality. The East however, had Spiritual lessons for the West as well. Then I had the understanding that if we could get East and West to merge in the middle somewhere, we would find perfect Yin-Yang balance. Part of the shift was the rising of a Yin-based consciousness and shamanism and the ways of the Ancients was a way to get there. I then saw a whole new dimension to it. The East is Yin - a highly feminine-based energy. They work in flow and harmony with the Moon and her cycles. Some of the most gifted souls I have come across have most certainly been from the East. The East and Africa! The East being Yin is often perceived as being dark; since darkness is the nature of Yin. However, darkness is not a bad thing. It is just expressive of the depths of one's power. So infinite we cannot see its end. The West is Yang, a male dominant energy and a very patriarchal aspect of that male energy. It was here that Lee-Anne made note of the difference in Spirituality between East and West. She expressed that, "The West is more rainbows and unicorns while the East is raw and authentic."

Africa seemed to sit in the middle of all this. We are neither East nor West. We are a culture all on our own. I thought back to insights I had been given while in Thailand. Keegan was a good friend of Chené's and I had spent a fair bit of time with him while there. Keegan proved to be a high-level shaman and on our first introduction, the intensity of his energy had me excusing myself as a massive wave of nausea and light-headedness had set in. It was during one of our conversations on his balcony that he explained Africa to me, "Africa is the ultimate matriarch. Mama Africa, shaped as the Elephant, is the one who holds the family together. She is our roots and where we are all descended from."

Suddenly I understood why I had been offered only Elephant bracelets when I had been looking for my Lion prior to leaving Cape Town months before. The Lion was not strength, he was courage. The Elephant was strength. Again, my lesson of compassion came to mind along with the rest of Keegan's lesson, "Africa is also heart shaped. We sit almost perfectly in the middle of the world. We are known for having rhythm, that is our heartbeat. The heartbeat of the world."

All of it made perfect sense. My conversation with Lee-Anne about East and West linked in with my teaching from Keegan and it all connected to Hilary's dream. I went home that evening to process all that I had come to understand and to ask myself some questions.

Lee-Anne's workshop the following day proved to be a very enlightening experience and added an amazing energy to the Full Moon vibe that was already around. It was still early and Lee-Anne arrived to setup. I received a message that one of the ladies was unable to attend, saying that she was ill. It happened to be the same lady that had objected to Reid attending.

"Well then, let Reid know he can join us. I don't see any issue with it," was Lee's response.

I messaged Reid who replied quickly that he would be over in a while to join us. The workshop was underway when he joined. As always, his energy was so soft and he blended into the workshop beautifully. He engaged where he felt he needed to and other times he seemed to be off somewhere else. I understood he was stepping between worlds. Learning in the earthly plane from Lee-Anne and then processing in the higher realms. He left towards the end and seemed upbeat.

He arrived at Mystics a couple of days later, looking sad. "Are you okay, Reid?" I asked concerned.

"Yeah. I just - I don't know... I just feel really emotional," he had not been the first man to say that to me that day. So I just figured it was something in the planets. He returned the next day and shared something with me, "I met up with a friend last night and we had an interesting chat. She explained about something called Kryon. It's where one awakens their inner Goddess."

The Universe still did not cease to amaze me. Out of all who had attended the Goddess Empowerment workshop, the single man attending was the one who was the most empowered. I messaged Lee-Anne to let her know the beautiful result. The understanding I gained was that this man was initially denied access to the workshop. In doing so, a woman was stopping a man from embracing his Yin aspect; something most women ask for! No one has the place to say where one is allowed or not.

Lee-Anne's workshop had gone magically, and as a thank you she had gifted both Matt and I a drop of LSD. It had come from South Africa and was apparently the cleanest she had come across. She informed me that she had left it on her altar since she had received it; so it was given with pure intentions, gratitude and blessings. Matt and I had agreed we would keep them aside and pick a day to take it together. Perhaps that would get us to sort ourselves out with one another. I was then gifted something else. Reid had come back in a bit later to say thank you and gifted me a [6]Changa joint. This was the second time I had received Changa from Reid. On my first experience, many weeks before, I had seen Matt shapeshift into a Lion; confirming the relevance of his tattoo and how he tied into my path. Matt had been shown another world by a Being of Light – a vision he felt resonated with the shift.

I found myself sitting with deep questions, two forms of psychedelic medicine and my set of cards. I asked about my path of shaman and drew The Chariot, Death and the Nine of Swords - the normal self master stuff, importance of transformation (the Death card) and the last card put something into perspective for me: my path is only as hard as I make it. It was a reminder of one's power and abilities. I then asked about doing a psychedelic journey. Surely I was not meant to take both? Tôm had mentioned previously that he was feeling the call to do a Changa journey. He had come into Mystics shortly after Reid had given me the Changa. I knew I was meant to share that with Tôm. I was still unsure of having so much medicine handed to me. I pulled the Nine of Wands, Five of Pentacles and Two of Cups. The trips where both healing and neither should be done alone. I then asked about my mushroom journey that I had done in Cape Town. The missing parts had been on my mind since the whole addiction issue had come up prior to my leaving for Thailand. I drew the Queen of Wands and the Eight and Five of Swords. I had not been in my complete strength at that time. Strength is the position I would have needed to be in, in order to have seen the full experience.

If I had been shown everything back then, it would have likely instilled confusion and fear. Perhaps it was fear that had stopped me from seeing. Fear also makes you unhealthy! I still felt I had unanswered questions, but knew I would receive the needed insights soon.

A few nights later, Tôm came round for his Changa journey. We chatted for a while and then he told me he was ready. I handed him the joint and I watched as he slipped into the realm of spirits. I watched as he was shown all he needed to see. I smoked on the joint as well and watched. I had no hallucinatory effects or journey. Just mild nausea and the shakes. As shamans, we are there to create and hold space for others. We do this so that they can do what work is needed; while feeling safe and secure to explore as far as they need to. I was not there to journey, I was there to watch and hold space. Tôm left after a couple of hours of deep conversation and I settled in for an early night. I had an uneventful sleep and woke the next morning as normal and started my day. Matt came around to fetch me. He was still giving me a bit of space and had been staying with Joe. As the morning progressed, I began to feel out of alignment. I put it down to maybe being the Changa and used some mind over matter. We needed to pick up some things on our way into Mystics. Stopping at the store close to me, Matt noticed I was not quite right, "You doing alright there Tam?"

"Yeah, sort of," I said as I dropped my keys for the third time.

"Take the day off Tam, you're obviously not managing. I'll run Mystics today, it's alright. Take the day off."

He drove me back home, checked if I needed anything else and headed to open Mystics. Summer was back in full swing and it was strangely a clear blue sky day. This is actually a rarity due to the high level of pollution in the city of Hanoi. I lounged around for a bit, lost with what to do with my day off.

"I could always drop my acid from Lee-Anne. I do have the day off after all. So why not take the day off?" was my thought as I chewed the gummy sweet that Lee-Anne had dropped the LSD onto. "Let's see where this goes," was my last sober thought as I headed into my journey with an open mind and no expectations. As the acid started kicking in, I realized just how pure it was! Then I heard what sounded like someone knocking on a door. "Wow this acid IS good," I thought as the clouds painted on my ceiling began to swirl and move. Then I heard Tracy calling outside, the knock on the door had actually occurred! She was calling for Ollie to come and open for her. They had both recently moved into the same house as me. It had felt like strange timing as well. I found it odd, yet synchronistic that they were in the same space as me once again. I came downstairs, perhaps a little shakily and unlocked the front door for Tracy. She looked at me and I looked at her, both perhaps a bit strangely; and then a very odd experience began to happen.

"Do I look okay?" I asked.

"Yeah, why? You feeling okay?" She asked, a bit unsure.

"Yeah I'm just tripping," I answered. Dealing with the body shakes induced by the acid, I was trying to explain that I was okay; that I was still there and had not flown the biscuit to outer space. I still had full sense of what was going on, but I felt strange. Not acid type strange either. She asked what I meant, "Do you need something? A hug maybe?"

Then she asked if it felt like something needed to come out. This question here was the trigger!

"I think I need to sit down for a moment, but carry on," I said as I sat down on the edge of the couch and listened. She had walked into the kitchen and carried on speaking. Her words seemed to flow, like they were coming from another place. I was seated with my back to her and looking out our front door as tears began to roll down my cheeks. She began to speak about emotions and release. It was strange - I was not feeling any specific emotions, but the tears were there. Then as she spoke further, my first realization occurred. The understanding of being broken. I sat and listened to Tracy with tears streaming as I felt the brokenness that she and I both carried inside. Yet I also understood that being broken was okay because it meant we could repair and rebuild. The conversation ended with her words, "Maybe that's just me." She placed a smoothie down in front of me and disappeared upstairs. I felt the need to move to the corner section of our L-shaped couch and sat there allowing everything to flow. The process that followed was a series of understandings. Understandings I had experienced before, but where? It was when I told myself it was okay to just sit in the corner and cry that I understood. My consciousness was slung shot backward in time to almost a year prior - to the moment I woke up sobbing in my mushroom journey, with the understanding that it was okay to sit in the corner and cry. I knew where I had gone during the moments I had 'slept' in my mushroom journey. My soul had traveled to the future, sat down on a couch in a home I would move into months later and had a conversation with Tracy. A conversation that would trigger much-needed understandings in order to progress on my path and find healing - healing with Ryan and healing with Matt. It was quite the sensation to sit in a space I had sat in before but had not known the circumstances of. My physical body was reacting to the experience in the exact same manner it had a year before. All my sobbing had caused my sinuses to block up. The understanding that the block in my sinuses was me holding onto anger and frustration pushed my consciousness forward and I felt my soul reaching out. It started with Ollie and Tracy who were home with me. Then it began to reach out further to friends close by. I then felt myself reaching out for Matt and understood the cause of my frustration. I was still holding onto anger and resentment towards him for what had happened while I was in Thailand. The feeling that passed through me next I can only attempt to explain. The understanding of Matt, who and why he is, flowed through me. We are all imperfect, we are all just human. He had never intended to hurt me. I could see the full picture; I could see everything and everyone. All connected, all one and the same in beautiful imperfection. Matt was still the genuine, honest soul I had met months earlier. He had just gotten lost along his way. In finding forgiveness with Matt, I found my healing and forgiveness with Ryan. I had the clear understanding that we will all make mistakes and that no one is perfect. I knew it was senseless to hold onto my resentments towards Matt. They were hurting me, not him. What he had done was not okay and he had crossed lines. Yet his intentions were not to hurt me. I could not hold anger towards him. What was I to be angry for? For a past experience that did not define that person? A lapse in common sense and poor judgment? This is where and how we learn. I felt my connection with Matt heighten and my heart open. I knew I could be okay with him.

Much the same way I did a year before, I began to focus on the room around me. I sat and watched the swirls of color and geometric patterns forming along the walls. I knew that Ollie was going to be giving me some sort of grounding soon. African grounding! Then I noticed how warm and sunny it was outside and the sun started to call me, much like the fire did on the night of my mushroom journey. Making my way upstairs, I knew my mushroom trip to the future was done and I could carry on with my acid trip - which in itself was a beautiful experience. I was on our upstairs balcony when Ollie offered me some coffee. Coffee sounded amazing and I happily accepted. I had sent Liz a message earlier that morning to share the experiences I had been having. I took a moment while waiting for my coffee to listen to her reply, "I do think some grounding is needed. Coffee comes to mind."

I had to stop listening for a moment and just absorb the beauty of the collective consciousness. I shared the collective joke with Liz and thanked her for sending the message ahead to Ollie. With my grounding cup of coffee in hand, I sat and watched the swirls of patterns once more. Enjoying the midday sun, I felt peaceful and connected.

"I really am lucky. Others have to go via substances to see this world and feel this connection. I have this while sober."

In the moment of acknowledging my gifts and how blessed I actually was, I found a new sense of gratitude for who I was at my core. Then the sanctuary of my room called. I returned, closed the door and lay back on my bed. I then sat up and looked at myself in the mirror and watched myself aging rapidly. "Don't go with that sadness in your eyes," I said to myself. I was not feeling sad, however. In fact, quite the opposite. It did raise the emptiness that had come up in my very first reading with Vũ. A rush of understandings on where that emptiness came from ran through my mind. I found peace with the emptiness. I understood that the emptiness was a lack of connection. When I was not connected or in alignment, I felt empty. My attention was then drawn to the music that was currently playing. I had left my YouTube to run at random and a Psybient style set was playing. The track that was playing had a recording of a man giving a speech. He was talking about purpose, doing bigger things and changing the world. I recognized it as the well-known speech Jim Carrey had given at his graduation in 2014 from MIU. His words struck me: "So many of us choose our path out of fear disguised as practicality. What we really want seems impossibly out of reach and ridiculous to expect. So we never dare to ask the Universe for it. Like many of you, I was concerned about going out into the world and doing something bigger than myself, until someone smarter than myself made me realize that there is nothing bigger than myself. My soul is not contained within the limits of my body. My body is contained within the limitlessness of my soul. As that shift happens in you, you won't be feeling the world, you'll be felt by it. You'll be embraced by it. Now I'm always at the beginning, I have a reset button and I ride that button constantly. Once that button is functioning in your life, there's no story that the mind could create that will be as compelling."

I could not deny my purpose any longer. I knew I was not done with my own shift, but by maintaining my flow, the rest would be easy. It was time for me to do something bigger than myself, it was time to be myself. I knew my purpose was big, but that it was not bigger than myself. Then further insights flowed through my consciousness.

"Bring awareness to the Feminine. Spread compassion and unconditional love. Do this through the Collective Consciousness by raising your vibrational frequency. By doing so you will raise the frequencies of others." The 'how' was being explained to me.

"Your vibrational frequency is not quite optimal yet. You are still missing insights." My health came to the fore and my focus went straight to my chest. My month in Thailand, and I believe, shifting stagnant issues had helped to clear up my chest infection. I still had a lingering cough, but it had drastically improved.

"Why do you struggle to breathe in the joy of life?" The question rang through me. This I would only be able to answer more than a year later.

Here the insights stopped and I felt my journey ending as I stepped back into reality. I knew I was done processing all that I could and spent the afternoon relaxing with Ollie. Later that evening, I knew Matt would be done at Mystics and it would be time for us to reconnect. I sent Matt a message asking if he would come by. He arrived a short while later and I opened up to him. I expressed everything that I felt and spoke my truth. I explained that I understood he had never meant to hurt me, that it was never his intention; and that I could not hold any resentment or judgment towards him.

"Do you think we could try again Tam? I know what I lost and I know how stupid I was to let you go. I know it will take time to earn your trust again. I get that; I will give you as much space as you need. Please just give me another chance."

"I don't know if I can, Matt. We are okay, but I don't know if I am ready for a relationship with you just yet. I'm scared to be honest. You have a dark side Matt; it really scares me," I confided in him.

"Please trust me Tam, I would never intentionally do anything to hurt you. You mean too much to me."

I asked him to give me some time and we could see how things went. My authentic self wanted to reach out and tell him yes. My fears however, went into overdrive and stopped me from embracing a relationship with Matt.

Our conversation soon moved to the plans for the evening and I asked him if he would take me to the Old Quarter. I knew I needed to be there and I knew my family was there. We arrived a little while later and went to a new place that had opened up the previous December, Maze. As

I had intuitively known, family members were about. I arrived to find Tôm and Joe sitting out front, along with a few members of my South African family. With Ollie and Tracy living in the same house, my two worlds had merged even more over the last few months. More family arrived and I soon found myself sitting with members from both my families - my South African and what I called my Hanoi family. These two worlds mingling and interacting so naturally. What had brought Ollie and a few other South Africans out there was that Imcia had started working with Joe. I had met her a few times in Mystics and she had attended the Goddess workshop as well. I adored her light and vibrant energy. A Green Witch for sure, Imcia was all crystals, plants and connection with Mother Earth. I was surprised when I found her working in a bar. She explained that after the workshop she had come round the corner for a drink and the workshop had inspired her to make a change; so she had asked for a job. I knew Joe consistently struggled to get female staff in, so she was pretty much hired on the spot. She had been there a few nights already and was loving it. She had offered to introduce Ollie to the owner and to discuss him potentially DJing there. It was so strange and yet so natural to watch my worlds mesh together. I spent a couple of hours with everyone and then grew hungry and tired.

"You want to get some dinner and come home tonight?" I asked Matt. He looked rather confused for a second, then skeptical, "Are you sure?" I assured him I was okay with it. It was strictly friends only, but he was allowed back into my space. We arrived back with dinner and chatted for a long while. I had missed my best friend. It felt good to reconnect with Matt again. I really believed it was just as friends, though. That lasted another hour as Matt and I went from being broken, to friends to a couple in the space of a few hours. My authentic self knowing that it was correct and okay.

21

Declined

The next morning we chatted about where we were and what we wanted. I put boundaries in place, "I'm not asking you to stop drinking, just drink less." Matt agreed and said he respected my boundaries and things went alright for about a day.

"Hey, can I go have a drink with Zain later?" Matt asked.

"Why are you asking me? And no! I asked you yesterday to please stop drinking every day and here we are," I could feel myself getting frustrated. What was frustrating me most was that he was asking me to move my boundaries. Boundaries I had just put down.

"No you're right, I won't go." Matt and I did this backwards and forwards dance for about three weeks. He would push my boundaries and I would stand my ground. On occasion I would reach a breaking point and just storm off. It was one night that I did this that Matt showed a side I had not considered before. He had been drinking and was starting to test my patience. There was nothing wrong with what was happening, but it was just triggering me. Then I lost my cool, grabbed my bag, did not say a word and walked out the door. Moments later I heard Matt calling for me. I stopped and gave him a moment to catch up.

"What the hell Tam! What happened? Why did you just run off like that?" he asked.

"I can't do it. I can't do the drinking and where it goes. I know I said I don't mind you still drinking, but I do mind. I'm struggling with it. I'm struggling because of what happened. I'm sorry Matt, I am trying to move on. It still triggers me badly though. Maybe it's still too fresh."

"No, you're right Tam, and I should not be drinking now anyway. There are more important things I need to be focused on. It's just really hard - I enjoy drinking. I'm also not coping too well with my own visa story. It's stressing me out a lot."

On returning from Thailand, I had learned that Matt had overstayed on his visa. This had been a big cause for a lot of his stress and his downward spiral. It was the main reason he had refused to come with me to Immigration when my visa issue popped up. Matt had been trying harder, I could not fault him on that.

"I will drink less Tam, I will keep trying. I need you to do something for me though. Please talk to me, don't just run away. If you are too angry to talk at the time, then tell me that and then when you are ready we can talk. Just please talk to me, so I know what is happening and where I can be better if needed. Please promise me you won't just run off like that again. It hurts when you do that."

I had never considered how my actions had hurt him. We continued to try, our ups and downs were fairly consistent, though. That was until I lost it completely.

Matt, as much as he was trying, would still push my boundaries. I still had nights where I dealt with his Shadow and nights where he did not come home. It all came to a head the day before Chené was set to arrive. She had left Thailand and had chosen to spend a month with me in Hanoi, with a stop in New Zealand and then she was heading back home to South Africa. I was excited to see her and spend the month with her. However, my excitement dwindled somewhat after a massive fight between Matt and I broke out. Matt had once again asked me to move my boundaries and once again I had gotten angry.

"If you are out drinking then rather stay somewhere else. I don't want that in my space." I heard nothing back from Matt for a while. We had been fighting over messenger chat. He had wanted to go for a few drinks with Zain after we had recently had a fight about his drinking. I had once again set new boundaries and once again he was pushing them. I was feeling lost on what to do with Matt and his drinking. He just never seemed to be able to get it under control. Intuitively I chose I chat to Ollie about it and he shared some solid advice with me: "You know Tam, alcohol is not the Devil! It is what people do with it that makes it good or bad. It's their intentions behind why they are using it. I get Matt though, I know that sometimes it is easier to deal with life that way. I was doing it for a while. The lifestyle here does not help either. He needs to set himself boundaries. He must find a balance and then counter the drinking time with something more productive. It will take some getting used to, just like with anything new."

Ollie's advice was helpful. I had shared it with Matt and he agreed to set his own boundaries to see if that made a difference. He set the boundaries for a change and what he proposed was fair. His boundaries did not last long either and I reached my breaking point. When Matt finally replied to my message, I knew he would not be home. The conversation was left at that and as I suspected, Matt never came home that night.

The next morning I woke up, took out his suitcase and packed his stuff. He had never fully moved out of my space since I had returned from Thailand. It was now time for him to go. I knew he would still need help, however. I messaged Zain explaining I could not help Matt anymore; that I was kicking him out and that he would need somewhere to go. As much as I was angry and fed up, I still cared. Zain said that he respected my choices and that he got that Matt was not always easy to deal with. He then said that he had never seen Matt like this with anyone, though. He was talking about the good changes he had seen in Matt. He had never seen him make this much effort with anyone. He advised that I think about it first before making a final decision. I was just so tired! I arrived at Mystics with Matt's suitcase in hand. Across the street was a small local restaurant. We had become friendly with the woman that ran it. She spoke no English, but with mine and Matt's broken Vietnamese, we had chatted a few times. She was standing out front when I arrived and she looked at me with the suitcase and seemed to know that something was up. I went inside to find that Matt was sleeping upstairs. On the nights he went out drinking, he stayed at Mystics. This was not particularly healthy either. I woke him up abruptly and told him his stuff was downstairs.

"What? What do you mean?" he asked hungover and half asleep.

"I'm done Matt, you are no longer welcome in my space," was my short reply.

"You can't be serious Tam?" he asked and that was that. My anger hit boiling point and came out in full force. I shouted furiously while I set up Mystics for the day. I opened the front doors and continued to shout at him about how he had messed up and hurt me. The woman across the street was now standing on the sidewalk watching in interest as to what was transpiring across the street. An angry woman is an angry woman, no matter the culture! She knew Matt had done something very wrong and seemed rather amused at our domestic dispute. It was not until I had a mop in my hands and I was angrily cleaning the floor, that she came over and seemed to start helping with the setting up. Perhaps she was coming over in case I decided to murder Matt with the mop. She said something in Vietnamese which we could only assume was, "Is everything alright here?" We both told her it was okay and proceeded to carry on shouting at one another. I told Matt I was taking Mystics away and that we were completely done. That was when he grabbed his keys and left. He sent me a message later on; which I ignored as I went about my day. I then closed up and went home. Chené arrived later that evening to rather unexpected news.

The last she had heard, Matt and I were doing good and she was looking forward to finally meeting him. She had heard so much about him already. We spent the evening catching up on things and had an early night. She was set to come with me to Mystics the next day. We got up early and I treated her to a traditional Vietnamese breakfast before we headed to Mystics. Matt not having anywhere else to go, had spent the night there. Poor Chenè had come for a month's visit and had arrived to chaos.

"Matt this is Chené, Chené this is Matt. Excuse the very awkward meeting - this was not quite what I had in mind a few weeks back."

Matt asked if he could talk to me for a bit. I had calmed down from the day before and agreed. I agreed once again to give him another chance. I could not fault that he had actually been trying. He explained that it was hard for him, that he had never really known the sober life; that it was new for him. I could not disagree with what he was saying and my authentic self knew I was being unfair and uncompassionate. We once again set boundaries, this time together. We began to establish a balance again and things between us flowed naturally and once more, the lessons around loyalty and brotherhood came back to teach me.

In the month that Chené was there, we had numerous enlightening encounters in Mystics. It had become the healing space I had always envisioned. Family like the Benz and li Kai rui would come in frequently for a drink and a deep chat. Tôm and Joe were regulars as well. The insights and knowledge that flowed through Mystics was magical. If anyone was feeling out of sorts or needed a safe space, we were there. I found myself working regularly with high level souls needing direction back to their paths or assistance with healing. Luke, who had become a part of the family, was there daily too. We would engage in deep conversations or he would chat with the various high level souls coming in. Luke was the one to reinforce the lessons of brotherhood and loyalty - lessons I had been given months previously by the US Marine I had met in Base. Luke often spoke to me of the high rise construction he did back home in California. The high risks with that type of job were obvious. He explained, much as the Marine had months before, that at those heights you only have one another; that you are dealing with life and death. One wrong move and the life of someone else can slip from your hands, literally! Having this lesson repeated to me was synchronistic with everything I had been going through with Matt. The understanding that in hard times you hold on tighter. That is not when you let go and then offer a second chance. One wrong move and you have no more second chance. The encounters we had in Mystics over that time reinforced everything I knew about the shift into a Yin-based consciousness. I knew I had much deeper insights and one final shift to make. Matt and I were starting to become burnt out, however. Holding the space of Mystics on a daily basis was draining us. Matt still had his worries over his overstayed visa and I was coming up for my visa renewal. It was something that sparked an anxious feeling inside of me as I felt the next inner shift coming.

It was time for me to renew my visa and I had chosen a different travel agent to work with. We had submitted my application with enough room so should it be declined I would have time to sort my life out. My concerns around my visa began to grow, particularly as the days passed and I heard no news. I had applied for my renewal a week previously. Visas were usually processed within a couple of days. I spoke to Matt about my concerns and he said something that surprised me, "If you don't get a visa Tam, I'm coming with you. It doesn't matter where you go, I'm coming with. I'll find a way to sort out my visa."

I could not believe what I was hearing. Matt had been making a lot of effort, but I had never expected that from him. My biggest worry was that I was going to be declined and I would lose Matt all over again. I knew in all honesty that I would be leaving Vietnam; I just did not know if I would be losing Matt along with it. I had waited almost a week before I heard something. It was not good news! Immigration was refusing to give me a new visa. The travel agent told me she would try something else for me and that I should not worry. I was worried! The constant nagging on Matt's visa and that voice had become persistent, "He needs to go home!" By the weekend prior to my visa expiring, I broke down. Matt told me that if my visa renewal came through, he felt he should leave Mystics for me to run on my own. He felt it would be better to do his own thing. I do not know why this triggered me so much, but I shouted at him about feeling done with everything and stormed out - something Matt had asked me NOT to do!

I walked off my frustration, arrived back home and went and hid on the upstairs balcony. Chenè found me a little while later, sobbing. I told her everything that had happened, the issues with Matt's visa and my concerns about mine being declined. She chatted with me for a good hour and shared some very beautiful wisdom with me. She assured me that no matter what happened with my visa, I would be okay. If I needed to go home for a bit, she would be there if I needed her. We had been a bit disconnected that last week or so. I had so much going on and she had found a love interest with Joe. She had spent a fair bit of her time with him. A part of that was due to the madness that was going on in my space, but it was also to do with the romance that had blossomed quickly between them. She chose to share something with me that day about her and Joe. She had been asked by a friend why she would put effort into someone if she knew it was going to be temporary. She had replied that, "It does not matter how long a person is around for. You love them in that moment. You make the most of that moment. Nothing in life is permanent and we have no guarantees on anything. So why not make the most of what you have right now?"

Her words sat with me and resonated strongly. I began to feel more grounded and rather bad for how I had acted towards Matt. Then all hell broke loose – Ashy messaged me, "Tam I am worried. Matt has messaged me that he has taken some of my stock for personal use. I'm running a bit low on stock and cannot really let him take it. I cannot get hold of him now, please can you sort it out for me?"

I was furious when I read her message. I knew what had happened. Matt had once again not dealt well with circumstances and was hitting the bottle. I immediately tried to get hold of Matt, which I succeeded in doing, and a fight broke out within seconds. I insisted that he come home or tell me where he was. I knew he was in self-destruct mode and I knew the potentials and risks. I then received a message from Luke that he was with Matt in the Old Quarter, that he was okay and not to worry. I could tell that Luke was drunk as well, however, and that did not do much to ease my worry. I finally tracked them down and Chené and I headed to the Old Quarter. In that time, Matt had headed home. We arrived to find a rather intoxicated Luke, but he still had complete control of his faculties, as he put it. He explained that I had just missed Matt. Luke chose that moment to remind me of his work back home and how he missed the bond with his brothers. I knew I needed to make things right with Matt. I knew there was something more to Matt and I than just friendship and relationship. I had known these things for months. It was now time to speak my truth.

I left Chenè in the Old Quarter with Luke and Joe who had arrived shortly after we did. I knew she was in safe hands. It would also give me and Matt space to talk. I arrived home to find a rather angry and frustrated Matt waiting for me. We started talking, we then started fighting and then for a change, Matt lost it with me, "I'm sick of this! If you want me gone just tell me, I can't do this backwards and forwards with you anymore."

I began to plead with him not to leave as an old co-dependent habit surfaced. He became angrier and suddenly picked up a bottle off the lounge table and threw it at the wall. The explosion of angry energy set my shakes off. I had stepped away from him and he assumed that he had frightened me.

"Why are you shaking Tam? I'm sorry I did not mean to scare you."

"You didn't scare me, your energy is just intense. I can't help it, I don't know how to control them. Don't ever think that I'm scared of you."

Something about this triggered my angry side and I lost my cool. The situation just kept escalating until Matt reached a point.

"That's it I'm done! This is what my life has always been. I will always run after people, but when I fuck up, people just toss me aside. 'Fuck him he's just an addict! He's a junkie, a nothing!' All I ever asked from you is that you talk to me and you can't even do that for me! I mess up and you just run. I'm tired of it Tam. It fucking hurts," he yelled as he turned to punch the wall behind him. I felt like I had been punched. The harsh reality of what I had actually been doing with Matt was far from okay. With my brother Jadie I had learned that tough love was the solution. If the person kept repeating their cycles, you had to have a cut-off point and say, 'no more' - even if that meant cutting that person out of your life. This is exactly what I had done with Jadie years before. That was until I arrived in Thailand to stay with Chenè and Jadie had messaged me out of the blue. We had engaged in a bit of consistent contact since then, but then the contact dwindled and fizzled out. I saw in that moment that I was repeating the same cycle with Matt - the cycle of giving second chances and if that person kept disappointing me, then the chances had to end at some point. I saw everything that was wrong with that way of thinking.

"You're right Matt and that is not fair of me. I cannot base our relationship on me always giving you second chances. If I'm going to be with you, then I must be with you. I know you're not perfect, but fuck, neither am I. I also know you've been trying. It's not like you haven't been. If you had not done anything then it would be a different story. I'm sorry Matt.

The way I have treated you is not okay. No more second chances, I won't base our relationship on that anymore. I love you and I want to be with you. That I do know."

He assured me that he was not going anywhere and once again he assured me that if my visa was declined, he would come with me no matter where I went.

The Monday arrived and my current visa was expiring that Saturday. I felt myself reaching a point of frustration. When I had received the initial 'no' the week before, I knew I should have just accepted it and taken charge of the next steps. However, everyone around me spoke over me and I landed up waiting some more. By that point, however, I did not even want a visa for Vietnam anymore. I was feeling burnt out and exhausted. My soul was starting to call for a stretch and reassessment of life. In the last few weeks I had been questioning my work and the mediums I used. My biggest questions were around me reading Tarot for others. Since I had come back from Thailand, I had worked with a lot of high level souls. I had also worked with some not so high level ones. I had been asked a run of low vibration questions and I was just feeling tired of being seen as just a Tarot Reader. I felt like I was more than that. That feeling that change was coming was intense and I knew the change was strongly focused on my work and my path. I finally heard back from my travel agent later that afternoon, "I am sorry Tam, there is nothing I can do for you. Immigration will not give you another visa."

Even though I had known this was going to be the case, the shock still hit hard. It was now time for Matt to decide what he was going to do about his overstayed visa, particularly if he truly intended to come with me to wherever I was headed to next. Matt had been talking about a man that he had met a few weeks back, Mr Lee. He had said Mr. Lee seemed to be an important man in Hanoi. He had also expressed his feeling that this man could help him with his visa. Matt was very nervous to approach Immigration about his overstayed visa and I did not blame him! He had overstayed nearly a year by then and his stress was over the possible consequences he would need to face. Matt had spoken to Mr Lee the first time I had received a 'no' on my visa renewal. He had told Matt he would look into it and see if he was able to do anything to assist me. That Monday when we closed Mystics, our cat Tom was looking rather unsettled. We had acquired Tom from Ashy not long after I had returned from Thailand. It had been a strange exchange and Tom had proven to be a strange cat. We had arrived at Mystics one morning to find another cat in the space. Ashy already had two that were permanent residents there. These furry goofs had often sat in on my sessions and frequently on the person I was seeing for the session. The Mystics cats were special for sure. Tom even more so. That Monday he was unsettled and had been following Matt around most of the day. When Matt tried to leave, he followed him outside and sat down behind Matt's bike so that he was in the way.

"I don't think Tom wants me to leave. I think I'm meant to stay."

Matt and I had been working on his drinking and he had started asking himself why he wanted to drink. He was basing his drinking decisions on his intentions instead of his wants.

"Do you want to stay because you want to drink or is it because you genuinely feel like you are meant to?" I asked him openly.

"I think I'm meant to. I do want a drink, I won't lie, but it feels like it's more than that."

I agreed we could stay and see what happened. When it started getting close to midnight, I started getting tired and I began to grow frustrated. "I'm tired let's go, maybe you were wrong."

"I don't think so, I really think we should stay, but okay if you want to go, we can go," Matt ceded and we left shortly after. I was woken up about an hour later to my phone ringing. It was Ashy's business partner Quân. "Tam Oi! Sorry it is so late, but Mr Lee is here and he wants to speak to you and Matt. Up till that point Matt had not spoken to Mr Lee about his visa, only mine. Matt knew it was time to open up and ask for help. We arrived back at Ashy's around two-thirty in the morning. Ashy's was empty except for Quân and Mr Lee. We first chatted about my visa. He advised that I would need to leave Vietnam for a few weeks and then reapply. He assured me that I would have no problems. Then we told him about Matt's overstayed visa. Matt was honest and explained how it had gotten so bad.

"That is not good Matt! That is not good at all! Tam's problem is an easy one, but yours - yours is very difficult. You have to go and see Immigration and tell them the truth. The truth about how you ran out of money to renew your visa and then you met Tam and fell in love. You stayed because you loved her and you were scared to lose her. Now she is leaving and you want to go with her, but you have no money. Tell them you are very sorry and that you did not mean to be disrespectful of Vietnamese law. Then you will have to see what will happen. I will see from my side what I can do to help you."

I could see a huge weight lifted off Matt's shoulders. He was nervous about Immigration, but he trusted Mr Lee and trusted his advice. Something about what Mr Lee had said about disrespecting Vietnam struck me. The ancestors came to mind once again and I questioned if this was why they were in an uproar. Because Matt had been disrespectful of the country and its ways? Something about this seemed to add up. There was still that voice, "He needs to go home."

The next morning Matt went to Immigration and owned up to his overstayed visa. He tried to explain that I was leaving that Friday and that he needed to leave with me, but unfortunately Immigration had their processes and we were not sure how long the process would be. I had no choice but to leave on the Friday. We agreed we would head to Laos and then figure life out from there. Matt and I were hopeful that he would be able to leave with me on the Friday. We spent that week finalising things with Mystics and packing up our lives. We did not know how long we would be gone for. We were hoping for three months maximum and then we would be back. Vietnam was home for both of us and our family was in Hanoi. When Friday afternoon arrived, Matt went to see Immigration. He arrived back at Mystics half an hour before I was due to leave. We had our friends meet us there so we could say our farewells. When Matt walked in I knew I was leaving on my own.

"I'm still being processed. They are working out my fine; once that has been paid and processed, I can leave. I don't know how much the fine will be though."

The amount for the fine was our main concern. A year's overstayed visa was going to incur a hefty penalty. We did not know what would happen if he was unable to pay his fine. We did know that within the next week we would have an answer and I would know for certain if Matt was coming to Laos. Our friends were getting a bit rowdy and seemed to think that we were having another farewell party. I lost my cool and shouted across the space, "That is it! Everyone out, I have twenty minutes to figure my life out and to say goodbye to the man I love."

I did not exactly have a graceful farewell with my family, but I was too distressed to think about anything else. I had not made any real plans for when I arrived in Laos. I had never been there before and knew very little about the country. I did not even have accommodation booked. I had twenty minutes to figure life out with Matt and make last minute plans. I split the last of our money between us. "I keep seeing five million, so I'm going to give you enough to cover your costs for the week and then an extra five million. I don't know why it just feels right." I took the balance and then it was time for me to leave. I once again said broken-hearted goodbyes to Matt and got on a bus to Laos.

22

Liminal Skills

*"**Liminality** - the quality of ambiguity or disorientation that occurs in the middle stage of a rite of passage, when participants no longer hold their pre-ritual status but have not yet begun the transition to the status they will hold when the rite is complete"*

Limbo - a space and place I had become quite familiar with. I had seemed to do a fair bit of waiting for life to happen. This time I was prepared for the liminal space I knew I was going to head into. I spent a rather uneventful twenty four hours on a bus from Hanoi to Vientiane, the capital city of Laos. For many, I am sure you are wondering where the heck Laos is. It is a landlocked country that borders Vietnam, Thailand and Cambodia. It is also possibly one of the prettiest countries in South East Asia. I arrived and checked in to my hostel. I had been placed in room number two. A sunny room with owls painted on its wall. I knew it was time for quiet reflection and finding my balance. I had left Hanoi in quite the rush with only a few days to sort my life out. I assessed everything I had actually packed for myself. I had clothes, a notebook and pen and two books: The well-known Alchemist by Paulo Coelho and a thirty-day motivational book that had been given to me by Chené before she left Hanoi. For the first time in twenty-odd years, I did not have a set of Tarot cards with me. My questions around my work with the cards was sitting foremost in my mind. I had done an immense amount of work already, but I knew I was nowhere near finished. I had found my way back to my roots and the path of Witch. I had achieved my role of High Priestess and had moved into a shamanic path for certain. My abilities had become the strongest they had ever been. I just intuitively knew things, had strong clear visions and I had started having highly vivid dreams. My knowings had become clearer where I could see a situation exactly as it would play out. The rest were strange, highly symbolic visions. I had come to better understand the Moon and how her cycles were my cycles. I also knew it was time to become more than just a Tarot Reader.

I reflected over my years of reading for others. I saw where I could have done better and the unhealthy cycles of those seeking traditional and predictive-style readings; readings I was more than capable of doing, yet I began to see how others had misused this side of my gift. I realised how they had been trying to hand their responsibilities and issues on to me. It was no wonder I had reached a burn out with Mystics and a burn out with Tarot. I had been working with far more high level souls since returning from Thailand - souls I knew were going to be some of the facilitators for the coming shift. Yet I was still seeing the traditional clients too. I did not want to do this any longer. I had far surpassed that level. I also came to realize that I did not have any real fulfillment on a personal level. My life had become predominately a service to others. My life had become purpose. Which is not entirely a bad thing, but it did make for the emptiness that Vũ had first raised with me nearly two years earlier. I then understood that personal fulfillment was actually a foreign concept for me. I did not know how to achieve this. I then began working through the motivational book. Perhaps this would give me some insights and answers. Thank you Chenè! The book was more than helpful. It ran me through a series of questions - questions that would give me the answer to personal fulfilment. I learned that personal fulfilment came from self love and self worth and it tied in with being of service. But being of service for the right reason! Was I offering a service that provided value to others and what were my intentions behind doing what I did? I understood why I missed the personal fulfilment. I was being of service - but not to my fullest capacity. I was still not finding the answer as to how I wanted to work and how I could work better. What I did know however, was that I did not want to read Tarot for others any longer. I was also questioning where my home was and where I was meant to settle. I was feeling rather displaced in the world, not having Hanoi as home any longer. Matt was not dealing too well in the country next door, either. I could feel and see it every step of the way. I knew when he was out drinking, I knew who he was with and I knew when he was seeking solitude to just avoid everything. The stress of not knowing the amount of his fine was a big trigger for both of us. Being in a state of knowing, it meant I could also see where and what he needed to do to get his process finished. I struggled to communicate with him without sounding like I was nagging or that I had lost my mind. Instead I talked around my truth and dropped hints. Then I would become frustrated when he went the opposite way. Finally, by the Thursday morning we got an answer for the fine.

"My fine is [7]five million and apparently I don't have any penalties. I'm picking up my passport tomorrow and I'll be on a bus by the evening," Matt had messaged me to tell me the news. I just smiled at the fine amount, understanding why I had seen the five million.

The next day Matt was finally on a bus to Laos. We spent our first couple of days taking a break. It was something both of us needed. We had chatted a bit about what we wanted and what we could do. The only thing that had become solid was Matt's insistence that he find work and that from there we would be okay. From there we could figure out the rest. I had told him that I was going to stop reading Tarot, that I was still figuring out what I wanted to do. He said it was alright; that he would take care of things while I worked it out. We both believed we would not need to wait too long before we could get back into Vietnam. This was what we both wanted and our plans worked around us being able to get back there. Staying in South East Asia seemed liked the best solution. We did not see the need to go back to either of our home countries. Matt least of all. Going home was the last thing he wanted. From my side, there was not much to go back home to. We just needed to see which South East Asian country would be our best option while we waited. Something inside of me nagged at me, though and that voice continued, "He needs to go home."

We found there was very little going on in the capital city and had been advised to try Vang Viene, a small town further up north of Laos. Matt had been up there before a few years back and agreed it could be a good option. We arranged for a minibus and left the next day. Our funds were starting to run quite low and Matt's stress with finding work became quite apparent. We arrived and I soon learned that Vang Viene was a tiny semi-developed town that functioned mostly on the tourist trade that came through to see and experience the exquisite landscape. I also soon learned that one could find absolutely any drug they could think of in a fair number of the small bars around the town - everything from Methamphetamine to LSD to Opium. There seemed to be an unspoken rule in the town: you could have almost anything you wanted and get as messed up as you liked; you just could not take anything away with you! The town itself unsettled me somewhat. Since arriving in Laos I had a feeling of being unsafe. A feeling I knew was rooted in the fact that I was a woman and the world worked differently for me.

We had checked ourselves in to a peaceful bungalow a few minutes' walk out of the town. Here I felt settled and safe. It was here that I worked out what I wanted to do and how I wanted to work. While I had been in Thailand with Chené, I had signed up for a Mindfulness Masters course. I had started it while in Thailand and had worked on it only a few times while in Hanoi. With all the ups and downs that had been going on, I had not yet completed the course. In fact I was still only a little way in. Yet something about this course was right and the parts I had worked through already resonated strongly with the teachings I already had. I was a teacher and teaching was what I wanted to do. I knew that the Mindfulness course was a big part of this. I knew I needed to finish that course and I knew that teaching and mentoring was where I was meant to head to next. I was no longer a Tarot reader. I had given a month's full notice so that any of my past clients could have a last session with me. I had about one week left when we found that Laos was just not going to work out for us. Our funds were very low by this point. We had spoken to a few of our friends about the other countries around us and almost everyone had said we should try Koh Phangan in Thailand. Everyone I had spoken to said it would be perfect for me with my work. Matt was likely to find bar or hostel work as well. We were advised that this could be a bit difficult for him however, but we were running out of options. Matt had been talking to his parents a fair bit over that time. He had been working through his old issues and had begun letting them go. It still took a lot for him to ask for their help, but we had run out of options. I had not had any interaction with Matt's parents. I knew he had mentioned me, but I understood they did not know much about me at all; which unsettled me a bit as they were inadvertently helping me as well. Matt and I had agreed we would head back to the capital of Vientiane. From there we would try and apply for visas for Vietnam first. If that failed, then we would head for Thailand. We returned to Vientiane and went to the Vietnamese embassy that same day. They took our forms and passports and told us to come back in two days time. I had taught Matt a lot around manifesting. He had helped to manifest me home from Thailand and we were now hoping to manifest our visas for Vietnam. Two days later, our passports were handed back to us and we were told we could not be processed. They could not give us anything more than that and Thailand became our next stop. That voice continued to be persistent: "He needs to go home."

We arrived in Bangkok around six in the morning, somewhat sleep deprived. We had taken the train across the border. The train itself had been comfortable and a great way to travel, but the Arctic-like temperature and neighbours that sounded like they were cutting down trees with chainsaws in their sleep, had made for a rather sleepless night. We negotiated a semi decent rate with a tuk-tuk driver to take us to the infamous Khaosan Road so we could book the next stage of our travels. Being first thing in the morning, we obviously needed to use basic facilities by the time we reached Khaosan Road. However, we quickly learned the Land of Smiles was actually rather unfriendly and the smiles were fake. We were either greeted with disrespectful words or complete disregard. We were left feeling a little stranded on the sidewalk of Khaosan Road while we waited for places to open so we could book our tickets. Sitting on the sidewalk, I looked down the stretch of the infamous road and then looked and Matt, "I don't like the vibe here, it doesn't feel right."

It was like a dark undercurrent ran beneath the tar road, with an almost mocking voice saying, "Yes [8]Farang, welcome to Thailand."

Matt's response of, "I feel it too, I don't like it either," made my uneasiness more concrete and I knew what I was feeling was real. Thailand was not what it portrayed itself to be and I began to question if we were doing the right thing.

We decided to take a walk down the street to see what travel agents were there. We were fortunate enough to come across one that was open at that hour and we were able to book our tickets to Koh Phangan. While waiting for our tickets and change, I wandered off to finally have that pee I so desperately needed. I was gone all of a minute only to return to a somewhat uncomfortable looking Matt.

"You alright?" I asked.

"Umm yeah except for the Lady Boy that just appeared right in my face and asked if I wanted a drink!"

Apparently, the proximity was close enough for him to see the fresh start of some beard stubble beneath the heavy layer of make-up. Matt looked somewhat bewildered and was more than happy to venture off to see what all the hype was about around Khaosan Road. The agent had offered for us to leave our luggage there so we could explore the areas in close proximity, unhindered. Although I do not believe the word unhindered is an accurate term to use - not when the floating market is open and there are sights to be seen and every tuk-tuk driver is insistent that we should go. In the space of five minutes we had been asked "Hello, tuk-tuk? Where are you going? Floating market?" numerous times while they shoved printed images of 'places to see in Bangkok' in our faces. We had at least another eight hours of this to deal with while we tried to pass the time waiting for our overnight bus. As the city of Bangkok came to life, more street vendors flocked to the streets to force their wares onto travellers, from roasted scorpions on a stick to torches with built-in tasers which were happily crackled dangerously right in people's faces. It was clear that Bangkok was all about making as much money as possible with little regard for respect and common decency. A truly sad effect of Westernisation in what should have essentially been a country steeped in rich cultural traditions. It appeared that the 'Zen' aspect of authentic Thailand had been lost. Where thought and consideration were only given to achieving financial value in terms of a Western currency and a willingness to do whatever it took to achieve it. Upon doing some research, we discovered that most of the 'impossible to refuse' bargain deals were actually elaborate scams that had caught other foreigners off-guard and had cost them a pretty penny. We were more than relieved to get onto our bus at the end of a very long day and head for what was meant to be the perfect place to go: the tranquil island of Koh Phangan.

My unease sat with me throughout the bus ride to Surat Thani, the mainland port of Thailand. We had stopped at a small travel agent's office to get the bus and tickets for the next stage of our journey. Matt had ordered some breakfast and was waiting for his change to arrive. His food arrived and in the middle of it, so did our bus. We were quickly hurried on board and were on to the next stage - our ferry ride which would take us to the island. Matt and I were both a bit grumpy and tired but in good spirits. Until Matt realized he had not been given his change! It was a large amount of change as well. He had given the woman a large Thai Baht note as that was all he had and was meant get a large amount of change back. When he realized what had happened, that dishonest side of Thailand reared its ugly head once again. Things down-spiralled from there. We arrived at the pier of the island and were instantly harassed by a handful of taxi drivers. All of them charging exorbitant fees. While we had been in Bangkok, I had messaged a South African friend of mine that I knew was on the island. Garth had told me where he was staying and recommended we head there. When we had left Bangkok, I had lost wifi and my connection with the world. I did not receive his message offering to meet us at the pier and help us get to the place he was staying. We finally gave in to a semi decent fee and climbed into our taxi.

We were dropped off about fifteen minutes later next to a dirt road and a sign with the name of the place we were staying at. We assumed we were meant to head down the dirt road and went for a walk. We finally found the reception area and were greeted in an unfriendly manner. We booked ourselves for a single night as we were now once again very low on money. I had money that I had stashed away in Hanoi from a few last sessions and funds in my PayPal account. Both of which would take a good day and internet access to get hold of. When the places we were booking into told us that a deposit was required, that was where we became stuck. We did not have enough. "Then we can give you the room, but no internet access or food is included." We were not bothered with the food, it was the internet access that we needed! We pleaded with them, explaining our situation and they handed us a one hour internet usage voucher. We were then shown to our bungalow and moved our stuff across.

It was while moving our stuff from the reception to our bungalow that I heard a very familiar voice call out, "Well hello there!" I turned to see who it was and saw my friend Garth. He had been in Thailand for a few months already. He was a very welcome sight indeed! He asked why I was looking so unhappy as this was not how he remembered me at all. I explained the events of the last few days and he understood. He then went to speak to the owners of the place as he had come to know them pretty well. He vouched for us and paid our deposit. We were finally given the rest of what was supposed to be included in our room rate. We spent the afternoon catching up and Matt and I had a much-needed rest.

That evening we sorted things out so I could get hold of the funds I had saved. It took some effort and bit of planning, but by the next afternoon we worked it out and we were looking alright for a while. We then set to learning a bit more about the island and our options. We soon learned that there were not many options for Matt and I realized that that my friends did not know me very well. Koh Phangan essentially has two sides. The lively party side where the famous Full Moon parties are held and the Zen side - home to a vast number of healing centres, yoga studios and retreats. When I began to look into them properly however, I found a situation far from what I was looking for. It was mostly tantric-based workshops and high-end hippy-style yoga training and retreats. Something about the energy there felt dirty, artificial and far from healing. This was not my space! It was then that I realised how many of my 'friends' saw me. They saw me as a gypsy-infused, yoga-styled Tarot reader. A hippie! I was beyond disheartened with my realization and that feeling that I was meant for so much more reared up again. I was on my last few days of reading Tarot and I was looking to move more into my teaching and mentoring. Once again that realization of the impacts of the Westernisation on what should have been an immensely beautiful spiritual energy came to light. Thailand had become a watered-down version of its true self which had led to spaces being created that offered fake and superficial Spirituality in order to make a quick buck from Western tourists. Then Matt and I ran into a well-known Thai scam and Thailand became a nightmare.

Garth had recommended a bike rental place close by that he had used before. He had never had any issues and Matt landed a decent deal. The bike was a typical rental with the usual scrapes and bumps. The woman had rushed through the process and being a referral, Matt had not stopped to take photos of the bike before he left. For anyone traveling and renting overseas, do yourself a favor and don't repeat our mistake! Matt and I had begun looking into Cambodia as another option as Thailand was just not working out. Siem Reap was then recommended to us and we felt like we had a bit more direction. The more we looked into Cambodia and Siem Reap, the more it seemed to be a better option. Matt and I agreed he would find work and get us settled. He assured me that I did not need to worry and that I could focus on finishing my course and deciding my path from there.

It was the day before we were set to leave for Cambodia. Matt left early to return the rental bike and seemed to be gone longer than he should have been. I was getting concerned when he returned - furious! The woman at the rental place had told him he had crashed the bike, showed him the scratches and bumps that were originally on the bike, and told him he needed to pay the equivalent of about $450. The bike was not even worth that much. Matt had tried to talk to her reasonably. Having sold and rented bikes in Vietnam with Nhât, he was familiar with prices and how things worked. He had also not caused the damage she was pointing out. The downside to all this, was that Matt had left his passport with her as security. This is generally not done, but seeing as it was a trusted situation, Matt had not given it a second thought. She then told him that $260 would be fine and he could have his passport back. Matt flatly refused. It was just blatant extortion! This was when she got angry with him and told him to go away and come back later. We both went up to talk to her, I also tried the common sense and tactful route and soon saw why Matt had come back so angry. This woman was insane! She finally told us that we had to pay $150 and that was that. We then threatened her with the police only to be laughed at and told to go ahead.

We took a taxi into town and tracked down the police station. From what we had been told and had researched, we were looking for the Tourist Police as they handled any problems for tourists on the island. We walked into the police station and spoke to the man at the counter. He seemed to not speak much English, looked at us disapprovingly and called another man over. We explained what had happened and we were told, "We cannot help you." We were both shocked and taken aback at his response. This was a police station, correct? "You really cannot help us?" Matt questioned as respectfully as possible. "This is not your country!" was the man's final reply before walking out the door. We sat there for a few moments, stunned, when another man came in and showed us where the Tourist Police office was. We hoped we would get a better response there. We were greeted by somewhat friendly men and they listened to what had happened. Our claims of being scammed were brushed aside and it was clearly just a misunderstanding. They asked if we had photos of the bike from when we had picked it up. This was our downfall!

"Then there is not much we can do to help. We can negotiate a rate that is fair for both you and the owner. If you had proof that the damage was there already, then it would be a different story."

Matt and I both felt disheartened but hoped we could get the amount reduced to something that was not ridiculous like $150, which was about the total value of the bike. They drove us over to the bike rental place and chatted to the woman in Thai for a few moments. The man who seemed to be in charge came over and explained that she would not settle for less than $120. If we wanted to dispute it, we would need to go back to the police station and open a case. We were told this would land up being a lengthy process and not really worth the time. We grudgingly gave her the money and Matt was given his passport back. Before we left, the man in charge asked to take a photo with Matt. Images like these were used to market how well the island worked and that justice was given to all. It was another reminder of the darker, false side of Thailand that we had felt when we first arrived. It was the final sign that Thailand was not where we were meant to be. That night we both slept very uneasy.

The whole situation with the bike had unsettled us and that feeling of not being safe hit me hard! I barely slept at all that night as much as Matt tried to reassure me and held me close, I just could not break that unsafe feeling. We were both sad to say our farewells to Garth. Matt and Garth had seemed to form quite a friendship with one another in the short time we had been there. We were not sad to be leaving, though. We had a flight booked from Surat Thani to Bangkok and from there we would catch the bus to Siem Reap. We arrived back on Khaosan Road to book the bus only to find that we would need to wait till the morning when the next bus was leaving. We booked our tickets and set off to find a hostel close by. We found a reasonably priced one which unfortunately backed right onto the chaos of Khaosan Road. We both hardly slept at all that night. Khaosan Road is well known for its wild parties and the sounds of the street beneath our window ensured we both got little to no sleep. We boarded our bus the next morning and were well on our way before we both dozed off for a very restless trip. My feelings of unease and not being safe still sat heavily with me.

We had been traveling for a while when we both woke up. Our bus soon pulled over to the side of the road, across from a small restaurant. We were both somewhat drowsy and trying to see where we were. Our bus was then boarded by an official-looking gentleman, "Good afternoon ladies and gentlemen. You are now at the border crossing of Thailand and Cambodia. Please bring all your important items with you - passports, phones, money and any other valuable items and please come with me."

We were ushered off the bus and into the small little restaurant where we were given arrival cards for Cambodia and asked for our passports. We were told the amount for our visas in Thai Baht and being somewhat sleep deprived, we did not stop to check the currency converter to see what that amount came to in US Dollars. We handed our passports and money over and the men disappeared somewhere for a good twenty minutes. Something wasn't sitting right with Matt and myself as we woke up a bit more with the passing time. Matt suggested we check the currency converter as he just wasn't trusting the situation. The amount they had asked us for was not correct!

When the men returned, we questioned them about why the amount was so much higher than what was stated in the Cambodian Immigration website.

"It's my government's fee, Cambodia is a poor country, so they raise the amount. It is the correct amount to pay. It's just how the government works."

Feeling somewhat unsettled by the large price difference, but unsure if it was actually the case or not, we went with it. Our passports were finally returned to us and inside was a three-month visa for Cambodia. This put our minds at ease and perhaps the larger fee was because we had received a three month visa as opposed to a one month visa. We were ushered back on the bus for the next part of the process. It was explained that we would be heading to the border crossing next. Before we could cross however, we were told that we needed to change out all of our Thai currency for Cambodian Riel. He advised that there was only one ATM in the town of Siem Reap and that now would be a good time to draw out however much one felt they would need for their time in Cambodia. Matt and I only had cash on us and so moved on to exchange our Thai Baht. We were rushed through the process of changing money, not really having the chance to check the amounts correctly. We were then moved onto the next section, which was Customs and Border Control. Here we would stamp out of Thailand and cross over into Cambodia; where we would receive an official stamp in our passports. We stamped out of Thailand and into Cambodia and checked our passports.

The three-month visa had been stamped canceled and a thirty-day stamp given instead. Matt was furious and I was feeling very unsettled. We did not arrive on very good terms with Cambodia.

We arrived at the bus station about half an hour outside of the town of Siem Reap. We were told we would be given a free tuk-tuk to our hostel in town. We were somewhat relieved to be off the bus, but we were both very on edge and did not trust the free tuk-tuk. We had not actually booked anywhere to stay as yet, either. We wanted to get into town first, have something to eat and then see what we would be doing. We told our driver that we had not booked anything yet and that he could just drop us off in town somewhere central. He said he could take us to some hostels he knew, that he did not mind. Something about it did not feel right. He seemed very insistent that he take us to our accommodation. We agreed, but did not feel right about it. Matt then told him that we rather wanted to eat and research places; and that he could drop us off somewhere central again. Our driver suddenly pulled over and got out looking angry. It took us a moment to figure out what had made him angry and we saw the other side to our bus scam. The ride was free but you were then tied to your tuk-tuk driver. He knew where you would be staying and he knew you would likely want to go and see the sights and temples. It was a smart tactic, I could not fault that, but it also made for very pushy tuk-tuk drivers. He drove us into what looked like the outskirts of town and pulled over. He told us this was as central as we could get. I was bewildered by what I saw. Siem Reap was nothing more than a small town, still fairly underdeveloped, but clearly growing. A lot of its main roads were dusty and the majority of its back roads were dirt. This was not what I had expected at all. I did notice an abundance of ATM's however, and pieced the rest of the scam together. We had been scammed multiple times between two countries all in the space of about 72 hours. South East Asia was pushing us hard!

We were both exhausted! We found a restaurant not too far from where we had been dropped off. We ordered some food, asked for the wifi details and hunted for a hostel. The restaurant was mostly empty when we arrived as it was early evening and not quite dinner time. A couple with their young child came in and took up a table on the other side. I recognized the South African accent straight away. I was feeling very unsettled about being in Siem Reap. I had felt nothing but unsafe since the incident with rental bike in Thailand. Our journey into Siem Reap had just amplified that.

"I think I should go talk to them and ask them what they know about Siem Reap. I don't feel very safe here. If anyone is going to know if a place was safe or not, it would be a South African." Matt agreed and I went over and chatted to them. I soon waved Matt over to come and join us and we landed up having a long conversation with them. They put our minds at ease about Siem Reap. They said that traveling with their son, they always checked the safety of a country before they went there. They had only been there a few days, but so far they had loved it and found it to be very safe. This put me at ease and the good conversation lightened our moods. We had told them about our adventures so far and they could see why we were skeptical. They made a few suggestions and recommendations and gave us a vague layout of what was where in the town. It seemed simple enough to navigate and there was apparently an entire street that was just bars - called Pub Street. They had seen a number of Westerners working there and were optimistic that Matt would find work quickly. They chatted to us about things back home and other places they had traveled to. We spent a good three hours chatting before they retired for the night and we headed out to our now booked hotel. We had found a very reasonably priced hotel not far from where we were.

On our walk there, we happened to walk past a place with an owl as its logo and then a little further down was a place with an elephant.

"See, we are in the right place. Those are definitely signs!" said Matt looking a lot more upbeat than he had earlier on in the day. We arrived at our hotel and were checked into room number three.

23

The Mindful Spider - Lessons in Toxicity

Siem Reap is home to one of the largest temple sites in the world, Angkor Wat. Sitting atop [9]ley lines, this site is known as one of the earth's power centers and is revered as a sacred site. It would be here that Matt and I would spend seven months and I would experience one of my most intense transformations. It would be here that I would endure a bite from the Cosmic Weaver - Grandmother Spider herself, as I transitioned from shaman to crone. In ancient lore of the Wise Ones, there are three stages of progression for a woman - Maiden, Mother and Crone. These stages are in line with the phases of the Moon and are meant to denote the pivotal life stages of a woman. They are not age specific, however, so do not let the names mislead you. The Crone, also known as Wise Woman in other traditions, is said to be the final stage when one acquires their wisdom. A title of honor reserved for those who had faced severe challenges and stepped into their full power. It was in Siem Reap that I came to understand that if I could shift in discomfort, I could shift in anything. Over these seven months, I began to develop mindful practices and shifted my dynamic in my relationship with Matt. It was over these seven months that Matt would experience his own shift and our relationship would progress to the next level. I would also encounter certain women that would prove to be pivotal teachers in Yin and activists for the shifts.

I did not notice the spider bite at first. Not until Matt noticed and pointed it out. Since arriving in Siem Reap I had felt strange and displaced from reality; hence me not noticing a nasty spider bite on my ankle. For a few days I struggled with it and then the Full Moon hit and a severe transformation state set in. High fever, body shakes and feelings of delirium wracked me through the night. Matt was out working a shift at a local bar, but by the time he returned home he was ready to take me to a hospital. I refused as I fought off the fever and shakes. "You need to heal yourself then Tam," Matt's words pierced through the delirium and I knew he was right. I summoned up mind over matter, reduced my fever and eased my shakes. I then let Matt help me change the dressing on my bite and dozed, exhausted as he held me. The following morning I sent Liz a photo of my ankle and asked for her insights. She confirmed it was a spider bite and then flowed into speaking to me about Grandmother Spider. Liz explained that she is the 'creatrix' in some of the Native American cultures. She went on to explain that the spider represented the Feminine and our ability to create life; that we chose the life we wanted to weave. The spider is associated highly with the number eight - eight legs, eight eyes and is described as being the shape of the infinity symbol - a symbol associated with Magicians and a symbol that I had come to associate strongly with myself. At the time I knew the bite was a wakeup call, I assumed it was a call to step into my power and start creating my life as I wanted it to be. What I did not understand at the time was that is also a calling to step into Crone, that I had shifted into my last phase and all I needed to do was see it and own it. As I progressed with my time in Siem Reap, I noticed my visions getting clearer and my intuitive knowings becoming stronger.

My spider bite began to heal and I had managed to complete my Mindfulness Masters course. The spider bite and completing that course were like tipping points for me. The spider reminds us to be mindful of the fact that our thoughts create our reality. My biggest learning from my course was that we can only take responsibility for ourselves and our own thoughts. The lesson of one only being able to take responsibility for themselves and how they responded to life, was the key. It was here that I came to fully understand that a relationship cannot be one based on second chances. It was a realisation I had previously awoken to in Hanoi, but the course lecturer had put this more clearly: he explained that if you are going to be with someone, then be with them. But you cannot have conditions or judgments. Your partner is your partner. You began a relationship with them for a reason. If that reason was to change them, then you are not in a relationship with that person. Instead, you are there for who you believe they should be. If the person you are with is not working for you, that is also okay. Then move on, have enough respect for both parties to not stick around in the hopes they will become who you want them to be. Be with your partner for who they are. If you do not like who they are, be with someone you do like. Matt I liked! There was also far too much synchronicity on a higher level for me to dispute our relationship. Matt and I had a purpose as a couple. I had felt this for a while. I knew it tied in with my soul purpose, the shift and the rising of Yin-consciousness. I knew it was time for me to shift my dynamic further in our relationship. I had begun to see where my own toxic behaviour had been at play and where I needed to step up and take responsibility for my actions. This was not about being harsh or judgemental with myself. Rather, it was seeing where I could be better. The fact that my course had given me much learning that could only make me better than I was, was the icing on the mindful cake. I had not been giving my best to our relationship. In fact, a fair bit had been me reacting to old triggers and patterns. This was not who I was at my core, though. Everyone at their core is compassionate, non-judgmental and unconditional with their love. It is society, culture and our pre-conditioning that forms beliefs and behaviours that are hurtful, selfish and judgemental. Having awareness of my shadow aspects was so vital for me to begin my process of being intentionally better. I had to understand every aspect of my nature and why I was the way I was; why I reacted the way I did. Those who know themselves, can master themselves - that is the ultimate lesson of the Chariot card. It takes wisdom to know how to put the knowledge into practice. It is also wisdom that tells you it is all about the practice. Matt was who he was and I loved him. It was time to embrace everything that he was. It was time for me to practice compassion and unconditional love with the man I really did love.

Shortly after all my awakenings and understandings, I pulled some cards. I wanted to better understand why we were in Cambodia. The Hanged Man came up and intuitively, I understood that sacrifices needed to be made in order to obtain enlightenment and growth. Pulling the Six of Wands for me specifically, was an indication that self-mastery was close or perhaps it indicated that self-mastery had been achieved already - I just needed to see it. For Matt however, I pulled the Five of Wands, the card of Strife. The number five cards in the Tarot usually indicate a challenge and for Matt, who was learning to master his Magician energy and his drinking, I could see why he got this challenge card. We had been chatting about his gifts and how he was learning to use them better or rather put them to better use; and I knew part of what the challenge was: controlling his love for alcohol, where he placed his energy and how he used it. While I had been in Thailand with Chené, I had done some inner work around addiction to assess if there was anything else I could understand about it. It was there that I had the insight of addiction and manifesting. Addiction is like manifesting in reverse. It's a want so strong that you would do anything to get that next hit. That next cigarette. That next drink. We take the power to manifest what we want but channel the energy in the wrong direction and for the wrong things. Be careful what you wish for! And because manifesting is so easy, getting that next fix is just as easy. Your life is falling apart around you, yet you'll have the means to get what you want, but your wants are blurred behind insecurities, self-doubts, traumas and your inner demons. Essentially, one is manifesting through the murky waters of toxic Yin. Our shadow is our Yin. How we are using that power is the question. In that moment when all you want is to feel is numb, no pain, no worry; you manifest what you believe you want for yourself - oblivious to the repercussions of your adverse manifestations. Once in the rabbit hole, all you can see is the downward spiral and so forget to look at where you have come from. This is perhaps where one starts to lose their gratitude. Blinded by the unending tunnel in front of you, you forget that you have put yourself there in the first place. You have done this through the power of manifestation. If one can manifest that next hit with such ease, imagine what one could manifest if they shifted that energy to manifest more positive things - starting with manifesting oneself out of the rabbit hole. I could see the full capabilities of Matt's power. I could not doubt that when intoxicated, his abilities and levels of understanding peaked and he was in fact very tuned-in; much the same as I had seen with Dené and many other Magicians. I thought back to the conversations I would have with Dené. Conversations around how he does his Magician thing, but how it takes a couple of beers to get there; how he still struggled to achieve altered states and be in his power whilst sober. My understandings from the months before around many not being able to achieve connection without substance, interlinked with this idea. What I had seen happen, not just with Matt, was Magicians pushing past the point of connection and the substance controlling them instead. The sharpness of the Magician mind occurred to me and I understood that if they can learn to work with their gifts mindfully, whether sober or not, they could probably cast their magic further than they ever believed possible. I knew they would be able to create a new world. The aspect of addiction and use of substances in the creation of that new world would become a much bigger factor as my journey to understanding the shift and Yin-based consciousness continued.

Siem Reap was proving to be the quietest I had ever been in my years of doing my work. I only had a handful of sessions while I was there. The souls I saw, however, were high level and pivotal to the shift. Alyson and Lori were two that stood out the most for me. During our time in Siem Reap I had continued to feel unsettled and unsafe. Looking back, I believe these feelings had a lot to do with the history of Cambodia, but were also indicative of the toxic effects of Yin. Alyson had triggered my unsafe feelings more intensely. This was not done on purpose. It was a combination of the energy in Siem Reap, the similarity between there and South Africa and the brutality of what had happened to her. When I arrived to meet Alyson for her session, I was greeted by a warm and lively lady. She seemed familiar, but Siem Reap was a small town. It was not until we had begun our session that I connected the dots. I had seen a post weeks prior from a woman sharing a brutal attack she had experienced. It told of how a man had climbed up into her second story apartment in the middle of the night. She had woken up to see a stranger's face in front of hers and the weight of a man on top of her. When she moved to struggle, that was when the beating started. She had managed to fight him off somehow and as much as she came off second best, she had survived to share her story with others. The centuries of abuse against the Feminine reared up in front of me. What struck me with Alyson was that she had endured a nightmarish experience and instead of it breaking her, it made her stronger. Alyson had gone on to share her story with others, not to instil fear, but to share courage and strength in the face of adversity. I had watched the impact she had made over the months and I cannot dispute her place in the shift; as well as her place in assisting others to step into their Yin and raise themselves as well. Alyson became my first lesson in learning that as much as the Feminine had been badly abused over the centuries - particularly by the patriarchy - we still had a choice in how we responded to that abuse. We could either grow and be better or we could let it make us angry and resentful.

Lori is fierce, compassionate and knows how to make things happen. She has spent her years in Cambodia building and managing an NGO that works with families affected by the Khmer Rouge genocide that shook Cambodia in the seventies. She shared with me her story of how it had begun, some of the hardships and heartbreaks she had experienced and how she had seen communities rise up and start healing. The rise of a Yin-based consciousness came into our discussion as she mentioned that her team was predominantly women and that the women in the villages they worked in, were the ones making the difference. She saw women in a culture that was pure patriarchy rising up and finding their power, but not in a hostile manner. Rather it was their strength in compassion and their ability for non-judgment and forgiveness that was causing their shift. Seeing how Yin could rise in the face of adversity and horror, I knew the shift was happening and I knew it was something we as Humanity could complete. It all lay in how we responded to the years of abuse and how we chose to change. There was one more thing that Lori shared with me, it was around her heritage and ancestry. She was almost an exact split between Native American and [10]Quaker. I had picked up a strange inner conflict with her and now understood why. The horrific past of the indigenous cultures of North America at the hands of the White settlers had caused an inner turmoil and battle within her for years. Tapping into that turmoil, I felt the destruction and chaos imposed upon those indigenous cultures and felt anger and a massive sense of loss. There was something else, though. This secondary insight I shared with Lori: if she could find healing and peace within her, she could begin to facilitate a healing process for her ancestry line as well. Then I felt them, her ancestors, all of them nudging her to find forgiveness as this is where her peace lay. It was a bizarre experience for me and one that would become a crucial insight for me later in my journey.

Throughout our time in Siem Reap, I continued my new mindful practices and as I shifted, Matt began to shift as well. He also started a new habit of giving me the ring he wore on his little finger. On his drunken nights he would slip the ring onto my finger while I was sleeping. The ring only fitted on one finger - the one where an engagement ring sits. Every morning he would then ask for it back saying it felt too weird not wearing it. He did this on and off for months until he finally asked me the question and the ring stayed put. We had been in Siem Reap a good six months and we had been discussing where we wanted to go next. We both knew we needed a change and a move from Siem Reap. It was an intuitive knowing from both of us. We had, over the months discovered that we had both incurred a minimum of a one year ban from Vietnam and that returning there anytime soon was off the cards. Neither of us had really settled into Cambodia, both of us finding the energy there intense and uncomfortable.

"Marry me and come back to the States with me Tam. We can settle there for a while and then decide what we want to do."

Without hesitation I said yes. We agreed to get married in South Africa, sort out my spouse visa and then settle in the United States. Marrying Matt I knew was correct, and not just because Madame I had seen it happen all those years ago in my very first Tarot reading as a teenager. I never once questioned this knowing. Getting back to South Africa and getting married posed somewhat of a financial problem, though. We settled on staying in Cambodia for another year so we could save up. It was in that same week that a post came up on my Facebook feed with a simple abundance spell, it had been shared as planetary alignments were in favor for some extra powerful abundance energy. I took it as a sign and asked Matt if he wanted to do some casting for our future. He agreed and we set to looking into deities that aligned with abundance. The Hindu deity [11]Lakshmi came up consistently in our search and choosing to go with the flow, we chose to work with her. We both decided what it was we wanted to manifest - I had settled on manifesting the means to take Matt back to South Africa for his birthday. I was looking at his birthday in a year's time as this was when we had planned for traveling to South Africa. I felt it was a good alignment and cast my intention while asking for a blessing and assistance from Lakshmi. We finished our ritual, both of us feeling solid in our manifesting and both of us looking at our manifestations coming to fruition within a year's time. It was not long after this that we chose to leave Siem Reap and relocate to the coastal town of Otres. We were both feeling very done with Siem Reap and were beginning to feel very stagnant. Otres had been suggested to us a few times in the weeks before, so we set plans and were due to leave for Otres in a few weeks. We had given ourselves some extra time in Siem Reap as Tôm was coming down from Hanoi for a visit. Our time in Otres would prove to be shorter than we expected, though!

Seeing Tôm as always, was magic, Magicians, full moons and cats. We spent the few days that we had together catching up. He and Matt got up to the usual shenanigans, but the days flew past quickly and Matt and I were on our last day in Siem Reap. We said our goodbyes to Tôm, once again not knowing for sure when would see each other again and we got on a bus for Otres where we spent a total of ten days. That was about all I could manage.

Upon arriving, the unsafe feeling that I had in Siem Reap intensified tenfold and as the days progressed, it reached a breaking point. It was here that I saw an aspect to Yin I had not seen before. It was an insight however, that was crucial to fully understanding the shift into a Yin-based consciousness. In true Yin fashion, the lesson was heavy! Matt took up work at the hostel we had checked into and I found work in a small, offbeat bar owned by an older woman named Jess. She told me the pay rate, which I negotiated with her and told her that I did not drink. She upped my rate by an extra $2 and I agreed to start that Friday. I did not feel too good about it at all, but I pushed the feeling aside and let Matt know I had found work. I had been struggling to get my normal work going and Otres was proving to be quieter than Siem Reap - my work had come to a standstill! Matt asked me if I was sure about taking the job with Jess, he did not seem comfortable with something. I told him I was sure and worked my first shift a couple days later. My shift went alright, but I did not feel comfortable or safe while there and I instantly wanted to avoid any man that came in. This feeling persisted over my first three shifts, but I continued to push it aside and instead spent my time chatting to Jess. Our conversations, however, always seemed to land back up around men, abuse of women, the severity of patriarchy and how messed up the world was. Jess seemed to have a fear in her eyes whenever I looked at her. It was on my third shift that she had a bit too much to drink and I learned she was in fact desperate to get out of Otres. She felt trapped and unsafe. She spoke about how the town a year ago had been completely different. Now it was fast becoming a shadow of its former self.

It was the night of my fourth shift and the night of the Full Moon. I was sitting at the bar of our hostel as Matt was working his shift. A group came in and sat down next to me at the bar. I landed up with two men sitting next to me. The one man turned to me and passed a lewd comment making out as if it was just joke. I felt my hackles rise! Matt was on the other side of the bar, out of earshot. I knew if he had heard what had been said, he would have told the man off. "That was highly inappropriate," I told him in a manner that implied I was not impressed at all. I excused myself and went to speak to Matt on the other side of the bar. I was heading out for what would be my last shift. That unsafe feeling had been amplified by the comment that had been passed back at the hostel. When I arrived for my shift, that feeling was intense! That night I was sexually harassed by different men from different countries; all of whom believed it was okay to either make lewd suggestions or speak to me in a disrespectful manner. By the end of my shift I was done! Done with that bar, Otres and Cambodia. I was ready to go home. I returned to our hostel and told Matt about what had happened and that I was ready to leave. Something in me triggered hard that night. Everything around the abuse of the Feminine and Mother Earth just seemed to rise up inside of me and I became almost manic, "All you men do is abuse us. You just take from us and treat us like garbage." I do not recall all I said to Matt after that, but I know it was heavy and that I was not just speaking for me. I was speaking for the Feminine as a whole. Then the realization set in that unhealthy, toxic Yin was destroying the world, not men! I saw that men and women were both unhealthy in their Yin. They were misusing it for unspeakable things. I knew and understood that all of us had been abusing our own Yin aspect. It was no wonder we were abusing one another. Amma's kirtan and my intense reaction to it reared up and I finally understood why I had reacted the way I had. I had begun scratching at the surface of my own toxic behaviour back then already in Cape Town. I had misinterpreted my reaction, however, and assumed it was abusive men I was picking up; when in fact it was the abuse of all of us.

Matt and I had been moved into a dorm a few nights earlier as the hostel had gotten full. Matt was working a shift downstairs and the dorm room had only men checked into it. It was just how it had happened to work out. I could not sleep. I was terrified in case one of them tried something while I was sleeping. I do not believe I have actually ever been in that much fear before. That night I felt the fear of every woman. Women who were abused on a daily basis; women who had been raped and were reliving their trauma constantly; women terrified to speak their truth out of fear. I felt scared and angry! It was not okay, none of it was okay. I cannot tell you what it was about Otres that triggered me that night, but by the next morning, I had not slept and I just wanted to leave. I was panicked and distressed and had packed my bags. I was so insistent that we had to leave. I did not care where we went as long as it was away from there.

"Okay Tam, I'll sort something out. You don't feel safe here and that is not okay. Let's do it, let's go to South Africa, get married and sort out your visa for the States. There I know I can keep you safe. I know I can look after you there," Matt then took me back upstairs with all my stuff. He climbed into bed next to me and held me close.

"I've got you, I promise I won't let anything bad happen to you," was the last thing I heard him say before I fell into a deep, heavy sleep. I woke up later that day to find it was early evening already. I also realized it was the day before Matt's birthday. I must have been awful to deal with earlier and right by his birthday. I came down to apologize and Matt told me that he had spoken to his parents. They were going to help us and he asked me when I wanted to leave. I wanted to leave straight away of course, but I would not let Matt spend his birthday in an airport of all places. We agreed we would spend his birthday in Otres and then leave the next morning. We would be in South Africa in three days time and Goddess Lakshmi had come through a whole year earlier than intended.

24

Owning the Crone

When you know what you want, manifesting is incredibly simple and sometimes surprisingly quick with the turnaround. What aids this quick manifestation is alignment: alignment with the self and alignment with what is meant to be. Believe me, I speak from experience that when we are manifesting something that truly is not for us, it will not come to fruition no matter how much energy you throw at it! But manifest something that is in alignment with yourself and most importantly, the Collective, the turnaround time can look like a complete miracle. This was our case as Matt and I had made our last minute plans and were now in Kuala Lumpur, Malaysia waiting to check in for our flight to Cape Town, South Africa. Our initial plan of spending another year in Cambodia had been fast tracked, much to my relief! Intuitively I had known that we needed to leave and had we stayed, I believe things would have become harsh very quickly. There was an instant shift in my energy upon leaving Cambodia and within a short time of being in Kuala Lumpur, I began to feel more grounded and allowed my intuition to take the driver's seat once more. Over the couple of months that followed, we both lived on sheer faith and allowed our process to flow as it should; not giving the small challenges along the way a second thought. Not even when one arrived to test us almost instantly as we were checking in for our flight at Kuala Lumpur airport.

"Do you have your exit ticket with you?" the woman at the check-in counter had asked Matt. We had looked into his requirements for entering my country and nowhere had we seen anything about an exit ticket and expressed this to her. I explained that he was my fiancé and he was traveling with me back to South Africa. She asked us to wait a moment and went to have a chat to the captain of our booked flight. She returned a moment later and told us to wait and that he would come talk to us in a moment. A few minutes later the captain came over and greeted us. He looked at our passports for a moment, handed them back while smiling at us warmly and said, "Welcome on board." He then signed off some paperwork and gave the all clear to the woman at the check-in counter.

"Maybe we are meant to be doing this then," I joked looking at the very obvious 'welcome message' that had been passed on. This cemented our faith in knowing that we were doing the right thing. Matt was officially coming home with me. We arrived roughly fifteen hours later in Ethiopia for a short layover. I was back in the same airport I had been in more than two years before; where I had felt Africa running through my veins and Africa had shared some stark messages around gratitude with me. I felt her once more as we were greeted by a spectacular African sunrise. A sunrise just as exquisite as the one I had seen two years before. I took a moment to acknowledge Mama Africa and then nudged my very sleepy fiancé in the ribs and pointed out the large window in front of us.

"I think Africa likes you."

He smiled through his sleepiness and we boarded our final flight to Cape Town. I felt my intuition kick into overdrive and I knew without question that the next stage of our journey together was meant to be. All we needed to do was trust the process and flow with it.

A few hours later, we arrived to the mid-summer heat of Cape Town, and were trying to find a way into the city. My South African simcard no longer working, made ordering an Uber difficult and I was stuck on figuring out other options. I think reverse culture shock had set in and perhaps I'd left my common sense on the plane. After about an hour of trying to figure my own country out, I reached out to Dené intuitively and within a few moments he had ordered us an Uber to his place.

I had arranged for us to stay with very good friend of my mom's, Rose. Staying with her had been an intuitive decision as well. I may not have worked my country out yet on a practical level, but I sure as hell was going to trust my gut. This was my home turf after all and I had come back a whole lot wiser and fully aware. We spent a couple of hours with Dené while we waited for Rose to finish work and come fetch us. Dené was the first of friends and family back home to meet Matt. I was excited to see him and to introduce him to Matt. It had been nearly two years since I had left Cape Town and there was a fair bit of catching up to do. However Dené was Dené and talk turned to music quickly. Always enthusiastic to teach someone new about mixing music, I left Matt in the capable hands of Dené and sat on his all too familiar couch to ground myself back home. Dené had taught me a grounding technique before I had left.

"You create marker points for yourself. Places that are safe spaces. Then when you need to, you connect to it and ground. No matter where you are in the world, you can tap into these spaces."

I stole a few moments to do just that, except I was already sitting in one of my safe spaces. After I had left Ryan, Dené's space had become a sanctuary for me. It had been a safe space to work through a much needed part of my healing process and journey. I settled in and began grounding myself back home and reconnected with my roots. I felt connections reaching out to those close by, then they extended out further. Much the same way I had done on my acid trip in Long Bien; when I had reached out on the collective and reconnected with Matt. I reached out and reconnected with everyone, felt where they were and where they were at. I then brought my awareness back to the present moment and knew I wanted a shower, food and needed a good night's sleep. From there we could figure this marriage thing out. Rosie arrived a little while later and we were soon settled into her home for a couple of weeks and our planning began.

Our first few days we spent researching, making relative appointments and understanding the processes and legalities of marriage, along with the processes and requirements for my spouse visa. I had intuitively reached out to the woman that had married my older sister Kim a couple of years before in the small coastal town of Port Shepstone where my parents lived. I had never met Diane in person, but something about her energy resonated with me. I had reached out to her to ask for her guidance on the legal aspects of marriage. She proved to be more than helpful and even offered to do our legal marriage for us. She advised, however, that the Home Office in Port Shepstone was heavily backlogged. This spurred our decision to rather do our legal marriage in Cape Town and things ran smoothly until it came to booking a date for our actual marriage. We had opted for the simple route of doing our legals at Home Affairs and having a ceremony at a later date. For us, getting our legal marriage done was the main priority. We knew that there would be a bit of a wait for my spouse visa and we wanted to begin my visa process as soon as we could. We had been for our interview with the immigration side of Home Affairs. This was a standard formality for any South African marrying a foreigner. Our interview process went smoothly and we had been approved for marriage. The woman who had interviewed us informed us that they had no available dates for us to have our marriage finalized at that office. She then suggested we try the other Home Affairs offices in Cape Town and see if they perhaps had dates. We spent a fruitless few days trying before deciding it was time to try something else. Diane had been on my mind constantly and my intuition knew she was meant to marry us. I shared with Matt and he instantly agreed, his own intuition giving him the same message. I reached out to Diane who responded almost instantly that she was able to marry us the following week as we had already been approved by Home Affairs for marriage. She sent us a list of the documents she would need, including our approval form from Home Affairs that stated we could marry. I felt a moment of unease, but then I stepped back into the flow and I knew we would be okay. We went back and spoke to woman that had interviewed us and explained our situation. At first she outright refused saying that she was not allowed to send approvals to offices in another Province. She could only send it to another Cape Town office. Not allowing the speed bump to deter us, we explained that we were not trying to mess with this system and explained about wanting start my spouse visa process as soon as possible and she understood. She was not happy about it, but she agreed to help us. She agreed on condition that she would send the approval directly to Home Affairs in Port Shepstone. I gave her the email address Diane had sent me for the person responsible at the Port Shepstone office. She questioned if the email address was correct as she was sure there was a character missing. I was not able to get hold of Diane at that moment and told her that if there was a change, I would let her know. She then advised that she was going on leave the next day for a week and would only be back the following Thursday. Something in the gut gave me a nudge, but I pushed it away quickly and we set off to make arrangements for the next stage of our journey.

We had planned to spend a month in Port Shepstone so Matt and my family could get to know one another better and so I could catch up as well. I had not seen my parents since I had given them the news that I was leaving Ryan and heading for Vietnam. We spent our last couple of days in Cape Town finalising arrangements for our ceremony, which we had agreed would be in Cape Town. The plans for our ceremony had come together pretty smoothly. Lee-Anne was back home in Cape Town as well. We had messaged to let her know we were there and getting married.

"I have the perfect place for your ceremony. My family's home has a space on it that I am looking to use for workshops and ceremonies and I would love to offer this space to you two."

I still love this strange Universal exchange. We had offered Mystics to Lee-Anne for her Goddess workshop the year before. She was now offering us her family land to use for our ceremony. We both knew it was the correct choice and gladly accepted her offer. Her Mom had offered to help as well with the finer details like seating, tables and decor. Between the four of us, we had our ceremony logistics sorted out pretty quickly. We had asked Liz if she would officiate our ceremony and once again things lined up. Liz asked a few questions to understand the elements and what we wanted for the ceremony. From there she put together the wording and the structure for us. There was nothing else left to do but get on a bus to Port Shepstone. It was time for Matt to meet my family.

My family took to Matt instantly.

"He is just so you, my love!" were the happily whispered words of my mother the first day she met Matt. Up till then, despite our ups and downs, Matt had genuinely fitted me perfectly in every way and he was now fitting in perfectly with my family. I had learned before coming down to Port Shepstone that my whole immediate family was currently home, including Jadie. I had started chatting to Jadie again a few months back while I was still in Siem Reap, he had seemed to be struggling a bit and then he disappeared; this was a common thing for Jadie, something my family and I had experienced with him over the twenty something years of his journey with addiction. When I had grounded myself back at Dené's and I had reached out to reconnect with everyone back home, I had seen Jadie standing on a bridge and the scene had left me with an uneasy feeling, particularly when I had not heard from him a few months. When I learned that he was home with my parents and safe, I was relieved. It had been about five years since I had last seen him. He was looking healthy despite the new additional scars on his wrist, but he seemed to be doing alright. Jadie took to Matt instantly and I have to say that having my older brother's approval of the man I was marrying meant everything to me. As much as my journey with him had been a long and tiring one, he was still my older brother and his opinion did matter. Matt and Jadie got one another as well, both having had a rough journey with addiction and substance abuse, they clicked quickly and I saw a fond love for Matt grow quickly with him. I took the time to catch up properly with Jadie and shared all that I had learned about Spirituality, the shift and addiction over the years we had been apart. Our conversation then shifted to how Jadie had been doing and he caught me up on the years I had missed. Not much had changed, he still swung between being sober and going off the rails. He then shared something with me, "I'm just so tired and so lonely! I've burned every last bridge I had and I have no one left except for mom and dad, and they have one another. So I'm really just feeling so done with everything. I'll be turning forty in a couple of weeks time and I have nothing to show for it. I know I have to be sober, I have to be done with this journey, but it's just so hard! I'm just so tired..."

We chatted for a good while longer and throughout that conversation the feeling that my brother's life would be short-lived sat strongly with me. This was not a new feeling for me, it was something I had felt for years and through most of it I spent waiting to receive that phone call that anyone who has an addict in their life dreads, but expects. Jadie just wanted to be done and he had made numerous attempts to make that happen, but the Universe would not relate and give him the peace he desperately sought. It would not give him the easy way out.

The couple of days that followed our final arrangements for our legal wedding went smoothly, except for one piece of very important paper! The approval from the Cape Town office had still not been received by the office in Port Shepstone. We discovered that the email address had been in fact been incorrect and we did everything we could to get hold of the woman at Immigration. It had also completely slipped our minds that she was on leave for a week. It was Thursday and we were down to the day before we were meant to be married. Our attempts to reach the woman in the Cape Town office had come up short and Diane had advised she would not be able to marry us without that approval form. My intuition, however, assured me that everything would be okay and to reach out to Diane and ask her to contact the woman in Cape Town. It was mid-afternoon when Diane contacted us and let us know she had sent an email to Cape Town and had received a reply - along with our report! I knew without question she was meant to marry us and I had known all day that she would get that report. Diane put together a very simple, yet meaningful legal ceremony for us and Matt and I were officially husband and wife.

We spent the remainder of the month bonding with my family and finalizing the paperwork for my spouse visa. Over that time, as much as I loved being with my family, a feeling of disconnection with South Africa sat strongly with me and I knew it was no longer home. I did know for certain that I was back for a reason and that reason was not just for marriage and visas. I knew it had something to do with my transformation into Crone, my roots and the Ancients. This is where psychedelic plant medicine would come into play for the last time. Matt and I had acquired mushrooms before coming down to Port Shepstone, we had found a day where we had very little to do and agreed it was the correct time to take a journey. As my mushrooms set in, however, I began to feel very unwell and then very old insecurities began to surface. I suddenly found myself at the doorway to the ancestors being questioned on why I was there. I immediately felt an anxiety increase and quickly stepped away from the door and for the first time I experienced what one would term a 'bad trip'. I do want to interject here and say that there really is no such thing as a 'bad trip'. Psychedelics and mind-altering substances will always show you what you need to see, including the shadow aspects. This was my case as I found myself working through and being tested on old patterns and insecurities specifically around relationships. I felt I was being tested on my strength and I knew that I needed to push through those lingering layers so that I could step into Crone and my marriage with Matt fully. What felt like an extended period of time passed and I found myself back at the door of the ancestors "Why are you here?" I was asked once more.

"I'm here to ask for your blessing, I will be leaving soon to build a home in another land and I know I cannot simply up and leave and not first ask for your approval. This would be disrespecting my roots and the land that I was born on."

I felt their approval almost instantly and my 'bad trip' was over in a second. My intuition once more assured me that Matt and I were on the right path and that my spouse visa would come through and I would be making a new home in South Carolina in the months to come. My journey with plant medicine, however, had come to an end; I knew this without a doubt and I still have that knowing to this day. The few times I have attempted to work with the plants since then, I have received nothing but an upset stomach! The only plant that continued to journey with me was marijuana.

As the month with my family came to an end, we left to return to Cape Town for our ceremony. A ceremony that would connect the Collective in a beautiful way. We both felt there was something much bigger to our ceremony than just ourselves. Upon returning to Cape Town and meeting up with Lee-Anne once more, she made mention of the fact that she was going to use the piece of land our ceremony would be held on, for healing ceremonies and retreats. The land buzzed with magic and possibility. She explained that our wedding ceremony would be the first one to be held there. She explained how love would become a part of the foundation for something bigger. We felt honored and humbled and there was no mistaking that us being married there was in alignment and our union was something more significant and bigger than both of us. We finished our last few plans and had a couple of days left when I fell ill. I had caught a chest infection, once again! This one flattened me nicely two days before our ceremony and with a few last things yet to get sorted. I managed, but by the eve of our ceremony, I was exhausted and feeling done with everything. I expressed that I did not want to do the ceremony anymore, but I understood I could not cancel at that stage. I knew not feeling very well was not helping, but the last couple of days had just felt very intense. Not in a bad way, specifically. Just intense. Matt who was mastering his gentleness with me, pulled me close to him and said, "Remember this is not just about you and me. We both know this is bigger than ourselves. We don't know what our ceremony will spark. Everything has been right up till now and we both know that this ceremony is as well."

I did know and I pushed some serious mind-over matter into it while acknowledging the understanding that the physical is always the last point of release. I had been through a whirlwind of a journey up to that point and I needed to release! It was completely worth the push and wow what a beautiful ceremony it was! I sat back for a moment to watch our guests interact. Some I had known since I was child, some Matt and I had met while in Hanoi and Siem Reap. Many were meeting for the first time. I have seen the Collective Consciousness at work thousands of times before; I see it in my daily life now; but that day I watched the Collective shift. There they were, people from different walks of life, beliefs and cultures, chilling out and having a chat. There were no judgments, only open and curious conversations. It was quite the sight to behold. Our ceremony that day had indeed been in perfect alignment and it gave me a deep insight into how the world would be once the shift was done.

With my spouse visa being processed and a rough idea of a timeline, Matt and I knew we would need a bit more of settled space to stay while I waited to be processed. Before we had left to see my parents, Liz had messaged me about a room that was for rent in a shared house. I knew the person renting the space as I had met him a few times before in passing. Ollie and Liz both knew Reggie well and both had spoken quite highly of him before; specifically in a spiritual sense. Ollie who was back home as well, had also mentioned the rental to us. I took it as a sign and once more alignment happened and Matt and I were soon settled in what was meant to be a temporary home. The wait for my visa was growing long, though. We had not heard anything new as yet - just that my application had been received and was in the first stages of being processed. Matt was also beginning to grow restless. He was looking forward to starting work again and to start building our life in South Carolina. Matt was with me in South Africa for around six months before he chose to head home and start working and getting himself settled. We agreed to take the process as it came and we would work visits out as we went. For the first time in nearly two years I was on my own and it was time for me to fully process and reflect on the journey I had been on.

Matt and I spent a total of five months apart. Over that time, I came to understand that I had moved from Shaman to Crone; that the last step was to step into this and own it. Over those five months I assessed myself, my behaviors, my boundaries and practices. As the weeks rolled on, I focused on bettering them. I found myself closing off old connections, re-establishing where my various friendships and relationships sat; and assessed what I wanted in life. Over those months I set to weaving a new version of myself. A version not much different to the person who was asked if she was genuinely happy more than two years previously. Being more settled, I acquired myself a new yoga mat, adjusted my eating habits and stopped smoking marijuana. I was completely clean and in full alignment with myself. Over this time Liz and I engaged constantly in conversations around the shift and a move into a Yin-based consciousness. We shared all that we had both seen and learned and we both knew the shift was in place. The toxic aspect of Yin, however, reared up strongly over this time. Particularly when a women's protest march had been arranged in the city of Cape Town. The march was in protest of women consistently being abused, justice not being served for those who had endured severe crimes against them and for women to express just how tired and angry they were. Something about the march triggered me and everything about it felt incorrect. I then began following the progress and conversations of women attending the march and the toxic aspect of Yin was grossly apparent! Women were turning on one another for having different views and opinions. Some were pro the death penalty for these injustices, while others shamed them for being cruel and no better than those that had incurred the injustices against them in the first place. The entire thing seemed to morph into a toxic war of angry voices now shouting at one another. That same understanding I had while in Thailand with Chené came through strongly. Women were rising but in the incorrect ways! They were rising through their toxicity and not their compassion. This understanding would continue to sit with me for the months that lay ahead. I, however, maintained my alignment and stayed strong within myself; that was until I applied for a tourist visa to visit Matt and my old visa anxiety got the better of me as I stepped out of alignment and into the world of sugar addiction. For a good couple weeks leading up to my interview for my tourist visa, I had the same persistent anxiety that I had experienced with my Australian visa application. Remember my words around manifesting and how if things are in alignment and meant to be, then manifesting is easy? If that alignment isn't there, however, the manifestation won't materialize no matter how much energy and willpower one summons. This became the case as the day for my interview arrived and my anxiety was in overdrive! I stumbled my way through what was essentially meant to be a simple interview and found my request for a tourist visa being declined. I would have to wait for my spouse visa before I would be able to step foot in my new home country.

Matt and his family agreed to come out that December to see me instead. I had not yet met my in-laws and we were all a little anxious to get to know one another. I also missed Matt terribly and the distance was proving to be a challenge for us both. By the time Matt had arrived for his visit, we had received news on my visa and my case began to move forward more swiftly. My meeting with my in-laws went smoothly and we seemed to all get along just fine. This put my mind at ease as Matt and I had agreed to stay with them for a couple of months once I got to America. Matt had been staying with them already, which had been a bit up and down as old issues and patterns surfaced between them. I felt we would be okay, however, as we were making good progress with my visa application and we both assumed we would not have much longer to go.

While Matt was there, Liz invited us to see a film with her - Down To Earth. The film struck chords with the shifts and rising Yin, but it gave me something I had not considered before. I knew this was something I would need to do before I went anywhere else. The film documented a family traveling to spend time with ancient cultures and tribes around the world. This included the oldest recorded culture in the world, the San, the one culture that is actually native to South Africa and believed to be the culture from which all other cultures are descended. It was here where I understood my missing piece. It was time for me to sit with the Ancients! My month with Matt flew by quickly and I found myself alone once again. It was early January and a few days after Matt had left that Reggie had invited me for a Full Moon hike up a mountain, not too far off from where I had hiked with Dené with Les years before - the same hike where I saw my owl. Reggie made mention of a sacred site and that the hike was being facilitated by a man who had a strong connection with the ancient San culture in Cape Town. Two San men would be joining us to share their knowledge on the plants and the mountain. I knew without question that I needed to go. We followed the group up to the top and I was greeted with an ancient sacred site that buzzed with an intense energy. This is where I would sit and watch the first Full Moon of 2020 - almost two years exactly since my experience in Mystics where the ancestors had come to chat with me and my experience had turned nightmarish very quickly. I reflected deeper on how far I had come and then our guide's words caught my attention. He was explaining the history of the sacred site and how it lined up with the sun on the solstice. He then spoke about the cycles and then he spoke on the shift into a feminine-based consciousness.

"This is beyond weird! Everything he is saying I am writing about in my book, " I whispered to Reggie. I had been writing the sequel to my original memoir and was set to publish and release the following month. I felt that this experience was a closing of a chapter and that my memoir would be complete.

"This must be good timing then and a nice synchronicity," was Reggie's reply. In the time I had stayed with Reggie, he had proved to be a rather peculiar soul - a high level Magician without question and very connected to the Collective Consciousness. On numerous occasions he would either say or give something to me that was perfectly timed. This experience was another one of those profound moments with Reggie. I sat and watched as the sunset and an exquisitely large full moon rose. I knew without question that I would be leaving South Africa once more in the coming months. I reflected on the lessons and practices I had acquired and reflected on my journey once more. That feeling of needing to sit with the Ancients sat strongly with me with once more and intuitively I knew I was not done with my journey. As much as that evening felt like the closing of a chapter, my journey was far from complete!

25

Toxic Christianity

It was February 2020 and I was set to publish the sequel to my original memoir and I had made arrangements to run a last few workshops and courses in Johannesburg and Cape Town during the month of March. Both Matt and I were sure that I would be heading to America in a couple of months time. The end of February arrived, I published my sequel and then the anxiety set in! Within days of publishing I had not sold a single copy of my book. This was a first for me and the author in me was devastated! I had known without question I was meant to write that book and share what I had learned about the shift, my journey, addiction and the Yin-based consciousness. My anxiety escalated from there and my gut began to shout at me that I needed to cancel my plans for Johannesburg and Cape Town. I did not understand what was happening, I knew I had to do it, though. Then Jadie went off the rails once more with his addiction, and my parents reached a breaking point with him. We arranged to help him get into a rehab in the city of Port Elizabeth. It was a place he had come across a few years earlier. In his drugged haze I could hear his authentic self speaking and assuring me that this was where he needed to go. Without any issues I was able to assist him and within a few days he was settling into rehab. My anxiety, however, was in overdrive and I cancelled all my plans for the month of March and took my book off the market.

Then March set in and COVID which had not reached our borders as yet, made its way to South Africa. My visa process was still flowing smoothly and I believed that I would be able to finish my process and get to America before anything too crazy happened. Two weeks later and one step away from the last stage of my visa process, South Africa shut its borders and the entire world came to a standstill; along with every American embassy around the world. Visas were no longer being processed and everyone worldwide went into lockdown! My sugar addiction intensified and I stepped completely out of alignment - the knowledge that I had no answer as to when I would see Matt again fuelling my disconnect. With borders being shut, Matt was not able to get to me and with the last stage of my visa process not completed, I could not get to him. I descended into a downward spiral and let everything I had learned over the last couple of years since leaving Ryan fall to the wayside as the entire world descended into what I now believe was a [12]Global Dark Night of the Soul.

For six months my entire life came to a standstill and I lived in a constant space of not knowing what the future might hold as I found myself caught in one of the most severe lockdowns in the world. South Africa was taking their lockdown restrictions to the extreme and each day the people found something else being taking away from them. I lived in a consistent space of fear and anxiety with the military and police often brutally enforcing lockdown laws within the country. I felt displaced, anxious and most days terrified for my safety. Over that time Jadie began what would be a one year long journey of sobriety and Matt and his old family issues began to resurface in extreme ways. Matt's relationship with his parents has mostly been a toxic one. With them being overbearing, co-dependent and controlling and Matt constantly pushing back and fighting to be his own person, he was finding living with them to be a daily challenge. This added to my anxiety as I knew he was back living with them as a way to help us get started with our lives in America. We had all agreed that Matt would stay with them while I waited for my visa process to be finalized and then for the first few months of me arriving in the States. My levels of guilt were extreme by the time lockdown hit as Matt would tell me frequently about how they had stepped into old habits and how he was struggling with living in their space. His dad's condescending manner and constant belittling, coupled with his mom's need to control his life, led Matt into a regular pattern of heavy drinking as a means to cope. I would often chat to a very drunk Matt, helpless to do anything for my struggling husband! By the time the American embassies reopened for visa processing, Matt was more than ready to move out his parents' home. By late August we were able to finally complete my visa process and make the final arrangements for me to fly over. By this stage I had developed a very unhealthy relationship with sugar, had gained unnecessary weight and my overall physical and emotional health was questionable. So when I arrived to live with Matt and his parents I was already so far out of alignment with myself. I was having regular bouts of severe brain fog as well as and intense anxiety and depression. My yoga practice all but diminished as I just had no energy to get on my mat. Then came the change to a standard unhealthy American diet along with the added stress of living in the toxicity of the relationship between Matt and his parents. My misalignment was amplified and I would consistently feel a severe lack of energy and a feeling of being intensely unwell. All well trying to set-up and establish my work in a new country and culture, it was even more challenging to be doing this in what is known as the Bible Belt; an area of the Southern United States marked for its intense and often toxic version of Christianity. The Universe had indeed chosen a bizarre space to place me. With my physical and emotional health being so bad, however, it took me far longer than necessary to fully understand why I was here and what I was meant to be doing. Then I met Linda.

I was nearing the end of my first month of being in South Carolina and I was in search of a space to work from. I was living in the town of Easley then, which is known to be extremely old fashioned in its thinking and the Southern Baptist faith dominated. A town where the type of spiritual work I do would not be accepted in a hurry. It was here in the middle of Easley, South Carolina that I was pointed in the direction of a Yoga Studio and told to speak to a woman by the name of Linda. When I learned there was a Yoga Studio close by, my faith levels rose somewhat and my skepticism about where the Universe had placed me eased. I contacted Linda and made an arrangement to meet with her in a couple of days; and man am I grateful that I did! Upon meeting Linda, I can honestly say I liked her instantly. She radiated authenticity and her studio space felt safe and welcoming. I was still somewhat skeptical about doing my work in the middle of Easley, but I trusted Linda and even through the fog of my misalignment and poor health, I knew the studio was correct for me. She showed me around and explained how everything worked and then she mentioned what would be the first synchronistic thing I had heard in months: she was running a Yoga Teacher Training course that would be starting the following February. Earlier that year, before the chaos of COVID and lockdowns, Tracy had been round for a visit and we got to chatting about our yoga practices and how we both wanted to expand on them and do a Teacher Training. Tracy was looking specifically at doing hers in Bali and I was considering India or America for mine. "I know I want to start mine next year February," were my words to Tracy. Now here I was a good few months later and Linda was telling me about her Teacher Training that was starting in February. I knew I could not ignore the synchronicity and I my intuition gave me just the slightest nudge and said very quietly, "You need to do that training." February would become so much more than just the month I would begin my synchronistically timed Teacher Training, though. It would be the start of a nine month long journey back into alignment, where the Ancients would begin to speak to me loudly about their prophecies and the shift, and I would unknowingly lose my very first spiritual mentor, Jadie.

Matt and I having reached a breaking point with living with his parents, made the move into our own space in mid-December and settled into our very first home together. Having spent the first part of our journey together in SE Asia and then a brief moment in South Africa, Matt and I had actually never had a home of our own together before. This new aspect to our marriage began to raise some challenges as I stepped into old habits and took on the role of housewife all whilst attempting - often fruitlessly - to get my business going. My health had deteriorated so badly that most days I struggled to focus and get through what I needed to and my brain fog would be so intense that driving was a frequent challenge. By late January my emotions were like a constant rollercoaster and I persistently felt very ill! I would be starting my Teacher Training in roughly a month's time and I knew that if I was going to get through a nine-month long intense curriculum, I would need to sort my health out. The trouble was that I had no understanding at the time of what was wrong with me. I had questioned the unhealthy diet and my high intake of sugar, but being so incredibly unwell, I just could not place where the illness was stemming from. I would be well into the month of February before I would get the answer.

In the midst of all my misalignment and poor health, I stumbled across an Apache Medicine Woman, Lauren, who would become my first interaction with the Ancients in America. I had come across Lauren in a

Women's Business group on Facebook and once again my intuition gave me a nudge and whispered, "You need to contact her, she has important things to teach you." With being so far out of alignment I took about an hour to send her a quick message asking if she would like to meet for coffee. Between my brain fog on one side and my whisper-quiet intuition on the other, I could not quite work out what the correct message was that I was meant to be sending to her. I felt the need to share that I believed she had something to teach me, but my poor health and high anxiety had me questioning if this woman I had never met would think I was totally insane for messaging her out of the blue to tell her she was a teacher of mine and that I would love to meet her. After a long process of typing, deleting and retyping, I finally settled on a message and hit send; hoping she wouldn't think I was bat shit crazy! Through my brain fog haze I felt that what I had sent was correct. Trying to work from an intuitive place whilst horrendously ill is an immense challenge! Thankfully, Lauren didn't think I was completely nuts and we arranged to meet for coffee around mid-February.

In-between me sending that message and meeting Lauren for the first time, I experienced my first snow ever and Jadie made contact with me again. While Jadie was in rehab, the only way I could chat to him was on the main landline for the rehab centre as he had no cellphone on which I could contact him directly. So when I left South Africa, direct contact with him was lost and I would only be able to pass messages along through my mom who would still chat to him regularly. Jadie had been making healthy progress in rehab and had settled in well. Despite a slip up here and there, he looked to be well on his way to recovery. Then a couple days before my first snow he contacted me out of the blue. He had been able to purchase another cellphone for himself and for a brief time I was able to chat him. Something in my mind kept telling me that something was amiss and as much as he was asking me how I was doing and genuinely wanted to know, I chose to say very little about the challenges I was facing, out of fear that it would push him back into addiction once more. We chatted a little each day up until my first snow fall. If one was to use a single word to describe snow, I would have to say it's 'peaceful'. My childlike amazement at witnessing snow for the first time had me standing outside in below freezing temperatures, staring up at the gentle flakes, taking in the calm and quiet that is synonymous with falling snow. In that moment, standing in the tranquillity of the falling snow, my state moved from being one of excitement and wonder, to a moment of overwhelming sadness. I did not understand where that feeling had come from and put it down to the rollercoaster of emotions I had been experiencing over the last couple of weeks. I pushed the sadness aside and went back indoors to warm up and message my parents and Jadie that I had seen my first snow. My whole family knew how much I had always wanted to see snow, a big item on my bucket list! So when my chance finally arrived, I was eager to share my experience. I contentedly messaged my mom and then began to message Jadie and something in me said 'no' and that feeling of sadness peaked again along with that same fear of pushing him back into addiction again. I chose to ignore this and messaged him regardless; the message never went through. Two days later my mom messaged me that Jadie was missing from the rehab. It appeared he had hopped the wall and had not returned. She expressed her anger and disappointment and we began our usual wait for Jadie to resurface, as he always did. Shortly after this, my Tarot based posters that I had up in my office began to fall off my walls consistently to the point where I would eventually stop trying to put them back up unless I needed them up. The times that I did remount them, within a few hours, they would be laying on my office floor once more. This bizarre occurrence would continue for another two months.

Mid-February arrived. I was set to meet Lauren for the first time and I was a week out from starting my Teacher Training; and I was still struggling severely with my health. I'll admit I was horribly nervous and anxious about meeting Lauren. Something about it felt massively intimidating, but our coffee date was happening and I was not going to cancel at the last minute - and I am still so grateful that I didn't! I found Lauren incredibly easy to talk to and within half an hour of meeting her, she had already given me something valuable. Prior to the lockdown in South Africa, Liz had sent me a link for a documentary that spoke about a world shift into a feminine-based consciousness. Without a second thought, I had watched the documentary and found that everything they spoke about had already been shown to me over the last few years. It confirmed and amplified my knowing that a shift was happening and it was a shift into a Yin-based consciousness. A shift that would bring about an age of compassion and unity. Liz and I chatted about the documentary afterwards and my understanding of the importance of Africa in the shift rose up for me once more. We spoke a bit more and then the conversation shifted to South Africa and Liz spoke about how it is known as the Rainbow Nation, yet it is still such a divided nation; my intuition kicked straight in and said, "You need to research the Rainbow People." Which I duly did after finishing my conversation with Liz. My search however did not bring up much about South Africa, rather it brought up search results for a prophecy that was spoken about in a number of the Indigenous cultures of North America; the prophecy of the Rainbow Warriors and Great Whirling Rainbow. The words from the Hopi and Navajo nations struck me strongly: "There will come a day when people of all races, colors, and creeds will put aside their differences. They will come together in love, joining hands in unification, to heal the Earth and all Her children. They will move over the Earth like a great Whirling Rainbow, bringing peace, understanding and healing everywhere they go. Many creatures thought to be extinct or mythical will resurface at this time; the great trees that perished will return almost overnight. All living things will flourish, drawing sustenance from the breast of our Mother, the Earth. The great spiritual Teachers who walked the Earth and taught the basics of the truths of the Whirling Rainbow Prophecy will return and walk amongst us once more, sharing their power and understanding with all. We will learn how to see and hear in a sacred manner. Men and women will be equals in the way the Creator intended them to be; all children will be safe anywhere they want to go. Elders will be respected and valued for their contributions to life. Their wisdom will be sought out. The whole Human race will be called The People and there will be no more war, sickness or hunger forever."

These words encapsulated everything I had been learning to understand over the years about the shift that was already taking place. My intuition had then pushed me to look into the San people once more and the migration of humanity out of Africa. It was here that I understood we all had the same roots, and that root began in Africa. So when Lauren began to tell me about a [13]Seminole Medicine Man who believed that the tribes would one day be reunited, the words I had read months before rang in my mind. "Does he feel that the reunification is just on the Native American level or does he believe it's a global thing?" was my immediate question. She replied that she was not sure, but went on to share another insight with me that proved to be even more valuable. She was explaining that each culture native to North America shared the same core belief - that the Earth was meant to be honored and respected. That they lived in harmony with Earth and were custodians of the land. They never saw the land or Her resources as a commodity or something that could be owned. What separated the cultures was their ceremonies, stories and their ways of daily life; all this became dependant on where they lived. Because they were all so tied to the land, they lived according to their surroundings and this impacted the type of rituals or ways that they would follow. Cultures that were desert based would hold rituals that invited rain while others would have ceremonies that welcomed the heat of the Sun. My knowledge of the migration of humanity out of Africa expanded in that moment and I began to see clearly where our disconnection from one another had begun to take place. Many of our ancestors had departed Southern Africa, while the rest had stayed. As they traveled north and began to disperse across the globe, they settled into new lands and the original ceremonies, rituals and stories began to adapt to their new surroundings. Names of things changed along with physical features and division began to occur. Fast forward a ten thousand odd years later and here we sit with a spiritually disconnected Western society, many of the traditions of the ancients long forgotten and a world at a constant war with itself. My first cup of coffee with Lauren would be the start of the Ancients truly revealing themselves to me. My diminished health and lack of alignment would hinder this learning phase somewhat, but my nine month journey with Yoga would get me back on track.

I was two days away from starting my Teacher Training and I was at my wits end with my health so I did something I had not done in years: I went to see a doctor. Over the years since living in Cape Town with Ryan and finding alignment for the first time, I had not been to see a medical doctor. I had no need to. When I had become ill in SE Asia, my fear of what the doctors could be like had prevented me from seeing any back then as well. But by the time Teacher Training rolled around, I was desperate and I also knew that if I did not understand what was medically wrong, I would be in for a very rough nine months of Teacher Training. It took consulting with two different doctors before I found out what had been ailing my physical health. My excessive consumption of sugar and junk food had triggered a massive yeast infection in my gut; something which left unchecked and untreated could potentially become something fatal! I was given a course of antibiotics and I knew I needed some serious lifestyle adjustments - which I began to make slowly. In between my two doctors visits, my first weekend of Teacher Training began and six new souls entered my life. Six individuals that would each step onto my path in their own unique way and would leave a massive impression on my life and my journey. One of them I had already met the year before, she had been to see me for a session to chat about purpose - another woman named Linda. To avoid some confusion here I'll be differentiating between the two Lindas as Guru Linda (the owner of the yoga studio and my Guru for Teacher Training) and my classmate as just Linda.

On our first evening together, we all introduced ourselves and as each one of us had our turn, three people in particular stood out for me: Joseph, Zack and Cherise. I instantly knew that Joseph and I would connect quickly. Something about him felt familiar and so much about him reminded me of Jadie. I then looked at Zack and Cherise, who I had learned were a married couple and knew that I would be making a connection with them soon as well. The remaining three women would begin to have an impact on me as the months rolled on: Linda who I already knew, Kelsey and Lori. Cherise and I made a brief, but impactful connection in our first evening as Guru Linda asked us to pair up with one another and discuss with our partner why we were doing Teacher Training, what we hoped to gain from it and what we needed in that moment. Cherise, who was sitting across from me waved me over and we began to chat. I shared with her how I had been struggling with my health and the impacts of that struggle affected me not just physically, but mentally and emotionally as well. I then shared how I was far out of alignment and that I hoped the nine-month journey in Teacher Training would help to restore that alignment once more. I told her how I had experienced authentic and complete alignment previously, but with the stresses of my spouse visa, 2020 lockdown and my unhealthy lifestyle had pushed me far out of alignment. I felt the tears welling up in my eyes as I shared openly with her. Cherise's soft, empathetic nature assured me that I was in the right place and that she had no doubts I would be able to find my health and alignment once more. Something in her energy made me feel safe to speak openly without fear of judgment or worry that she would think less of me for beginning my journey where I was. This would be the beginning of an impactful friendship and the start of finding my American family.

I did not anticipate Joseph and I connecting so soon and so intensely, though. The next day of training I found myself having lunch with him and our connection was immediately established. Throughout our lunch he reminded me more and more of Jadie: his mannerisms, quirks and the ways he expressed himself. The natural flow into deep conversations about Spirituality were almost identical to the ones I would I have with Jadie as well. Over lunch, we chatted on subjects that resonated strongly with the shift and I knew that Joseph was yet another soul who was pivotal to the change the world needed and that he would be helping to facilitate the shift. I also learned that he had attended Ministry School, but had eventually turned away from it due to the inauthentic way in which they were teaching and the harsh judgemental nature of both his teachers and the curriculum. Joseph who identifies as queer, found the school had little place or liking for people that lived the type of lifestyle he did. Once again, the harshness of Christianity reared its head as I became even more aware of the impact this was having on the world as it highlighted yet another pivotal aspect to the shift. By the end of our lunch, I had a strong love growing for Joseph and knew he was family for sure. The following weekend I invited him to have lunch with Matt and I, as I knew that he and Matt needed to meet as well. What was meant to be just a casual lunch soon morphed into an all night experience where I learned exactly where Joseph fitted in with the shift. I saw the intense similarities between Matt and him, and learned where he found a sense of peace and acceptance with who he was. Over the course of the evening, Joseph shared his personal experiences with the church and Matt found himself resonating strongly. Having grown up in an intensely religious home, Matt was forced to attend church and live his life in a way that aligned with the forced principles of Christianity. Matt, like Joseph had found this forced conformity to be highly inauthentic and had found himself pulling away from his Christian roots; instead beginning to form an intense resentment towards Christianity - which in turn, forced an even bigger divide between him and his parents. A big cause for this divide was his father's manner of forcing the 'good word' upon Matt and insisting that Matt needed to find his way back to Jesus, and that he would not be complete without doing so. There was one evening where I was witness to this. Matt's dad was telling him that he saw that he was lost in life and missing something - what he was missing was Jesus. This was one of many times that I stood up to my father-in-law and put him back in line. My exact words that particular evening were, "Who the hell do you think you are? You have no place or right to tell another person, particularly your own son, that he is not whole or complete because he has chosen to follow a different path to you. That is not your place to tell anyone that! How dare you force your conformist ways onto another?"

There were a number of other times where my father-in-law had tried to force his Christian views onto us and each time I slammed boundaries down and told him that was not okay! My experience in living in the Bible Belt was fast turning into an education on the toxicity of Christianity and just how much damage it had caused over the centuries.

The similarities between Matt and Joseph did not end at their Christian roots as they engaged in further conversations and found they had much more in common: their experiences with addiction, the struggle to step fully into who they were and how they both sought acceptance in the world. Our conversation soon flowed onto the subjects around the shift as Joseph began to share that he believed the world was in a birthing process, that a shift was happening and he was here to facilitate that birth as a [14]Doula of sorts. Everything he said, particularly about the earth birthing someone new and him being a Doula, resonated strongly. What struck Joseph was the calm acceptance from us about everything he was sharing, "You guys don't seem the slightest bit surprised by anything I'm telling you. In fact you're both really calm about all this!"

"That's because we know what you're talking about, I've been seeing aspects of the shift for years and Matt is well informed on everything I've seen. Plus both of us having our experiences together just amplified our knowing and understanding of what is happening in the world right now," I shared with him.

Joseph then began having intense body shakes, identical to the ones I had been having for a couple of years already. Shakes that seemed to be associated with one having intense shamanic experiences.

"I keep getting these and I don't know why. I'm sorry if they're freaking you guys out!" He confided.

"Don't be sorry, I have the same thing. I've learned they're linked to my shamanic awakenings and are completely normal," I assured him in a gentle manner; to which Matt added, "Yeah they're pretty common, I've seen Tam have them often. Especially in intense times or where she is receiving a lot of information or clarification on things from the spirit realm. You're completely okay man, you do you. You're safe here!"

Matt and I giving Joseph that much needed validation and insight into the fact that he was anything but abnormal, made him feel safe, seen and accepted - something he had desperately sought within the church, but had been denied time and time again. My conversations around toxic Christianity continued into the following week as I met up with Zack and Cherise for coffee and a walk.

By the time that following week had arrived, I had learned about my gut yeast infection and was already well into my course of antibiotics and beginning to feel more stable and grounded. My intuition had gone from a quiet whisper to being more audible and I knew without question that Zack and Cherise were important to my journey. So when they invited me for coffee, I knew instinctively that I was meant to go. The more time I spent with them, the more I liked them. Both of them had gentle demeanors and were far more enlightened than they gave themselves credit for. Our conversation soon flowed to the toxicity of Christianity and what my experiences had been like so far living in the proverbial Bible Belt. I shared what I had experienced to date, including the severe boundary setting with my father-in-law. Here they both resonated strongly and shared how both of their families sounded exactly the same as Matt's, in particular Zack's family. The more I got to know them, the more the similarities became apparent.

Toxic Christianity was now a firm aspect in the shift and rise into a Yin-based consciousness as I found it be the exact opposite of where the world needed to go. Something I had found to be insanely contradictory. Having attended a Christian junior school as a child and my own mom having instilled the core teachings of Jesus within me, my understanding of the teachings of Jesus were no different to the teachings of Buddha, [15]Yoga, the earth-based traditions of Wicca or any of the other faiths and belief systems out there. Yet what I was witnessing here in the Bible Belt, was the opposite of the teachings of Jesus. Where He taught compassion and loving kindness, I found judgment and a sense of being better than others because they had accepted Jesus into their life. Where Jesus taught acceptance and unconditional love, I saw a group of people who felt themselves exclusive and that the rest of the world needed to be saved or they would risk eternal damnation in the fiery pits of hell. Then there was the self-entitlement and self-importance element of the most prominent Christian belief system in the South; the Southern Baptists who frowned upon every other Christian and belief system out there; as they believed that they were the chosen privileged few who would make into Heaven while the rest of us were doomed to hell. All of this I found to be so far off from the core of what I knew the teachings of Jesus to be. Over the months that followed, the high level souls here to facilitate change and the shift, along with other highly gifted shamans and medicine people began to step onto my path; making my place in the shift more clear. I was here to help and guide those whose gifts were crucial to the shift so that they could fulfill their purpose and bring about the change the world so desperately needed. All of them were impacted negatively by the toxicity and hypocrisy of Christianity in the South and as I learned soon enough, in America as a whole. A nation that was founded on the core principles of Christianity and oddly enough a nation of immigrants that had originally been escaping religious persecution. They had transformed into a nation of hypocrites, who forced their Christian ways onto the Indigenous cultures already living in North America. Much the same as other White Christian immigrants had done throughout other countries and cultures around the world. The stark and harmful impact of Christianity was staring me in the face.

Here Lori, my fellow classmate became a light and direction for me in seeing that there was indeed a space for a unification of belief systems and that the Rainbow Warrior prophecies of Native America still had a chance. Over the months that I that sat next to Lori in class, I watched and observed her journey. Being strong in Christian beliefs, I had been curious to see where Lori's journey with yoga would lead her. As I watched her shift and transform with her practice, I saw someone who had strong beliefs become open to accepting new ideas and watched as she embraced the similarities between her faith and the yogic philosophies we had been learning and exploring in our weekends together. Lori's awakening and growth in her spirituality was truly inspiring for me. It gave the hope that we could indeed become unified once more, despite our differences in ceremonies and beliefs. We were all one and the same. The true meaning of yoga resonated with me and I knew the philosophies that yoga taught were accurate.

There are what is known as the Eight Limbs of Yoga and it is said that if one follows the limbs and integrates them into their daily life, they will surely find Samadhi or bliss: a place of authentic connection with the self and everything - true union! Through Lori I saw that this union was possible, not just on the individual level, but on the Collective Consciousness level as well. The teachings of Eight of the Limbs are identical to the teachings of Buddha, the philosophies of mindfulness and the teaching and ways of ancients. Live a life of balance, that is none harming, where you do not steal from others, where you pursue self-study and self-mastery and seek that ultimate connection with all. A connection that can only be reached if one finds true, authentic connection within them self first. I had already experienced this place of authentic connection more than once before and I was now reminded how important that connection was and I knew I had no choice but to step back into alignment with myself once more. I needed to do this not just for myself, but for the Collective as a whole. If I was not in alignment or in a state of optimal health, I could not expect to do the work I was placed here to do. I had to shift myself.

26

Stepping Back into Alignment

I was coming into my second month of Teacher Training and having tea with a new friend I had met. Shannon was yet another high level soul who had been negatively impacted by the toxicity of Christianity. There was something more to my meeting with her, though. She was the first of two people who brought the awareness that Jadie was still missing to the forefront of my mind. She had been asking about my own personal journey with Spirituality and Tarot, and I had been sharing how Jadie had been a big influence on my path - particularly in my younger years. I shared how he had endured a long journey with addiction and then she asked, "Where is your brother now?" The question hit me like a ton of bricks and something inside of me felt an intense discomfort, "I'm not actually sure, he went missing from the rehab he was in and we haven't heard from him since."

My response did not sit well with me and that uncomfortable feeling intensified. Later that week, one of my sets of Tarot cards chucked themselves at me, or so it had seemed. I had the set on the top section of my desk and when I stood up to get something from a shelf behind that, they landed on my laptop with a thud. They had been sitting on that top part of my desk for over a week already and had not been moved. I picked them up and asked in a gentle joking manner, "What do you guys want?" and proceeded to place them back where they had been originally. Only for them to fall back onto my laptop once more! My Tarot posters were still giving me uphill and were not staying stuck on my office walls either. I chose to place the deck on a different part of my desk where I was sure they would not be able to jump around again and that is where they sat for another week. My next Teacher Training weekend arrived and Joseph had asked if he could travel to class with me that weekend as his car was in for repairs. I happily obliged, and on our drive back from class at the end of the weekend, Joseph asked me the same question Shannon had. I had been talking to him about how similar he was to Jadie and had been sharing about Jadie's journey with his addiction.

"Where is your brother now?"

The question once again hit me hard and that intense feeling of discomfort reared up more strongly as I gave him the same reply I had given Shannon - that I did not know. Later that following week, my mom messaged me, sharing her concerns about Jadie and the fact that he had not turned up like he usually did. She said she was beyond concerned and was now considering opening a missing persons case. That uncomfortable feeling escalated and I agreed with her that something was not correct. Jadie had never, in all his years of normal addiction routine, gone this long without making contact. I offered to help where I could on my side and she shared that she was thinking of contacting an organization in South Africa that assisted with missing persons cases - The Pink Ladies. I agreed that it was a good idea, but my mom seemed to have the understanding that she would need to first open a case with the police in the town where Jadie had gone missing and that she would not be able to open one in Port Shepstone where she was living. It was already quite late in South Africa by this time and we agreed to continue our conversation the next day. Something about The Pink Ladies resonated with me and before I knew what I was doing, I was making contact and explaining our situation. Within a very short time, I had received a response from the woman that ran the organization, requesting more details and offering for us to move our chat to Whatsapp messenger for simplicity. Within a few minutes, she had explained the full process of opening a missing persons case and offered to assist with this process since she was based in Port Elizabeth where Jadie had gone missing. She simplified what my mom and I thought was a complicated scenario and by the next day a missing persons case was open and The Pink Ladies had begun sharing a missing persons post with their network. It was seeing their post with Jadie's face and details on it that solidified the experience for me; my brother had not just gone off the rails, this time he was missing and something was vastly different. That same day my mom shared that she had started contacting hospitals, police stations and morgues around Port Elizabeth to see if they had seen or checked-in anyone that matched Jadie's description. There was one place that came back and advised they had someone that matched that description, but because of COVID, they were unable to handle the body and do a full identification for her. She had asked if they could check if the person they had, had a specific tattoo on his back, but they refused and said they could not. She would need to either come in and look for herself or send someone on her behalf. My older sister Kim knew someone based in Port Elizabeth that was offering to help. He was a friend of her wife's boss that lived there - an ex-cop who had a lot of contacts and knowledge on how things worked. He had offered to go and see if the body in the morgue was in fact Jadie or not. He would only be able to do this the following week Tuesday though, as the weekend was starting and the following Monday was a public holiday, so all we could do was wait. When my mom shared this news with me, my intuition went into overdrive and Jadie began to talk to me.

I spent that entire weekend swinging between mourning the loss of my older brother who was my first spiritual mentor, and disbelief in what I was being shown, along with the instructions he was sharing with me. I was still far out of alignment and my faith in my gifts and abilities as a medium had dwindled drastically as I had slipped further into misalignment. Not knowing if I was losing my mind or if I was in fact communicating with Jadie, that weekend become an intense one and all I could do was receive the messages and instructions I was being given and wait for confirmation that following Tuesday on whether or not I had completely lost my mind. It began with a vivid vision of Jadie lying in a morgue, the color of pale blue and what appeared to be a severe head wound. Jadie then began explaining that he had been hit in the head and left for dead on a sidewalk. He then moved on to tell me that we did not need to focus on catching the person responsible, because this would be taken care of. He seemed to give me a moment as my mourning process set in and I broke down and wept for my brother. He then nudged me about the set of Tarot cards that were still sitting in the same spot where I had left them a week earlier. With shaky hands I intuitively drew a card. The set had dual imagery on it, with each card having a visual depiction of both upright and reverse meanings. The card I pulled was in reverse and the image only reinforced what I already knew intuitively. It was the Strength card with an image of a woman weeping over a coffin. "You're going to need to be strong in order to handle what you already know is coming next," I could almost hear Jadie clearly. I sat back down on my couch and continued to listen.

"Please don't bury me, I don't want to be boxed up in the ground. I need to be cremated and my ashes must go with mom and dad to the farm they are going to settle on. Here I want to be scattered so I can rest easy with my family close by. Please don't scatter me in the ocean I don't like it there! You need to come home, the family needs you and I need you to do some things for me. There needs to be two services: I want one for the family in Port Shepstone and another in Johannesburg. You need to do the service in Johannesburg! I want the family service to be on my birthday and please celebrate me. Please do not mourn my loss, celebrate me instead and don't hold onto the sadness of losing me. You need to tell mom and dad the same thing. I don't want you to be sad. I'm finally at peace, the peace I had so desperately been seeking for years, but was never allowed to have."

Throughout the course of that weekend, I continued to swing between thinking I had lost my mind and mourning Jadie. By the time Tuesday arrived, I needed the confirmation on whether or not it was in fact Jadie in that morgue. I messaged my Mom to see if she had heard anything as yet, to which she replied that they were still waiting. An hour later she messaged me the words I already knew were coming, "It is Jadie." My brother was indeed dead and my journey with my first spiritual mentor and teacher had come to an end. I went on to miss my third weekend of Teacher Training, Guru Linda assured me that everything was okay and that we would sort out the make-up classes when I returned from South Africa. I spent a week in South Africa with Matt, honoring Jadie's wishes.

Losing Jadie had pushed me back from my progress of stepping back into alignment and getting my health on track. I persisted, however, and pushed through the months that followed in Teacher Training. Over this time, one specific book spoke to me loudly. We had a set of books that was specified as required reading. Many of the books contained information and teachings I was already familiar with, but this one book in particular spoke directly to the shift and my pursuit of finding my alignment again: The Spirit and Practice of Moving into Stillness, by Erich Schiffmann. This is a book I highly recommend you to read, even if it is just the first chapter. There was one chapter that spoke the loudest to me, though. The author explains how, when we are in a place of stillness, we are existing at a higher frequency – in a space where we feel no inner conflict and we just simply are who we are. He spoke about participating fully in the moment we are in and I found the lessons on mindfulness I had gained a couple of years earlier were being repeated to me through this book. The author then went on to explain how many people are often ignorant of their true nature - their authentic selves – and that we often feel an inner conflict because we have been told throughout our lives that we are a certain way, when in reality, we are who we are, and the person that everyone else says we are, is not in fact us. He went on to further explain how everyone around us would appear to have these informed opinions of who they believed us to be and that many of us would believe these opinions accordingly, allowing others to define who we are. He then brought in the aspect of a yoga practice and how working with a practice of yoga, one can find a place of stillness, a place in which they could truly understand who they are, and not who the world has told them they should be. Everything I was reading related so strongly with me and why I was so far out of alignment. I had stepped so far out of myself and had become so concerned only with the opinions of others; becoming fearful of their judgments of who I truly was. The impact of moving to the Bible Belt and doing so out of alignment already, had only amplified my misalignment and I was not being authentically me. Instead, I had hid a lot of who I was, fearful of being an outcast and of not being accepted in my new space. In stepping out of alignment and fearing being shunned and disliked, I had handed over my power in a different way. Understanding this, I knew exactly how to get back to my alignment: I needed to step back into myself and start owning who I was without fear, shame or guilt impacting on my process. As I began to slowly shift back towards alignment, I began to learn more deeply from my classmates, while more and more people showed up on my path to share aspects of the shift that I already knew. They were showing up to reconfirm that I was who I was, and that I was here for a purpose. I needed to fully immerse myself in that purpose.

Kelsey then shared an insight with me. She had been chatting casually to the others in class about how she had no restrictions in life, and how she was able to live an open life on her terms. What she was saying resonated so strongly with me and instantly took me back to the space of pure alignment I had been in when I had arrived in Hanoi for the second time. I had nothing tying me down, no one else to answer to and I had been living a life very similar to the way Kelsey was describing. A huge of part of me began to long for that sense of freedom once more - that space where I could go anywhere I wanted and nothing could hold me back. But my unhealthy disconnect from myself interpreted my longing as something unachievable. Unachievable because I was married and had multiple responsibilities. I believed that I was tied down and that freedom was completely out of my grasp. This misinterpretation began to manifest strongly in my marriage as I started to struggle with finding balance in my home life. I began to question my marriage to Matt - whether it was in fact something I wanted and if I was there for the right reasons. At that stage, Matt and I had been living together for more than half a year and that I had found myself carrying out majority of the responsibilities around the home - mostly out of guilt because Matt had been supporting both of us of financially while I worked to get my business off the ground and generating some capital. Matt had also continued with his persistent drinking and had been dabbling with other substances as well. He had been dishonest with me a few times about his using as well and my disconnect with him intensified. It was not until the second last month of Teacher Training that I had a full on meltdown and the imbalances within my home life came to a head. A week before this happened, I had learned that Matt had been on a three week cocaine bender and had been lying to me about it. When I learned what was actually happening, I was furious! I felt like we had back-pedalled drastically in our relationship and I questioned my marriage even more. Matt then became ill with COVID and in the midst of my anger and frustration with him, I now had to be his caretaker. I then suffered a nervous breakdown - something I had not experienced in over ten years and I knew we either needed to make some changes or I needed to move. But the imbalances in our marriage and home life were fuelling my misalignment and poor health. Matt and I sat down and we began to work on finding balance in our relationship once more. This was something we had been lacking since before I had even arrived in America. Then in calling Matt out on his substance abuse, he called me out on mine. Along with my unhealthy dependence on sugar which I was still struggling to get under control, I had taken up smoking marijuana again. I was in the midst of giving Matt uphill about the fact that he believed he was incapable of doing his job without drinking. Matt had started bartending again a few months earlier. It was something he was genuinely passionate about, but it was also impacting his already unhealthy relationship with alcohol. I called him out on his addiction to bullshit about not being able to do his job sober, to which he then turned around and said, "What about you, your smoking? You said literally the other day how you need it to help you with your writing and work. How you can't work without it."

I had in fact said just that only a few days prior. The full reality of my unhealthy habits glared at me and with one week left of Teacher Training, I quit everything that was unhealthy: sugar, junk food, negative self-talk and marijuana. That week was hell for me as I struggled through intense sugar withdrawals - yes this is a very real thing and not something I want to experience again in hurry; in fact I'd rather not experience it again at all! When the last weekend of my Teacher Training arrived, my physical body was struggling to rebalance my blood sugar levels and readjust itself to a completely healthy diet. Then my classmate Linda took me through her final sequence and for the first time in over a year, I felt solid in body and in complete alignment with myself. For our final weekend, we each needed to create a final flow sequence that we would teach to a fellow student on our last weekend together. I had been placed with Linda and I am so grateful I was. Her final sequence was aligned to absolutely anybody and as she took me through it, I felt connected to myself, my body and my authenticity. She gave me the space to reconnect with myself fully, a space I had been missing throughout the nine months of Teacher Training. It was in my last weekend of Teacher Training that I finally found my alignment again. What had aided this was my own final sequence which I had developed for Yogis who had become disconnected from their practice. Mine was a sequence that had been inspired by Tamsin, Jadie's childhood friend that came round to help me heal when I had suffered my first round of Shaman Sickness at the age of sixteen. I had made contact with Tamsin again - with the loss of Jadie we had reconnected again after many years. I learned that she had completed her own Yoga Teacher Training and was now teaching as well. She had shared a post on her social media that expressed her gratitude for the space her yoga mat gave her - how it was a space where she could grow, transform, have a damn good cry and practice being her authentic self. This inspired my concept for my final sequence, coupled with my own disconnect with my practice that I had been experiencing for more than a year already. It was time for me to honour the space my yoga mat and my practice gave me. It was on my mat and in that space it provided, that I could find myself again. I graduated my Teacher Training still struggling with severe sugar withdrawals, but fully in alignment with myself.

In the weeks that followed my graduation, I met up with Lauren again. We had connected a few times during the months of my Teacher Training and each time I got to know her better. The more I got to know her, the more I realized just how identical we were. Lauren had become a mirror image of myself. As much as she was Native Apache, Lauren had not been raised as such. She had been adopted at a young age and had been raised by a white family - not far off from how I had been raised in an open-minded house - where she was allowed to explore any belief system she liked. Lauren had taken to the Bible and the teachings of Jesus from an early age, but having been left to explore these teachings for herself, she had seen very much the same teachings that I had; those of compassion, non-judgment and loving kindness. Later on in life, Lauren established that she was in fact Apache and had tracked down her blood family and began her journey to understand herself and her gifts. Just like me, Lauren was born with incredible gifts of foresights, prophecies, healing abilities and a large role to play in the shift into Yin-based consciousness. And just as I had experienced, she was raised in a Western culture that was disconnected from Spirituality, in a culture that could not teach her about who she was or explain that the bizarre experiences she had while growing up were actually normal for her. It was not until she began reconnecting with her culture and through the assistance of a Medicine Man, that she was able to truly embrace who she is. Lauren has become one of my biggest inspirations in stepping into and owning my power and gifts. My journey to get here has been long, often terrifying and confusing, but a journey completely worth taking as it has led me to meet so many teachers and amazing souls that I now call family. It has also led me to my Apache twin. We may be from different tribes, but Lauren and I are one and the same and we have a shared purpose; the purpose of assisting others to step into their power so that they too can facilitate the shift and change in the world. During these weeks following my graduation, I began to rewrite my memoir. As I worked through the past chapters, I was reminded of where we had come from and just how far out of alignment I had stepped - not just within myself, but within my marriage to Matt. In the loss of my health and alignment, I stepped so far away from the lessons that I learned about mindfulness and compassion in relationships. I realized that my not in being alignment had fuelled the disconnect between us and had sparked my misreading my marriage for something that tied me down and took away from freedom. With old lessons resurfacing to teach me once more, with my past self now my teacher, I was reminded of the core foundations for any relationship - the same core foundations that the shift into a Yin-based consciousness would need to be built upon: the foundations of non-judgment, compassion and loving kindness. Over those weeks, more and more souls arrived to share and reaffirm insights I already knew. Each one reminding me that I was not crazy, that the bizarre journey I had begun back in 2016 when I had left Ryan had been for a bigger purpose. That the journey was always meant to lead me here, to where I am now, sharing these same insights with you.

27

My Insights into the Shift and Final Thoughts

As I sit here, writing from a place of pure alignment, I know with complete certainty that my alignment is with myself and the core aspects of myself: my physical, emotional, mental and energetic aspects. I understand fully that my alignment is also impacted by my relationships with others, my immediate environment and most importantly with my faith in myself and who I am. Faith has been my biggest lesson. In the times where it dwindled and I questioned it, I would almost instantly step out of alignment and out of my power, or I would become susceptible to handing my power over to another person or even worse, to my own fears. I have, over the span of my bizarre journey, come to understand that alignment is a core requirement in facilitating the shift and changes that need to be made in the world. One cannot fully work to aid the shift if they are not completely within themselves. With the understandings I had gained from the book, The Spirit and Practice of Moving into Stillness, I know without question that energy and frequency are vital to us shifting into a Yin-based consciousness. The times where I have been in full alignment, my energetic frequency has been high and the souls I attract while in those spaces are vibrating at the same frequency as me. This is what we are primarily striving for in the shift - a shift in frequency from a low vibration to a higher one. It is here in this higher frequency that we can weave and create our new world; one built on compassion, non-judgment, unconditional acceptance and unity. Since my teenage years, I have studied numerous beliefs and philosophies and all of them share the same insights and teachings. Some are maps and guides on ways we can live our lives in order to achieve these insights and teachings, while others are reminders of why we need to shift in the first place. It truly does not matter what belief or tradition you follow, as long as you are following the core principles, that run through them all: compassion, non-judgment, unconditional acceptance and unity.

My interactions with the teachings of the Ancients have proved time and again that a move back to old ways - the ways that dominated before the ruin brought on by toxic Christianity, will be our salvation. A move back to living with the earth surrounding us and reverting to being custodians of the land instead of trying to own it. We need to learn to go back to nature and live according to Her cycles. Most of all, we need to go back to living in harmony with one another. The San people being the oldest tribe, our true ancestors, must become our teachers. We must become reunited as one tribe once more. Our ten thousand years of living in separation and segregation, often times forced, has led us to the massive disconnection we are now facing - the disconnection from our roots and our authentic selves. For thousands of years, we have allowed others to tell us who we are, to force us into boxes of conformity and slap labels upon us, telling us who they think we should be.

If you are still questioning how you can be part of the shift, then know that all you need to do is rip off those labels, chuck away your boxes of conformity and step into being your authentic self. There are many pathways that can lead you to back to your authenticity and a higher frequency. The Eight Limbs of Yoga, the Eight Fold Path of Buddha, the teachings of mindfulness practices and the true teachings of Jesus or any of the religious prophets; but most importantly, seek out your own inner guru.

I know that the shift is already taking place and the more of us that step into our authentic selves and move back into alignment, the faster the shift will occur. If you are working towards getting back to this place, be gentle with yourself, even if you trip and stumble and do the occasional back-pedal. I have done this numerous times, but each time I come back to my authentic self, I come back stronger in who I am. It's okay to stumble along your path, we are not seeking perfection here! We also have thousands of years of deprogramming to do. We have generations of baggage and trauma that we need to shift and heal from. We're going to make mistakes, we are going to get stuck, but it's okay because there will always be someone in the Collective who will step onto your path and show you the way back. Whether they are a known friend, a complete stranger or a new teacher coming in to teach you a needed lesson, you will always have the assistance you need at just the right time.

In moving into our next stage of a Yin-based consciousness, we must not forget the positive aspect of Yang! As much as we have been existing in a space of unhealthy patriarchy and Yang-based energy, we must step forward in a balanced manner. Otherwise, we will continue to the see rise of toxic Yin and we will be back to square one, just in reverse. In order for you to do your part, you simply need to become your authentic self - genuine, compassionate and living with due consideration for others and the planet on which we reside. We need to take the lessons of brotherhood and loyalty and become a single tribe once more. In becoming unified, this does not mean that we must all conform to a single way of life. Rather we must learn to embrace our differences, see them for what they are and learn to love those differences we each bring. That is because these differences are what makes us whole and unique. My journey has brought me an entirely new family, one that exists outside of my direct blood relations. My family spans continents and cultures and I am proud to call each one brother or sister. Life truly does take you to unexpected places if you let it, and love truly does bring you home. I can now say for certain that home is right here, this moment right here, this place right here. Home is where your heart is.

If you are working with or contemplating the use of plant medicines, I ask that you do so mindfully and with respect. This includes the massively abused medicine of alcohol. A return to ritual and ceremony is vital for our shift and as long as we continue to abuse these medicines, the more we will prolong our shift into a better world. Stepping into alignment requires one to be healthy and balanced. Existing in a space where people are not afraid to face their shadow aspects such as fear, addiction, trauma and insecurities. It also not about disowning these aspects either, but rather seeing and acknowledging them and understanding why they are there in the first place. We are not seeking to be saints that do no wrong, rather we are simply seeking to embrace and be ourselves.

We are in the midst of a massive shift - the birthing of a new way of life and living. We are truly existing in exciting times as we bear witness to the dawning of a new era. The era of authenticity, compassion and unity in accordance with the true teachings of the Ancients. As much as I am here to be a facilitator for the shift, I know without question that the shift can only happen on an individual level first. As each one of us shifts within ourselves, we will begin to shift the world. The shift begins with you! Souls such as mine are simply here to help guide you through that inner shift so that you too can be a facilitator of the global shift. As we begin to shift into a higher frequency, the world will know and see change; and peace and unity will once again be restored. I believe wholeheartedly that I will live to see this transition come to fruition as so many more of us are waking up to our authentic selves in droves.

Be the change you wish to see in the world, be the embodiment of compassion, loving-kindness and unconditional acceptance - for we are all one and the same. I leave you with the Zulu word for humanity and unity, Ubuntu - I am because we are.

Namaste, my loves, the light in me sees and honors the light in you as you continue to be the light and spark of divinity that you were always meant to be.

Footnotes

1. The term for a traditional healer specifically within the Zulu culture; akin to a Shaman
2. The symbol for infinity
3. An astrological transit where Saturn returns to the same position it occupied at the time of a person's birth. It is believed that at this time a person crosses a major threshold into a new stage of life.
4. Kirtan is the main practice in Bhakti Yoga and is a Sanskrit word meaning to call, praise, recite or glorify a certain Deity. Often done through singing and repeating of mantras and names.
5. South Africa is the second most dangerous country in the world is notorious for its extremely high crime rates.
6. Changa is the smokeable form of D.M.T, the active ingredient in Ayahuasca.
7. The equivalent of about $220
8. The Thai word for foreigner.
9. These are intentionally drawn straight lines between ancient and historic sites such as Stonehenge and Angkor Wat. It is believed that these alignments where seen by ancient cultures and that these structures were deliberately erected along these lines.
10. The first English settlers in North America that arrived on the Mayflower.
11. The Hindu Goddess associated with prosperity and abundance - not just financial. She is often referred to as Mother Lakshmi or Goddess Lakshmi and is highly revered within the Hindu culture and is known as the bringer of Light.
12. An existential crisis that leads one through the darker aspects of the self in order to find re-connection with the self and enlightenment.
13. Seminole are the Indigenous people native to the area of Florida.
14. A person who provides physical, emotional and educational support to expectant mothers before, during and after birth.
15. Yoga – a practice that forms a part of the whole that makes up Hinduism –

including other branches like Ayurvedic medicine and nutrition, music, science, mathematics and mantras

About Tam Dillon

When an insatiable interest in ancient spiritual teachings and divination formed in her teens, Tam chose to immerse herself in the path of Spirituality as part of her life's journey. She has since then spent her years studying, researching, refining, and practicing her spiritual path and teachings. She has studied and worked with various spiritual practices and modalities, from Western, Eastern, and African traditions; allowing her to be able to work with and relate to numerous cultures and ways of life. Thus creating a compassionate space, that is free from judgment for who she works with. Tam has over twenty years, "hands-on" experience with both the art of Tarot and various practices within Spirituality.

As a Tarot Master, Tam has worked with this enlightening tool in both her personal and professional capacities. Utilizing its ancient spiritual knowledge to assist those seeking transformative change, spiritual growth, and to better understand themselves. Tam began reading for others while in her late teens and moved to professional readings in her early twenties. Having discovered a natural psychic gift, Tam read Tarot from a traditional and predictive perspective for several years. Over that time she developed more therapeutic forms of working with the Tarot and in 2019 moved away from traditional Tarot reading to embrace a more therapeutic way of working with the cards in her Tarot Therapy sessions as well as focusing fully on teaching others The Art Of Tarot through her range of workshops and courses.

She has been actively teaching and sharing her knowledge of the Tarot, since 2007; and has consistently made it her aim to make the Tarot as simple as possible. So that more people can access its knowledge and gain a deeper understanding of their own lives and spiritual path. In 2019 Tam went on to publish her first Art Of Tarot Guidebook and has subsequently released the second edition of her Guidebook in May 2021. Having seen first-hand the positive impact that Tarot can have, not just on her spiritual path, but in her daily life, Tam has worked to find methods that make reading and working with Tarot simpler for anyone with a keen interest in learning to work with the cards.

As a certified Mindfulness Practitioner and Registered Yoga Teacher (RYT200), Tam teaches the Art Of Mindfulness and Yoga through her range of workshops and courses and integrates these empowering ancient practices into her Soul Sessions with clients. Having seen and experienced the transformative impact of these powerful practices for herself, Tam also offers one-on-one sessions for those looking to develop and grow their own personal practices. Tam began her Yogic journey more than ten years ago when a strong desire for balance and stress management became her driving force in order to cope with her high-pressure corporate career. This exploration of the Yogic path led her to explore the paths and practices of Mindfulness and Buddhism as well. These traditions and practices have been nothing short of life-altering and Tam enthusiastically shares her teachings and knowledge so that others may experience the transformative effects of these beautiful traditions for themselves. In 2021 Tam went on to complete her 200 hour Yoga Teacher Training and is now a registered teacher with Yoga Alliance.

Tam Dillon is a Spiritual Guide and Teacher that assists others with powerful transformations, empowerment and finding their authenticity; as well as sharing guidance and direction on spiritual journeys. Utilizing various spiritual philosophies and practices, Tam draws on her twenty-plus years of personal and professional experience to give you exactly what your Soul is needing. Tam is a highly experienced Tarot Master, Registered Yoga Teacher (RYT200) and holds a Masters certification in Mindfulness as well as certifications in Applied Modern Psychology, Counselling, and Life Coaching. Tam has an established practice in Greenville, South Carolina as well as an online platform through which she can reach out to students and clients across the globe – bringing them encouragement, knowledge, and solid practical teachings; thus empowering them to take an active role in their own journeys. For more than ten years, Tam has been working with clients and students. Assisting them with their processes, journeys, and transformations; utilizing various mediums and modalities such as Energy Healing, Crystal Therapy, Tarot, and Spiritual Guidance. Over the years her practice has shifted and transformed along with her. The one consistent, however, has been her purpose; to assist others with transformative change and empowerment.

CPSIA information can be obtained
at www.ICGtesting.com
Printed in the USA
BVHW090216211221
624508BV00020B/640

9 781736 588321